D1754177

Kyoto   Its Cityscape Traditions and Heritage

京の都市意匠──景観形成の伝統

CONTENTS

PROCESS: Architecture

	12.	**Introduction**
		Kyoto: Its Cityscape Traditions and Heritage by Masafumi Yamasaki

I Rakuchu Rakugai Relationships

- 18. Development of Rakugai Scenery and its Traditions
- 20. Rakugai Landscape and Zen Temples
- 28. Sagano—Symbolic Landscapes
- 32. A Sense of Distance and Juxtaposition

II Monuments—Urban Design Features

- 38. Placement of Monumental Structures in the Cityscape

III Streetscapes—Their Development and Buildings

- 46. Historical Development of Streetscape Styles
- 61. Extant Built Elements:
  Wachigaiya／Sugimoto House／Namikawa House／Ichiriki／Nishikikoji／Seifuso／and others

IV Traditional Streetscapes—Design Features

- 72. Traditional Neighborhoods—Commercial and Domestic:
  Gion Shinbashi／Gioncho South／Pontocho／Kamishichiken／Teranouchi／Nishijin／Sanneizaka／Gojozaka／Kamigamo Shakemachi
- 97. Traditional Neighborhoods—Religious and Imperial:
  Kibune Shrine／Shugakuin／Imamiya Shrine／Shinnyodo／Nanzenji／Shorenin／Nishi Honganji Jinaicho／Bishamondo／Daigoji／Seiryoji／Daikakuji／Ninnaji／Ryoanji／Myoshinji
- 102. Highway Streetscapes:
  Saga Toriimoto／Kuramakaido／Katagihara／Otsukaido
- 115. Fushimi

V Rivers—Urban Design Features

- 120. Kamo River
- 129. Takase River
- 132. Shirakawa River
- 134. Horikawa River, Kamiya River

VI Views—City and Environs

- 136. Cityscape Design and Features

VII Tasks—Present and Future

- 145. Toward a Modern Japanese Style City
- 152. Location Map

Front Cover:
Section of Ikeda Rakuchu Rakugai
Screen Painting

Back Cover:
Kiyomizudera Temple
A maple tree at Shinnyodo

表紙：
池田家旧蔵本洛中洛外図（部分）　林原美術館
所蔵

裏表紙：
清水寺（撮影　廣田治雄）
真如堂の楓

12.	序	
	歴史都市としての京都　山崎正史	

I　洛外の意匠

- 18.　洛外の景観形成と継承の伝統
- 20.　禅宗寺院の十境と洛外の風景
- 28.　嵯峨野
- 32.　洛中洛外の距離

II　モニュメントの都市意匠

- 38.　近世京都のモニュメンタルな建築配置による都市景観構成

III　町家と町並み景観の発展

- 46.　町並みの様式発展史
- 61.　京の町家：
  輪違屋／杉本家／並河家／一力／錦小路／清風荘／ほか

IV　伝統的町並みの意匠

- 72.　伝統的町並み：
  祇園新橋／祇園町南側／先斗町／上七軒／寺の内／西陣／産寧坂／
  五条坂／上賀茂社家町
- 97.　門前参道の町並み：
  貴船神社／修学院／今宮神社／真如堂／南禅寺参道／青蓮院門前／西本願寺寺内町／
  毘沙門道／醍醐寺門前／清涼寺／大覚寺／仁和寺／竜安寺／妙心寺
- 102.　街道の町並み：
  嵯峨鳥居本／鞍馬街道／樫原／大津街道
- 115.　伏見

V　河川の都市意匠

- 120.　鴨川
- 129.　高瀬川
- 132.　白川
- 134.　堀川と紙屋川

VI　京の眺望景観

- 136.　眺望の名所とその意匠

VII　現代の課題

- 145.　近代都市の日本的様式へ向けて
- 152.　本書掲載の場所・地域・位置図

PRO:Arch

No.116

Publisher:
Murotani Bunji

Editor-in-Charge:
Masafumi Yamasaki

Management Editor:
Michiko Yamada

Editorial Staff:
Miwako Ito, Yumiko Fujimaki,
Chiho Minamiguchi, Midori Mochizuki

Editorial Assistants:
Kyoko Shibazaki, Junko Hashimoto

Translator:
Bill and Lou Tingey

Cover Design:
Takahisa Kamijyo (Kamijyo Studio)

Published by
Process Architecture Co.,Ltd., Tokyo Japan

Printed by
TOPPAN PRINTING CO. (S) PTE.,LTD.

Executive and Editorial Office
1-47-2-418 Sasazuka Shibuya-ku Tokyo. Japan
Phone(03)3468-0131, Fax(03)3468-0133

Copyright © April 1994 by
Process Architecture Co.,Ltd.

All right reserved.
ISBN 4-89331-116-6

第116号
発行日：1994年4月1日
発行人：室谷文治
責任編集者：
山崎正史
編集監理：
山田美智子
プロセスアーキテクチュア編集部：
伊藤美和子, 藤巻由美子, 南口千穂, 望月みどり
編集アシスタント：
芝崎恭子, 橋本純子
翻訳：
ビル・ティンギー, ルー・ティンギー
表紙デザイン：上條喬久(上條スタジオ)
制作・写植：
㈱協和クリエイト, ㈲ユニット, 大西写植
印刷：TOPPAN PRINTING CO. (S) PTE.,LTD.
発行所：
株式会社プロセスアーキテクチュア
〒151 東京都渋谷区笹塚1-47-2-418
電話03-3468-0131 FAX03-3468-0133
振替 東京6-57446

取次店：
トーハン, 日販, 大阪屋, 栗田出版販売, 誠光堂

禁無断転載

Editor's Note

It was about the time that problems were first being raised in respect of the general appearance of Kyoto, and high-rise plans for both Kyoto station and the Kyoto Hotel were first being put forward, that the publisher of Process Architecture, Bunji Murotani, asked me if I would be interested in compiling a special issue on the cityscape of Kyoto. It was the kind of opportunity I had hoped for, especially as it came at a time when I was taking stock of the changes which had beset the city where I was born.

Basically speaking, this publication is divided into three main sections. The first reconsiders from a historical viewpoint the importance of the relationship between the central, historical areas of the city which were formally known as *rakuchu*, and the surrounding areas known in the past as *rakugai*, where the city meets the mountains. The second section which is made up of two parts firstly considers the central areas in some detail, concentrating on the background of the overall appearance of the city at an urban scale by looking at the placement of monumental structures within the city, and also by looking back at the development of the streetscapes of Kyoto, in an attempt to grasp the relationship of the historical appearance of the city and how it appears today. After all, however much people might say that the heritage of this ancient city should be preserved, it is pointless saying so without considering what the fabric of the city itself is actually composed of and what concepts and intentions where behind its planning. This issue, of course, presented an ideal opportunity to write about such topics. The third section, which itself is divided into four parts, presents those neighborhoods and areas of present-day Kyoto which I feel can still convey something of the heritage of the city to us. I have also outlined some of the problems facing present-day Kyoto, considered from the point of view of the inheritance of the historical environment of the city.

In the final chapter, however, I have attempted to decipher both the historical context (time context) as well as the scenic context (space context) of the environment of the region, and it is the point at which the axis of these two contexts intersect that I consider should be the common basis from where environmental design and architectural design discussions should begin. In point of fact, trying to provide such a way of deciphering the context most pertinent to Kyoto was one of the main reasons for compiling this publication and the whole volume has been founded on this intention. Furthermore, because I also wanted to provide information useful to the people of Kyoto who will already have considerable knowledge about the history of the city, the second section, in particular, may seem somewhat pedantic in the way in which the subject is handled, but I felt that circumstances demand such an in-depth investigation. A large number of illustrations have been included so that the reader might be able gain a better understanding of the overall concepts being dealt with here.

It may of course be difficult for non-Japanese readers and for those other readers who are not familiar with the topography and scale of Kyoto, to understand how the city is composed of central, basically urban areas and surrounding areas with a predominance of natural landscape. Because of the peculiarities of its location, for example, it is possible to drive out to an area only a matter of five or six kilometers from the center of the city to find that the weather is different there. While it may be fine in the center of the city, it may be raining or even snowing in the areas at the foot of the surrounding mountains. And once among the mountains proper there is even a feeling of being deep in a mountainous area, almost cut off from the world described by the city proper. It would therefore be as well to bear in mind that Kyoto is a city of such variations of weather and topography before reading and considering the material that is presented.

It would be a mistake, however, to think that those places with a rich cultural heritage presented here are the only ones which exist. There are of course many other places and individual streetscapes which it was not possible to deal with in this publication. The Katsuragawa river, one of the most representative in the area, for example, has sadly been omitted. But as the reader will I hope understand, time and space is always limited.

Unless otherwise indicated, the surveys of individual houses and streetscapes are the result of work done by the Conservation and Renovation Planning Research Association of which I am a member. It should also be noted that the names of any historical personages in the English text have be left in the Japanese style with family name first.

Finally, I would like to thank the many people who have cooperated in the compilation of this publication. I am most grateful for the permission which has been granted by various bodies and private individuals to publish works in their custody or ownership of immense cultural value. I would especially like to extend my heartfelt thanks to all those individuals who have supplied photographs of work from private collections and I hope they will accept my apologies for putting them to so much trouble. I am also indebted to Michiko Yamada for all her help and kind advise afforded me during the editing of this publication. To one and all, I extend my sincere thanks.

Masafumi Yamasaki

編集言

京都駅ビルと京都ホテルが高層化計画を相次いで打ち出し、京都の景観が問題として取り上げられるようになった頃、プロセス・アーキテクチュア誌の室谷文治氏から京都の景観特集を担当してみないかとのお話があった。京都に生まれ、景観の変化を見てきて日頃考えるところもあった私としては願ってもない機会を与えていただいたと感謝している。

本書は大きくは3つの部分から構成されている。最初に、京都はかつて洛中と呼ばれた歴史的市街地と、かつて洛外と呼ばれてきた自然に恵まれた低い山並みのある郊外地域の2者から構成されていることの大切さを歴史を通じて見直している。2番目にはその洛中について、モニュメンタルな建築配置による都市的規模の景観の物語と、京都の町並み形成の流れを辿り、現在の都市景観につながる京都の景観史を試みている。歴史都市の景観を継承すべきと言われはしても、これまでその景観がどういう経緯で形成されたのか、どのような意図が込められてきたのか、殆ど書かれたことがなかった。3番目には、私の目で探した現在の京都が持つ景観的遺産を紹介している。最後に歴史的環境の継承という視点から現代の京都が持つ課題を書き加えた。本書の最終章で書いたように、地域環境のもつ歴史的文脈(通時的文脈)と景観的文脈(共時的文脈)を解読し、その2軸の文脈の交差する場での発言として環境デザイン・建築デザインが行われるべきだと私は考えており、京都における文脈解読の手がかりを提示したいという意図が本書の構成の基礎になっている。既に歴史に関してはかなりの知識がある京都人にも情報を提供したいということから、特に2章など歴史記述に詳細すぎる点があるかもしれない。挿図を見ていただければ概略が理解できるように配慮したつもりである。

日本以外の国の読者には、洛中と洛外から都市が構成されていることへの着目が理解しにくいと思われるかもしれない。周囲を低い山並みで囲まれた京都は、都心部から車で10数分も周辺へ走れば気候が変化する。都心部は晴れていたのに山裾に近づくと時雨ていたり、雪が降っていたりする。まして山の襞へ足を踏み入れると深山の趣さえ感じられる。そういう気候の微変化がある都市だということを念頭に読んでいただければ幸いである。

景観遺産として本書で取り上げた場所は決してそれが全てではない。町並みでも取り上げきれなかった所が多々あるし、河川についても代表的河川の一つである桂川を書いていない。限られた時間と紙面でのこととご理解いただきたい。

本書に掲載した町並みや町家の実測図面は、特に示したもの以外は筆者も参加してきた保存修景計画研究会で作成したものである。

最後に、本書編集にあたって多方面の方々のご協力に感謝を申し上げたい。本書に掲載した文化財的価値のある絵画を所蔵する個人・機関の皆様には掲載への快いご許可と協力をいただいた。特に個人で所蔵されている方々にはフィルムの郵送などお手を煩わし、お詫びと共に心から感謝を申し上げたい。プロセス・アーキテクチュア誌の山田美智子氏には編集作業を通じて貴重なご助言とご助力をいただいた。記して感謝の意を表わしたい。

山崎正史

山崎正史
立命館大学理工学部環境システム工学科助教授。京都大学博士(工学)。

1947年京都市生まれ。1971年京都大学工学部建築学科卒。1974年京都大学大学院終了。歴史的環境保全計画、都市景観論を専攻。京都市産寧坂地区、祇園新橋地区、近江八幡市等の歴史的町並み保全計画に携わる。著書「歴史の町並み 京都編」(共著、日本放送協会、1969)、「新・都の魁」(共著、京都新聞社、1989)など。

Masafumi Yamasaki
Ph. D. (Engin.) Kyoto University Ass. Professor in the department of Environmental Systems Technology at Ritsumeikan University of Science and Engineering, Kyoto.

Born in Kyoto, 1947. Graduated from Kyoto University, Department of Architecture in the Faculty of Engineering in 1971. Completed post-graduate school at the same university in 1974, having done research on conservations plans for historical environments and the theory of cityscape planning. Involved in conservation plans for Sanneizaka and Gionbashi districts of Kyoto and for the city of Omihachiman, Kyoto prefecture. He has published a number of works including Rekishi no Machinami — Kyoto-hen," Historical Townscapes, Kyoto" (1969), and Shin-Miyako no Sakigake, "Kyoto — its History and Life-styles" (1989).

写真撮影
廣田治雄:pp.5→11, 15, 20, 29左上、右下、30左、31上、62上、64上、71、79下、80左上、82上、右下、94上、96右上、左上、102-103、109上、110上、111 左上、右上、右中、120-121上、121下、126上、127右下、128上、左下、129上、130-131上、130左下、133下。
京極スタジオ:pp.63上, 72-73, 81上, 137上, 141右下。

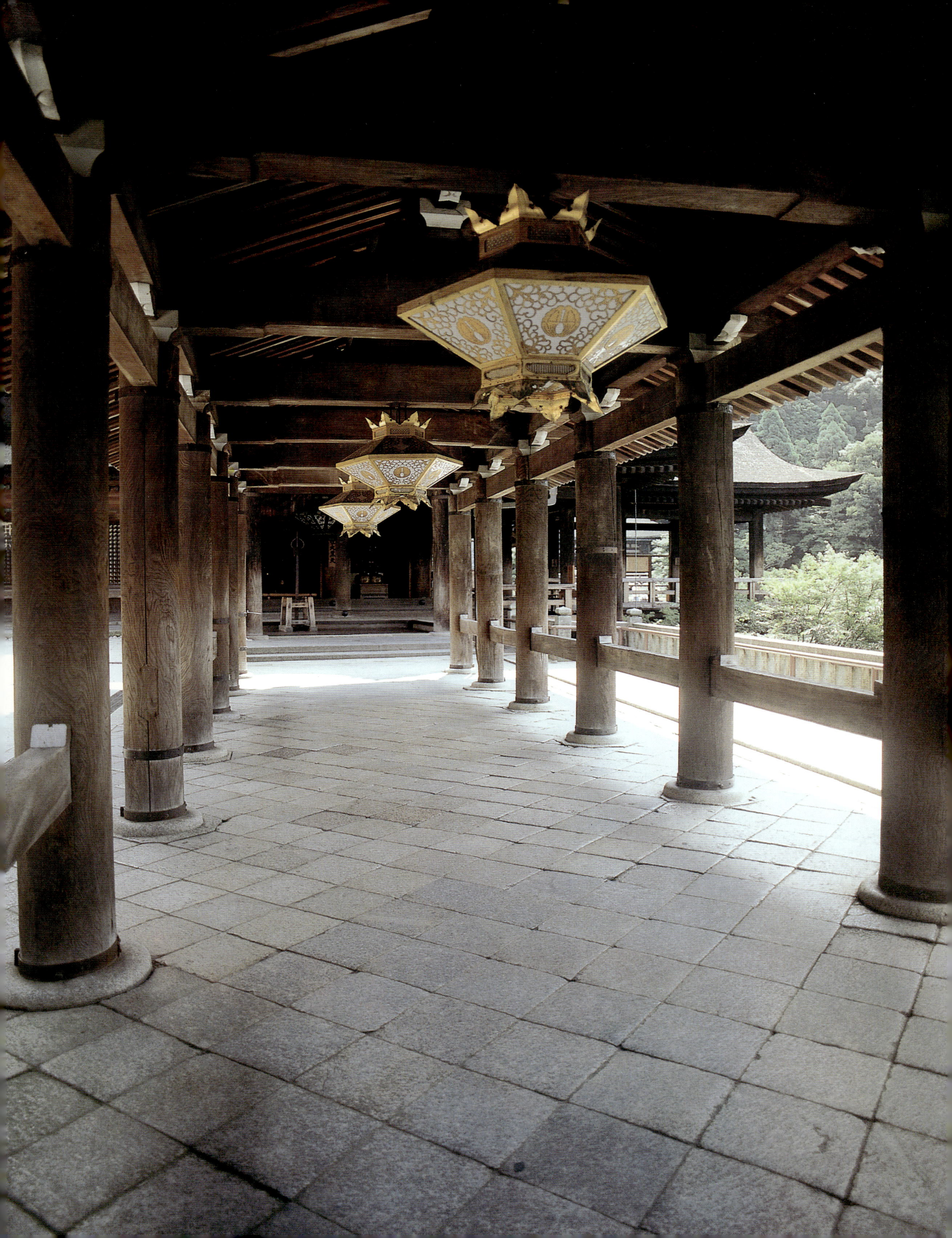

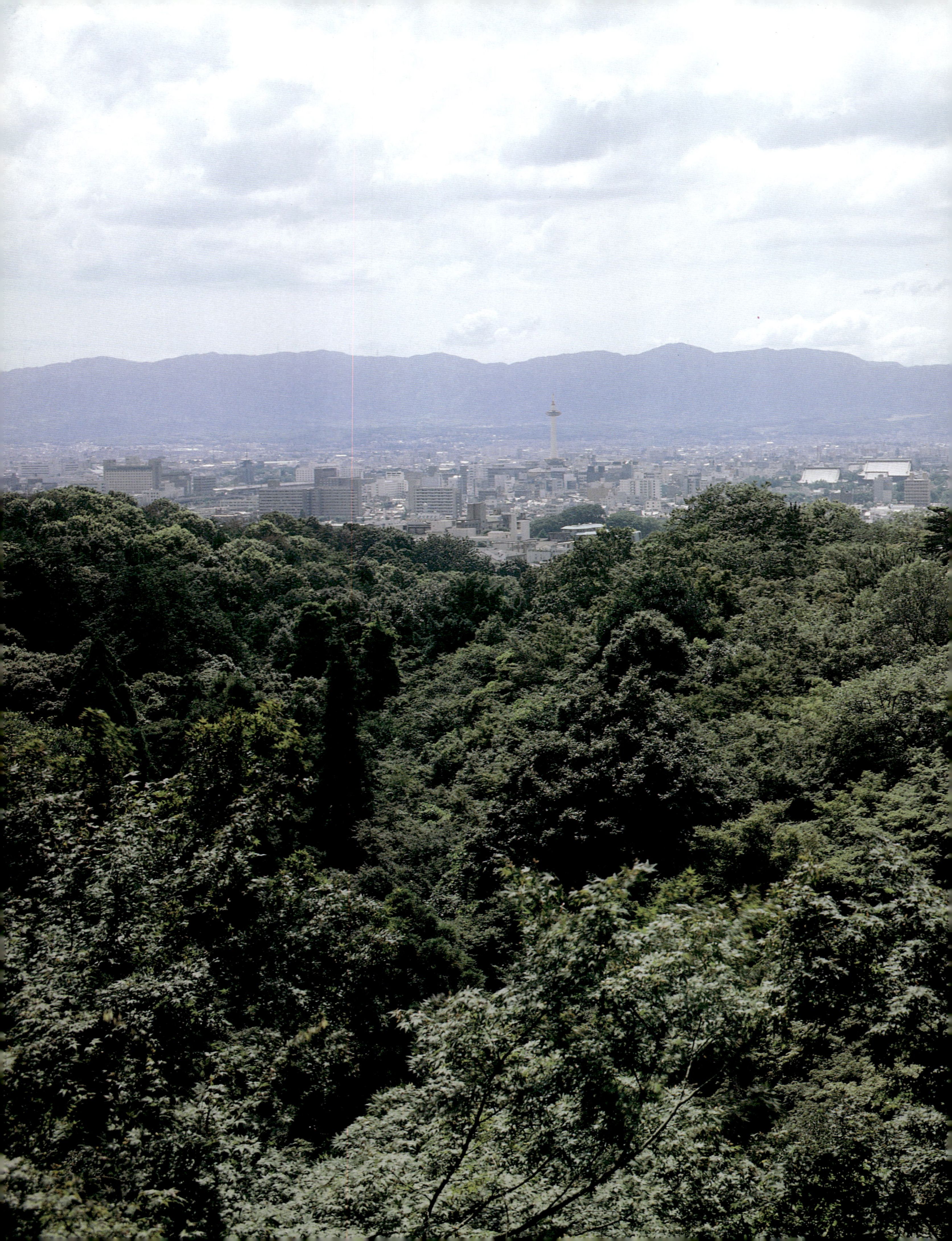

View from Kiyomizu-dera Temple　清水寺からの眺望

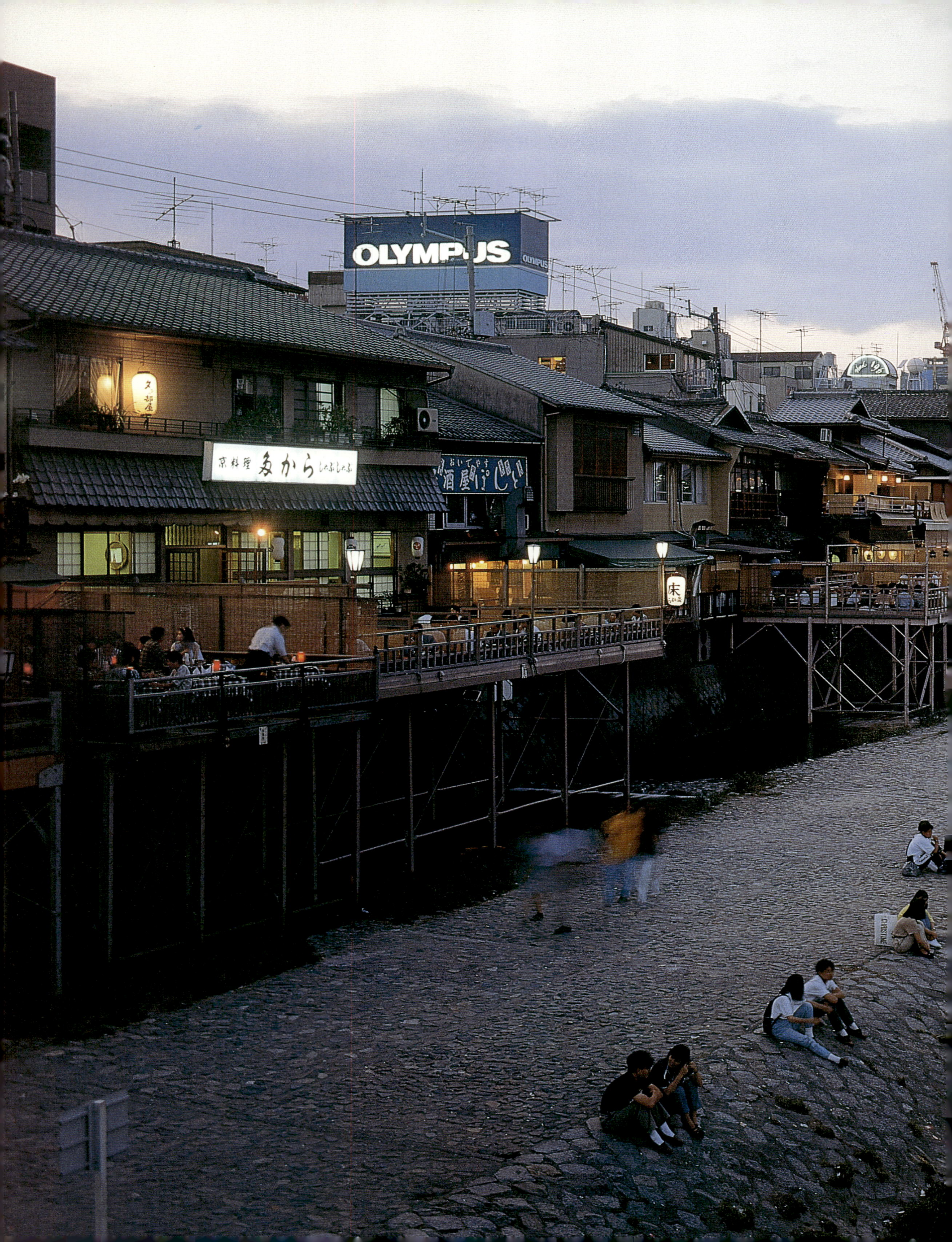

Kamogawa River 鴨川

Hirosawa Pond, Sagano　嵯峨野　広沢池

Introduction 序

Kyoto: Its Cityscape Traditions and Heritage
by Masahumi Yamasaki

歴史都市としての京都——求められる独自の道
山崎正史

This issue of Process Architecture is being published in 1994, the year which marks the 1,200th anniversary of the founding of Heian-Kyo, the Capital of Peace and Tranquility that we now know as Kyoto. This momentous occasion is an ideal opportunity to take stock of just how much of the heritage and tradition of this historic city is still evident today, using a large number of photographs and illustrations with which to make a general, visually orientated survey of some of the particular features of the historic fabric and overall appearance of the city.

Ordinarily, the title of this volume would make reference to the urban-design bias of its content. But rather than being concerned with an imported formative language of urban concepts associated with the planning and building of a new urban area, we will be attempting to decipher an inherently Japanese urban language derived from the history of Kyoto, with the hope and intention of considering its future within the parameters of an urban design discipline based on the context of that formative language.

First of all, however, we must take a brief look at the historical background of the city itself. In ancient times, the Imperial seat was at Heijo-Kyo in Nara until it was moved to Nagaoka. Then after only ten years, the capital was moved again in A. D. 794 and a new city was established on a grid pattern of newly constructed streets in the center of a basin to the northeast. Gradually the main built up area of the new Heian capital gravitated toward the east of this basin and then in the Middle Ages, Toyotomi Hideyoshi threw an rampart known as the Odoi around the city, which was also then divided up into narrow rectangular blocks. Although the Odoi soon disappeared, there were no dramatic changes which affected the general layout of the city after that, and it remained more or less unchanged throughout the Edo period (1600-1868). Much of the city was destroyed in a fire in the latter part of the nineteenth century, but the restoration work which was done after that mostly followed the pattern of the city as it was in the Edo period. After the capital was moved to Tokyo and in-step with the general spirit of modernization during the Meiji period (1868-1912), some basic urban facilities were constructed in Kyoto, including the Biwako Sosui, which was a channel to draw water from nearby Lake Biwa. Some streets were also widened to accommodate the introduction of streetcars and although many western-style buildings began to appear in various locations, the general appearance of the city as a whole changed very little right up until after the Pacific War and into the mid-nineteen fifties. In fact, it would not be too much of a distortion of the truth to say that the appearance of the city had remained more or less the same since the Edo period. The greatest changes in its general appearance took place during the twenty-year period from the mid-nineteen sixties.

Sadly, most of Japan's large cities including the capital Tokyo, were badly damaged during the Second World War, large areas being raised by fire. The task that confronted city planners after the war therefore, was the building of modern cities on the land which had been laid bare. Almost inevitably, the main trends in both architecture and in civil engineering in Japan since the Meiji period were largely geared to the introduction of advanced Western technology and the loss of a historic urban environment presented planners with an opportunity to realize the construction of modern cities. It could even be said that the system of architectural and city planning in operation after the war was arranged and geared to these prevailing circumstances. Consequently, if we consider in general terms the system of city planning at the time, we find that there was a tendency for city centers to be areas given over to commerce and business, where medium- to high-rise buildings stood shoulder to shoulder, with areas of low-rise housing surrounding them. But of course such a system was something of a contradiction in terms for cities such as Kyoto, Nara and Kanazawa, all of which had retained something of their heritage despite the hostilities. Looking back now on what happened after the war, such historic cities were completely disassociated from the mainstream of city planning being carried out in Japan at the time, and it would seem as though they should have followed their own course of development, perhaps even in isolation. However, it was not possible in Japan at the time for a regional city to have its own set of original city planning procedures. The same set of procedures which were applicable to a city recovering from the ravages of war, were also applied to historic cities. But on the other hand, it seems that there was very little resistance to these planning procedures from among the more historic cities and consequently, the same new set of values pertaining to modern city planning were applied carte blanche over the whole country and in time, even began to affect Kyoto.

Of course there was nothing wrong with wanting to 'modernize' the environment in which people lived in the sense of making it more hygienic, more comfortable and more practical. But the question is, was it really so necessary to destroy so much of the traditional environment and culture in the interests of modernization; and was the realization of a modernized city and buildings really impossible without dismissing the existing culture and environment which had developed over the centuries?

Ever since ancient times, people have conducted their lives within an environment which possesses a symbolic significance. It also follows

---

本書が出版される平成6年(1994)は，平安建都1200年にあたる．この記念すべき時期に，本書では，現在の京都に見られる歴史的景観がどのような伝統を持ち，継承されてきたのか，その歴史的経緯と景観の特質を絵図と写真を多用して視覚的に概観してみたい．

「京の都市意匠」というタイトルは普通ならアーバン・デザインと言われるものを日本語で置き換えてみたものだが，欧米流の都市概念と造形言語で日本の都市を「新たに造る」立場ではなく，京都の歴史の中から日本的な都市の造形言語を読み取り，その造形の文脈の上で今後の都市デザインを考えていきたいという意図と願いを込めてのことでもある．

奈良の平城京から長岡京に都が移り，それからわずか10年後の延暦13年(794)に平安京遷都が行われた．平安京は盆地の中央に碁盤状の新都として築かれたが，やがて市街地は左京に偏り，中世末には豊臣秀吉によって御土居と呼ばれた土塁で囲われ，街区を短冊状に割る都市改造が行われた．御土居は間もなく消失したが，都市の形はその後，江戸時代を通じて都市構造に関わるような劇的変化といったものはなく近代を迎えた．幕末に大火で京の大半が焼失したが，その時の復興は江戸時代の環境の姿を殆どそのまま再現したものであった．明治時代には軌道電車を通すための道路拡幅や琵琶湖疏水の建設など都市の基盤となる施設の建設が行われ，各所に洋風建築が出現したが，京都という都市の全体的な景観からいえば，太平洋戦争後も昭和30年代までは大きな変化があったとは言い難く，むしろ江戸時代以来の都市景観がその頃まで存続していたと言ったほうが事実に近いだろう．京都の景観が劇的に変化したのは昭和40年代以降のおよそ20数年の間であった．

不幸にも首都東京をはじめ日本の主だった都市の殆どが戦災を受け，一度は焼け野原となった．戦後の都市計画の課題は，そこに出現した更地，いわば荒れ地に，近代的都市を建設することにあった．明治時

Nakagyo Ward, Kyoto, 1952. The wide street running across the picture is Oike-dori after it had been widened and the Kamo River runs across the top of the picture.
昭和27年の京都市中京区全景．中央の広い通は疎開後の御池通，上方は鴨川．毎日新聞社提供

that the kind of environment in which people can share in the significance it possesses is, of course, one with a history, regardless of whether it is long or short. Furthermore, the history of an environment is characteristic of a particular area, a particular region and is characteristic, too, of a nation. Happily, now that a standard level of practicality and convenience has been achieved under the banner of modernization, we now live in an age in which there is a desire to express the cultural and historic aspects of an environment as well as the individuality of a region or a city. By my own definition, such a culturally impregnated environment is one in which the spiritual workings of people's minds are given shape and form. An environment is a stage for the enactment of history and literature; and places bedecked with traces of those actions, landscapes painted by famous artists and even the form of an environment or structures skillfully constructed by people in the past, are all examples of things which have strong spiritual links with people alive today. In Japan, it has often been claimed that conservation is not a question of form but significant more in terms of the inheritance of spirit. However, surely what we must turn our attention on now is a culture founded on an interchange between form and spirit, and a spiritual culture of which form is an integral part. One of the ideas behind this publication, of course, was to provide some basic pieces of information by which something new in the way of creating such a culturally rich environment might become possible, by attempting to describe some of the stories and background associated with the form of Kyoto as an urban entity.

代以来のわが国の建築および土木技術の動向は言うまでもなく欧米の先進技術を導入するという大きな流れの上にあり，歴史的都市環境を失ったことは近代的都市建設を実現する機会を与えるものでもあった．戦後の都市計画や建築に関わる制度はこういう文脈の上に構想され整えられたと言えるだろう．都市計画制度を概観すれば，都心部は中高層ビルが林立し商業・業務地区に専用化し，都市周縁部に低層住宅を配置するという方向が読み取れる．さて，こういう制度は歴史的環境を戦後まで継承した京都，奈良，金沢といった都市にとっては矛盾をはらむものであった．今にして思えば，これら歴史都市は日本の都市計画の大きな流れから離れて，孤独であろうとも独自の道を歩むべきであったかと思われる．しかし，地方都市が独自の都市計画制度を持つことはわが国では許されていない．戦災復興都市と同じ制度が歴史都市にも適用されてきた．また一方では，歴史都市がこのことに強い抵抗を示すこともなかったようである．日本中をおおった近代都市建設という新しい価値観が，ある時期からこの京都をもおおっていた．

　便利で清潔で快適な生活環境を実現するという意味での近代化が正しいことは言うまでもない．しかし，その近代化が余りにも伝統的環境文化を破壊しすぎてはいないか，都市や建築の近代化は伝統的な環境文化の否定の上にしか実現できないと言われてきたが果してそうなのだろうか．

　人は極めて古い時代から，象徴的な意味をもつ環境と共に暮らしてきた．人々が意味を共有できる環境とは，時間的な長短はあれ，歴史的な存在でしかありえない．そして，環境の歴史とはその国の，その地方の，その土地の固有のものである．こうして，利便性の追求という近代化の一定程度の達成の後に，環境の文化性，歴史性，そして都市や地方の個性への願望が各所で表明される時代を迎えている．文化的環境と私が言うのは人の精神的な営みが形態に表現されているよう

Muromachi Anekoji sagaru district in 1931
昭和6年の室町姉小路下ル付近の町並み　京を語る会提供

Muromachi Anekoji sagaru district in 1986　現在の室町姉小路付近

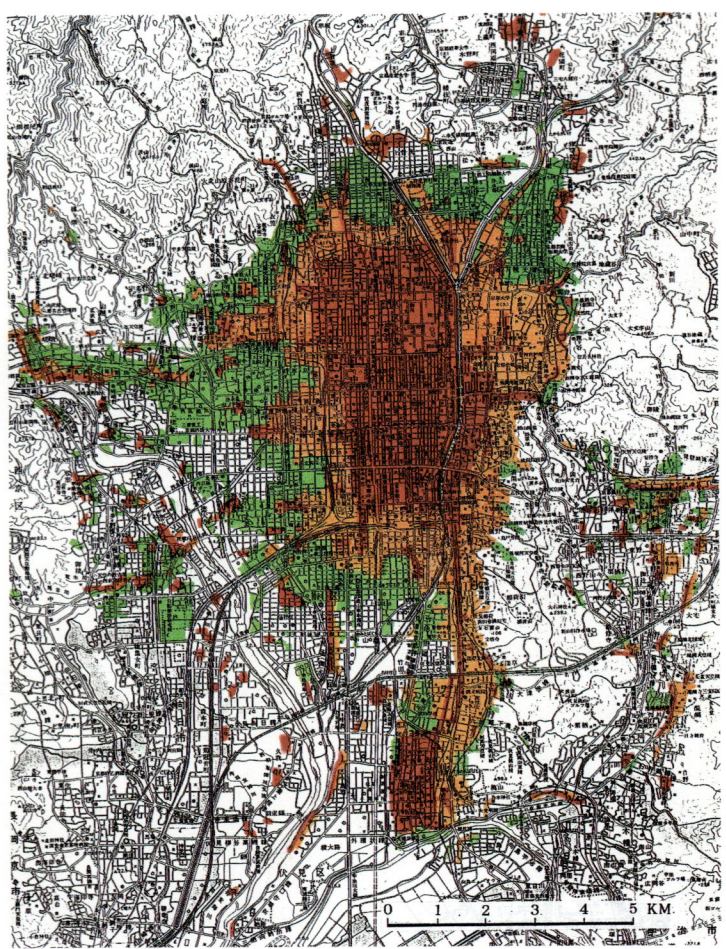

Urban development of Kyoto　Red: 1887, Orange: 1921, Green: 1965
京都の市街地の発展　赤: 明治20年頃、オレンジ: 大正10年頃、緑: 昭和40年頃の市街地

There are times when the way in which we perceive a piece of landscape is colored by having seen an old picture of it, or by having read an old piece of literature about it. In that sense it must surely be possible to say that there is a sense of history and culture in the way that we perceive that piece of landscape. Once again, one of the ideas behind the use of illustrations in this volume was so that it might be possible for the reader to decipher the sense of history and culture there is in the way in which we perceive a piece of landscape.

It was the well known city-planning theorist, Kevin Lynch, who stated in his popularly acclaimed book "What Time is this Place?", that it was fundamentally necessary for people to be able to gain an understanding of their position in the present as a section of time between the past and the future, and that people gained such an impression of time from the urban environment. In reality, of course, while people have a cultural presence, they also have a 'presence in time' and for that reason he was probably suggesting that people sought an expression of time and history from within the environment in which they exist.

When Kevin Lynch visited Kyoto some ten years ago, I was lucky enough to be able to take him to Sagano, located on the western edge of the city. We were walking along the lane from Rakushisha, the site of a poet's retreat, when he began to recite from memory in English, several haiku poems by the poet Basho. Lynch was anxious to know the correct pronunciation of some of the Japanese in the poems and I remember that he said he wanted to hear what the poems sounded like in the correct setting.

Similarly, if this publication is able to help the reader any small way to experience something of the deep sense of time there is instilled in various parts of present day Kyoto, I will be well please.

な環境である．歴史や文学の舞台となりその面影をとどめている地，画家が名作に描き上げた風景，過去の人々が巧みに造形した建造物や環境の形，これらは現代人と深い心の交流を生み出している．わが国では，保存とは形の問題ではなく精神の継承にこそ意義があると主張されることが多かったが，形と精神の交流としての文化，形と共にある精神文化を今評価すべきであろう．本書で京都という都市の姿に関する物語の描写を試みたのも，こうした文化的により豊かな環境を創出しようという新しい動向のために，基礎的情報のいくらかを提供したいという思いからに他ならない．

私たちは過去の文学作品や絵画から，風景の見方そのものを教わることがしばしばある．その意味で，風景の見方にも歴史性と文化性があると言えるだろう．本書で各所に絵画を挿入したのも，そこに風景の見方の歴史性と文化性を読み取って頂きたいという思いからである．

都市計画理論家として著名であったケヴィン・リンチ氏は，ある時期関心を集めた書時間の中の都市で，人は過去と未来の間に現在の自分を位置づけることができること，そういう時間のイメージを都市環境の中で人が持てることが根本的に必要であると主張した．その原著名も「WHAT TIME IS THIS PLACE？この場所は何時ですか」というものであった．人は本来的に文化的存在であると同時に「時間的存在」であり，それ故，環境に時間・歴史の表現を求める指摘であったといえようか．

十年程前，リンチ氏が京都を訪ねられた折り，筆者は氏に嵯峨野を案内する好運を得たことがあった．落柿舎から野を行く道すがら，氏は英語訳で暗唱していた芭蕉の句の幾つかについて日本語の発音を私に尋ね，句の響きを風景の中で確かめておられたのを思い出す．

現在の京都の各所で，その景観がもつ時間の深みを尋ねる時に，本書が僅かなりとも役に立てることができれば幸いである．

I
Rakuchu Rakugai Relationships
洛外の意匠

Machida Rakuchu Rakugai-zu screen painting depicting the cityscape in the first half of 16th century. 町田家旧蔵本洛中洛外図 景観年代16世紀前半 国立歴史民俗博物館所蔵

17

Rakuchu Rakugai Relationships
Development of Rakugai Scenery and its Traditions
洛外の景観形成と継承の伝統

Kyoto and its Natural Surroundings

The city of Kyoto and its surroundings were depicted in a number of screen paintings known as the *Rakuchu Rakugai* paintings, done between the middle of the sixteenth century and on through the following century. This period was perhaps the first in which an overall view of a city was taken as a main theme for paintings in Japan and it was also therefore the first time that such a cityscape had been depicted.

These paintings of course contain many interesting features. But, although they are a 'map' of the city itself which was known as *Rakuchu*, what perhaps we should be most concerned with is the fact that the relationship between the city and its environs, or *Rakugai*, is depicted. The city itself and the surrounding fields, foothills and mountains are, in other words, comprehended as a single entity. This means that any impression of the city was incomplete without the natural elements of the surrounding mountains and the areas of verdant countryside as well as the temples and shrines distributed among the foothills outside the city.

One other feature we should pay particular attention to is the fact that the *Rakuchu Rakugai* paintings also depict the changing of the seasons and they can also be read like a chronicle of the various events and festivals which took place throughout the year. It must be surmised, therefore, that the seasons and a year as a specific span of time, where both elements which could not be ignored when depicting an overall impression of the city. However, although the changing seasons are expressed as an integral part of some of the events which take place within the city proper, it is possible to gain a much richer impression of the wealth of natural scenery in the vicinity, from the depictions of flowering cherries and glowing autumnal tints of the maples shown growing there.

It is surprising to find how close to the built-up areas of the city, the scenery and depictions of religious buildings in what should be distant surrounding areas are shown in these paintings. Highly stylized gold colored clouds mask the areas between the city and its environs and by abbreviating the spaces and true distance between the two, the outskirts of the city are depicted as being within easy reach. This way of distorting the real distance between the outskirts and the central areas of the city is consistent in all these paintings and we must surely therefore interpret this as meaning that as far as people in those days were concerned, they were conscious of the surrounding areas as being close to the main parts of the city.

Development of Rakugai Scenery and its Traditions

Even before the founding of the Heian capital in the mountain flanked basin of the area known as Yamashiro, the land there was being actively developed by a number of powerful families: the Hata's in the west, the Kamo's in the north, and the Koma's in the east. In fact, it is recognized that it was the existence of these influential families controlling the outlying areas that made the use of a defensive wall around the city unnecessary. But that was not all, because members of the Imperial family and others of high rank also maintained villas and religious establishments in the surrounding countryside. To the west, for example, stood Sagain of the Emperor Saga, and the Seikakan, which was originally a villa for Minamoto Toru but later became known as Seiryoji Temple. To the east there was Shirakawain and Rikushoji temples located in the area known as Shirakawa. And then to the south we find Byodoin, originally the villa of Fujiwara Yorimichi located in Uji.

During the Heian period, which lasted roughly from when the capital was founded in 794 until 1185, one of the main festivals was the Aoi Matsuri, which is still held today. This colorful festival entails a procession from the Imperial Palace, first to the Shimogamo Shrine to the northeast of the Palace grounds, and then on to the Kamigamo Shrine located in the northern outskirts of the city. This festival can also be interpreted as something symbolizing the close relationship between the capital and its environs, particularly during the Heian period.

Later during the mediaeval times, a number of Zen temples and monasteries were established on the outskirts of the capital, particularly in the foothills of the surrounding mountains, consistent with the philosophical background of this new branch of Buddhism. Such religious establishments were sometimes set up on the former sites of such ancient villas. Two of the most well known are the Kitayamadono villa of Ashikaga Yoshimitsu which became the location for Rokuonji Temple, better known today as Kinkakuji, and the Higashiyamadono villa of Ashikaga Yoshimasa providing the site of Jishoji Temple, now known commonly as Ginkakuji. What remained of the expansive gardens of these villas was inherited by the following generations and these areas of arranged nature became a piece of cultural, environmental heritage layered with history.

The areas of Saga and Arashiyama on the western flank of the city are even today famous for their cherries, many of which were moved from Yoshino, south of Nara. This well known episode is documented in a collection of stories entitled *Godai Teio Monogatari*, and in the introduction written by the retired Emperor Gosaga to a collection of *waka*, or traditional songs going under the title of *Zoku Kokin Wakashu*.

If, as it seems likely that cherry trees had already been moved to Arashiyama by the middle of the thirteenth century, it means that the concept of actually manipulating landscape for effect, already existed at that time. The tradition of this kind of 'landscape gardening' was certainly not artificial but was much more of a tradition of 'creating landscape in the manner of nature' and these areas now constitute part of a heritage which lives on in the outskirts of Kyoto today.

Osawa Pond 大沢池

Arashiyama Shungyo-zu by Maruyama Okyo, 1780　嵐山春暁図　円山応挙筆（安永九年）逸翁美術館所蔵

洛中と洛外——京都は周囲の自然環境とともに成り立っている

16世紀中期から17世紀にかけて、京の町の全体を俯瞰して描いた洛中洛外図屏風が作成された．都市の全体像が日本の絵画において中心的主題となった最初の時期といってよいだろう．この頃、都市というものの全体像が初めてイメージされたのであった．

洛中洛外図には多くの興味深い情報が描きこまれている．中でも先ず、都市の図とはいえ、それが市街地である「洛中」でなく、「洛中」と、郊外の「洛外」の双方を描いた図であったことに注目したい．京という都市の全体像は、都市部と周辺の野山の、両者が一体のものとして把握され、イメージされたのであった．京を囲む三山の自然と、その麓に分布する諸社寺、緑ゆたかな田園地帯、それらなしに京はイメージされることはなかったのである．

もうひとつの注目される大きな特質は、洛中洛外図では一つの図の中に一年の祭事や行事と四季とが描き込まれたことである．都市をイメージし表現するとき、一年という時間と、移り変わる自然の四季もまた欠くことのできない要素だったのである．その四季は、洛中での諸行事によっても表現されるが、桜・楓の鮮やかな洛外の自然風景にいっそうよく味わうことができる．

洛中洛外図では、遠くにあるはずの郊外の社寺や景観が洛中の町なみのすぐ近くに接近して描かれているのに驚かされる．洛外の地点と洛中との間に金雲を配置して、その間の空間と距離を一気に省略し、町から手が届くほどの位置に洛外の名所を描き出す．洛中と洛外を実際より極端に近づけて描写するという特徴は、全ての洛中洛外図に見られる．人々の意識において、洛外は洛中に近しい存在であったと解釈すべきだろう．

したがって、いま、京都という都市のもつ景観的特色を、歴史的な文脈の中でとらえようとするとき、私たちは「洛中」と「洛外」の両者をみなくてはならない．

洛外の景観形成と継承の伝統

平安京建設以前から京都盆地には有力な豪族が開発を進めており、西に秦氏、北に加茂氏、東には高麗氏がいた．平安京が都市を囲む城壁を備えていなかったというよく知られた事実は、都がこれらの豪族の居住する平和な郊外地域に囲まれていたことを意味している．それだけではなく、皇族や貴族たちはすすんで都の郊外に別業や寺院を営んだのであった．西には嵯峨天皇の嵯峨院、源融の棲霞観、東の白川の地には白川院や六勝寺があったし、藤原頼道の別荘であった宇治の平等院など枚挙にいとまがない．

平安時代、「まつり」といえば葵祭を意味した．御所と上下の加茂神社を結んだ華やかな行列は、平安京とその郊外の密接な関係を象徴するものと読みとることもできよう．

中世になると、新興の禅宗寺院が次々に京の郊外に、特に山麓部に建立された．古代の別荘跡地にも寺院が営まれ、足利義満・義政の別荘北山殿・東山殿もそれぞれ鹿苑寺（金閣寺）・慈照寺（銀閣寺）の寺院となった．広大な苑地の跡地はその面影を残しつつ後の時代に継承されていったのである．庭園すなわち自然を素材にした文化的環境が継承され蓄積し次第にひろがっていった．

嵯峨・嵐山の桜は、吉野から移したと伝えられて名高い．『五代帝王物語』に「さて院（後嵯峨院）は西郊亀山の麓に御所を立て、亀山と名付、常に渡らせ給ふ．大井川嵐の山にはよしの山の桜を移し植えられたり．自然の風流求めざるに眼をやしなふ．まことに昔より名をえたる勝地とみえたり．」とある．また、『続古今和歌集　巻第二』の後嵯峨上皇の次の和歌の前書きも同じく桜の移植を伝えている．

「亀山の仙洞に吉野山の桜をあまた移し植ゑはべりしが花の咲けるを見て
　春ごとに思ひやられし三吉野の
　　花はけふこそ宿に咲きけれ　後嵯峨上皇」

13世紀中頃にはすでに嵐山に桜が移されていたか、少なくともそういう説があって、景色を作り演出するという概念は存在したことになる．このような景色をつくる伝統、といってもいかにも人工的な景色ではなく「自然の風流求めざる」ような景色を演出する伝統が、京都の洛外に受け継がれた．

Rakuchu Rakugai Relationships
Rakugai Landscape and Zen Temples
禅宗寺院の十境と洛外の風景

Oigawa River from Togetsukyo Bridge 渡月橋から望む大堰川

When considering the development and make-up of the natural landscapes on the outskirts of Kyoto, we must look in detail at the compositional elements of a Zen temple. They are made up of a number of elements known variously as *jikkyo* or *kyochi*, literally "ten stages" which are, as we shall see later, landmarks impregnated with meaning.

In Kyoto these elements were first established at the Higashiyama Kenninji Temple. It was in the Muromachi period (1473-1568) that a high-priest from Sung China visiting the court of Japan, moved on orders of the Godaigo Emperor from Kamakura to Kenninji Temple where he established what was known as the Higashiyama Jikkyo. Included in this composition apart from the more usual built temple facilities were such things as Mount Kiyomizu, the Gojo Bridge across the Kamo River, and the river itself, although they were all given Chinese-style names. Mount Kiyomizu is actually 1.5 km from the Kenninji Temple and the Kamo River and the Gojo Bridge were features of the view which could be seen from the temple.

Then, some ten years later in the Spring of 1346, Muso Kokushi - the posthumous name of Soseki (1276-1351), who founded Tenryuji Temple in Arashiyama to the west, established the Kameyama Jikkyo associated with this temple. These later became the most famous compositional elements of all those used in the arrangement of the environment of the many Zen temples and monasteries which were subsequently founded. In the case of Tenryuji Temple, the ten meaningful landmarks were: *Fumyokaku* - the Sanmon or main gate; *Zesshokei* - Oigawa River (Hozugawa River); *Reihibyo* - the Chinju Hachimangu Shrine; *Sogenchi* - the lotus pond in front of the priest's quarters; *Nengerei* - the summit of Mount Arashiyama; *Togetsukyo* - the bridge across the Oigawa River; *Sankyugan* - the stone over which the Tonase Falls tumbled on Mount Arashiyama; *Banshodo* - the pine forest on the southern slopes of the mountain; *Ryumontei* - a shelter on the banks of the Oigawa River from where the Tonase Falls could be viewed; and finally *Kichoto* - a pagoda-like tower on Mount Kameyama.

What is perhaps most important about all of these elements is the fact that even with the Togetsukyo Bridge, there are only five built structures, meaning that the remaining elements are all natural features.

First and foremost, such *jikkyo*, or meaningful landmarks represented the naming of elements from which the environment was composed. All the main features of the landscape were given new names, such as the way that Mount Arashiyama was called Nengerei, literally the "peak of the picked flower". The Togetsukyo Bridge which is now one of the popular attractions of Arashiyama was formerly known as Horinji-bashi and appears historically under that name as an identified element of the landscape.

Such naming, in other words, was a way of attributing specific meaning to the elements of the environment. The previously mentioned *nenge* of Nengerei, for instance, is derived from one of the teachings of Buddha, in which he uses a single flower as an example. This will be explained in more detail later, but this way of attributing meaning or significance to a scene, influenced the way in which people looked at and appreciated a landscape. An extreme example of this is the so-called Nangeto, literally the "tower of the south flower", which was one of the meaningful landmarks associated with Myoshinji Temple. The name was derived from the birthplace in China of the monk Rinzai and the pagoda of Toji Temple visible some distance to the south of Myoshinji was thus named and became understood as an element of Zen teachings.

These compositional elements of the landscape are therefore representative of the sense of culture there is embodied in what we fix our gaze on.

Another important point about these meaningful landmarks is the tradition for actually 'creating landscape'. In the case of the Kameyama Jikkyo of Tenryuji Temple, for instance, there is literary evidence to back up the fact that the choosing of elements was a way of formalizing landscape, as recorded in the *Taihei-ki*, a 41 volume chronicle covering the period from 1318 to 1368 and attributed to the monk Kojima, who died in 1374. Muso was actually responsible for artificially creating landscape, which included the moving and arranging of stones as well as the planting of trees: quite literally the art of landscape gardening. So even before the *Taihei-ki*, it would seem as though the *jikkyo* of Tenryuji Temple were understood in this way by Muso and others alive at the time, and it would seem reasonable to expect that they were also written about. Equally, it would not be unreasonable to say, therefore, that the establishment of such meaningful landmarks or compositional elements within the landscape also constituted a form of landscape gardening.

The same understanding of landscape composing elements which is apparent in the *Taihei-*

ki can also be found in the *Miyako Rinsen Meishou Zue*, a collection of illustrations of the more well-known scenes around Kyoto. The *jikkyo* landscape elements in this case are taken literally as meaning forests and springs - *rinsen* - and understood quite simply as landscape gardening. However, the *jikkyo* of Kenninji Temple and Sokokuji Temple are termed simply as *jikkei*, or "ten scenes". Then in the case of Myoshinji they are called *fukei*, or literally "landscapes". This way of understanding *jikkyo* as part of either a "garden" or a "landscape", was also evident within concepts of landscape during the 18th century, in the way that landscape was treated as a garden, in the way it was designed, and because of the way landscape was created.

But just what were these landscape elements for and why should they have been directly associated with Zen temples and monasteries?

It is said that apart from the Sutras and religious dogma of Buddhism, the part played by unwritten and unexplained teachings in which the essence of Buddhism is passed from a priest to his disciples in the way that Buddha did simply by example, is fundamental to Zen teachings and is summed up by *furyu monji kyoge betsuden*. This can perhaps be more easily understood in a highly abbreviated form as "what the mind thinks, the heart transmits". Muso founded his selection of elements for the Tenryuji Temple Kameyama Jikkyo on such Buddhist esoteric teachings creating what was referred to as "a place of esoteric teachings", or *Kyoge Betsugyo no Ba*, in a chronicle of the life of Muso - *Muso Kokushi Nenpu*. (The final character of *betsugyo* here is possibly a mis-transcription of the last character of *kyoge betsuden*. But as the original no longer exists it is impossible to confirm.)

The naming of Mount Arashiyama as the "peak of the picked flower" or Nengerei within the Kameyama Jikkyo, is suggestive of this particular method of association. But to understand this better we must consider one of the fables associated with the teachings of Buddha. Sitting before his disciples preaching, Buddha picked a single flower and showed it to them. This alone was enough for one of his followers to understand the significance of Buddha's teachings and a smile traced with the satisfaction of understanding rose upon the face of the disciple. This whole story is summed by the words *nenge misho* to which the name of Nengerei alludes.

Considered in this way, the "place of esoteric teachings" which was arranged by Muso at Tenryuji can perhaps be interpreted as a place directly communicating the teachings of Buddha, by inference rather than through words. If this is indeed the case, then such landscape elements are the very foundations upon which a Zen temple stands and it becomes clear that these temples, both as establishments of Zen teaching and academic learning, are not a reality simply because of the facilities and buildings standing in what we know as the temple compounds, but only become a reality when considered in conjunction with their surrounding environment.

The *jikkyo*, or meaningful landmarks are therefore part of a culturally appointed environment without which the Zen temples and monasteries would not be a reality and the surrounding natural environment and landscape was and integral part of that culturally appointed environment.

In fact, all of the main Zen temples in Kyoto had these landscape elements and any temples that were newly established during the Edo period were also provided with similar meaningful landmarks, many of which were located in the landscape outside of the temple compounds. Having been named and instilled with meaning, the environment was manipulated, even beautified in some respects and such places became famous enough for people to want to visit them. Such landscape elements as the Tsutenkyo Bridge and the valley under it known as Sengyokukan at Tofukuji Temple, were famous as places to view the autumn colors; and by the middle of the nineteenth century, large numbers of people from the Osaka area were making special visits to the temple specifically to see them. Nowadays, Saga and the Arashiyama areas of Kyoto are two of the most famous tourist attractions of the city.

Therefore, such places in the suburbs of Kyoto which have become famous and are traditionally recognized as highly meaningful landscape elements within the environment, are immensely important factors to be considered in any attempts that are made to develop and improve the landscape of the city now and in the future.

Such an attitude toward nature is evidence of how people down through history have sought to foster and arrange the natural environment to suit cultural and aesthetic inclinations, in a way that is different from the more functional manipulations of nature for the sake of agriculture and forestry. In actual fact, such trees as cherries and maples that would not normally grow well in the environs of Kyoto without a great deal of help, have been planted specifically to emphasize the changing of the seasons. A look at a present-day plant distribution map of the City of Kyoto, shows us that there are small pockets of various types of trees distributed around the edge of the Kyoto basin and it soon becomes evident just how much man has played a part in arranging this area of apparently natural vegetation. In the broadest sense, therefore, the environs of Kyoto developed as a 'garden' due to the attitude which was adopted toward nature, first during ancient and medieval times and then on through the Edo period until the present day.

Togetsukyo Bridge 渡月橋

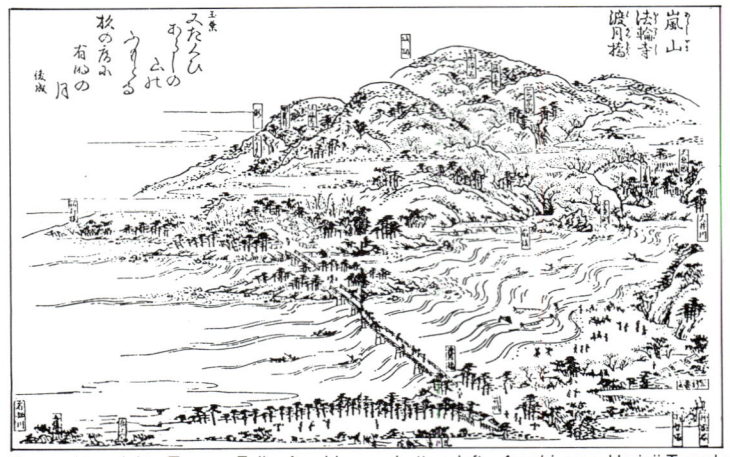

Top and top right - Tonase Falls, Arashiyama; bottom left - *Arashiyama*, Horinji Temple and Togetsukyo Bridge, *Miyako Meisho Zue*, 1780; bottom right - Togetukyo Bridge and Oigawa River during first half 19th century, *Arashiyamahana* by Inoue Kyuko

上・右／嵐山戸難瀬の滝
下・左／嵐山・法輪寺・渡月橋 『都名所図会』 安永九年刊
下・右／19世紀前期の渡月橋と大堰川 井上九皐筆 嵐山花

郊外の自然的景観の形成という観点からみるとき、禅宗寺院の立地について注目したい事実がある。禅寺の境内域を構成する「十境」あるいは「境致」と呼ばれるものの成立である。

京都で最初に十境を定めたのは東山建仁寺であった。時は室町時代初期、宋から来朝した清拙正澄は、後醍醐天皇の勅により鎌倉から京の建仁寺に移り、そこで「東山十境」を定めた。その中に寺院の施設とともに、「清水山」と、「第五橋」「鴨川水」と中国風の名で五条大橋と鴨川が入っている。清水山は建仁寺から1.5キロメートル離れているし、五条大橋と鴨川も寺院から眺望される景観要素であった。

それからおよそ十数年後の貞和二年(1346)春、嵐山に天竜寺を創建した夢窓国師が「亀山十境」を定めた。これは後年、多くの禅寺が定めた十境の中でもっとも有名な十境になった。

普明閣：山門
絶唱渓：大堰川
霊庇廟：鎮守八幡宮
曹源池：方丈前の蓮池
拈華嶺：嵐山の峰
渡月橋：大堰川の橋
三級巌：嵐山の戸難瀬の滝を落とす岩
万松洞：当山南の松林
龍門亭：大堰川畔にあった戸難瀬の滝を望む亭
亀頂塔：亀山の頂の塔

ここでも注目されるのは、このうち建造物は渡月橋をいれても五つであり、他は自然の要素だということである。

十境とは先ず、環境の構成要素に命名することであった。嵐山を拈華嶺と言いかえるなど、すべて新たに命名しなおしている。現在も観光で有名な「渡月橋」は旧名を「法輪寺橋」といったが、このとき十境のひとつとして命名されて歴史に登場した。

命名するとは、環境に意味を与えることであった。「拈華」という語は、釈迦が一輪の華を見せて教えを説いた故事にちなんでいる。景観に意味を与えることは、人の景観の見方に影響する。極端な例は妙心寺の十境に挙げられた「南華塔」で、これは臨済の故郷の名をとったものだが、妙心寺から遠く南方に眺望された東寺の五重塔を、身勝手にというべきか、禅宗的な景観に読み変えたものだ。視線そのものに文化性があることを、十境は示している。

もうひとつ十境が注意を引く点は、「風景を造る」という伝統である。先の、天竜寺亀山十境に関する『太平記』の記述を、ここで読みなおしてみよう。「この開山國師、天性水石に心を寄せ、浮萍の跡を事としたまひしかば、水に傍ひ山に依り、十境の景趣を造られたり。」とあった。十境とは景趣、景色の趣であり、それは夢窓国師によって人為的に造られたものであったという。さらに、「この十景のその上に、石を集めては烟嶂の色を仮り、樹を植ゑては風涛の声を移す。」と記している。ここでは「十景」と言いかえているのが注目される。そして、石を集めて配置する、植樹する、と文字どおり造園を行ったと伝えている。『太平記』の成立は応安三年(1370)頃以前とされるから、夢窓国師と同時代人によって、天竜寺の十境がこのように理解され、書かれたと考えてよいであろう。十境とは造園された景観であったといえるだろう。

十境について、『太平記』と同様の理解を示しているのが『都林泉名勝図会』である。十境が「林泉」の書に紹介されたこと、これは言いかえれば十境が林泉すなわち「庭園」という範疇で理解されていた、少なくとも庭園に関わるものとして理解されていたことを示している。ところが一方では、建仁寺と相国寺の十境が「十景」と変化して記され、

Sogen Pond at Tenryuji Temple against a backdrop of Arashiyama　天竜寺曹源池と嵐山

Kameyama *Jikkyo* associated with Tenryuji Temple, selected by Muso Kokushi, in 1346.
天竜寺の亀山十境　夢窓国師が貞和二年に選定した．

1. 普明閣：三門　Fumyokaku: Main Gate
2. 絶唱渓：大堰川　Zesshokei: Oigawa River
3. 霊庇廟：鎮守八幡宮　Reihibyo: Chinju Hachimangu Shrine
4. 曹源池：方丈前の蓮池　Sogen-ike: Lotus Pond in front of the priest's quarters
5. 拈華嶺：嵐山の峰　Nengerei: Summit of Mt. Arashiyama
6. 渡月橋：大堰川の橋　Togetsukyo: Togetsukyo Bridge
7. 三級巌：嵐山の戸難瀬の滝　Sankyugan: Tonase Falls
8. 万松洞：門前の松の木　Banshodo: Pine Forest on southern slopes of Mt. Arashiyama
9. 龍門亭：大堰川畔にあった音無瀬の滝を望む亭　Ryumontei: Shelter from which to view the Tonase Falls
10. 亀頂塔：亀山の頂の塔　Kichoto: Pagoda on Mt. Kameyama

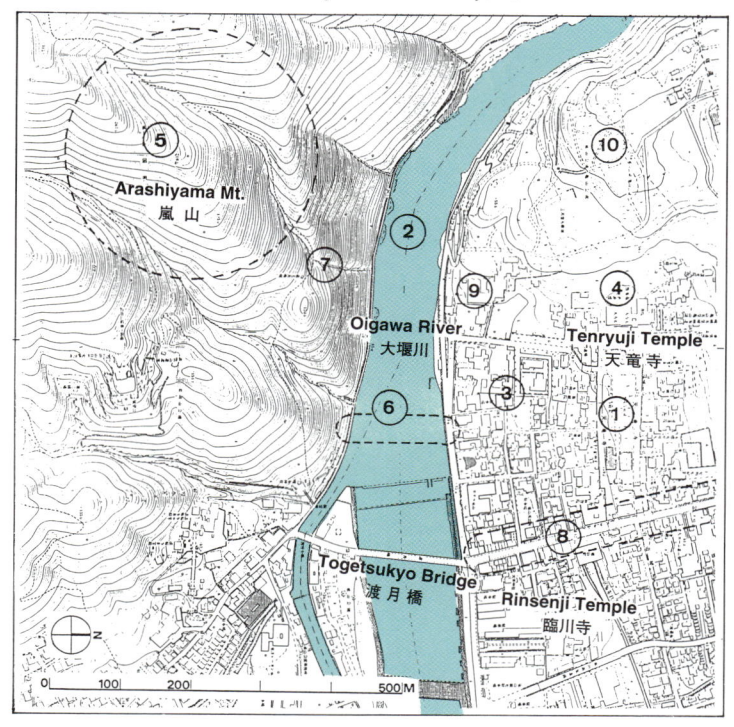

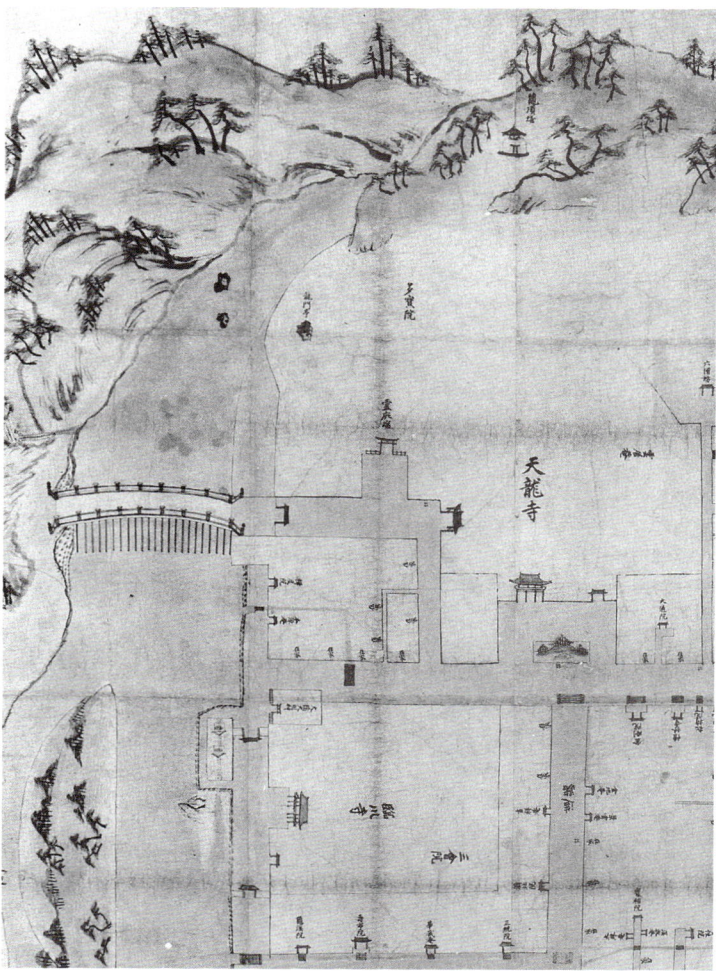

Oeikinmeiezu dating from 1426 showing the environs of Tenryuji Temple at the begining of the Muromachi period.
応永鈞命絵図　応永三十三年　天竜寺所蔵　龍門亭，亀頂塔，渡月橋などが描かれている．

寺院 Temple	峰・山 Mountain	川・峡 River	橋 Bridge	池水 Pond	岩・洞 Rock	建築施設 Buildings				その他 Other
南禅寺 Nanzenji	獨秀峰 半角嶺			拳龍池	帰雲洞	蘿月庵 愈好亭	曇華堂 (法堂)		鎮春亭 蘆萱林	綾戸廟
天竜寺 Tenryuji	拈華嶺 [嵐山]	絶唱溪 [大井川]	渡月橋	曹源池 [方丈蓮池]	三級巌 [戸難瀬瀧] 萬松洞 [南松林]	普明閣 [山門] 亀頂塔 [亀山山頂塔]	龍門亭 [戸難瀬瀧対岸]		霊庇廟 [鎮守八幡]	
相國寺 Shokokuji			天界橋 (蓮池)	功徳池 (蓮池) 龍淵水		祝釐堂 (輪堂) 覚雄寶殿	護國廟 (鎮守八幡) 妙荘巌	國通閣 (山門閣)	洪音楼 (鐘楼)	般若林 (総門前壇)
建仁寺 Kenninji	清水山	鴨川水	第五橋			慈視閣 (方丈上閣) 入定塔 (開山塔)	望闕楼 (山門之上) 神楽廟 (鎮守此神)	大悟堂 (僧堂)	群玉林 (衆寮)	無尽灯 (在禅居隠)
東福寺 Tofukuji		洗玉澗	通天橋	思遠池 (蓮池) 甘露水		妙雲閣 (山門) 潮音堂	選仏場 (僧堂) 成就宮		栢壇林 (衆寮)	千松休
等持寺 Tojiji				芙蓉池		清晏斎 (方丈) 妥帖庵 八講堂	香雲亭 (書院) 観音殿 故卿所寶雲閣		宗鏡堂 (僧堂) 聴雨	聚星 (衆寮) 万年松
興聖寺 Koshoji	六国見 (主山)			白鷺池 (面前蓮池) 妙香池 (正続院前)	虎頭岩	華厳塔 (在黄梅院) 法雲閣 (山門)	選仏場 (僧堂) 大光明法殿 (仏殿)		平等軒 (方丈) 妙荘厳域	直指庵 (法堂)
妙心寺 Myoshinji	萬歳山 [仁和寺山] 鶏足嶺 [北山]	宇多河 [東流]	度香橋 [南門前]	高安灘		百花堂 [玉鳳院内] 拈華室 [開山塔]	斎宮社		南華塔 [東寺塔]	旧籍田 [寺内花園]

十境の各要素の下の（ ）内は『和漢禅刹次第』（15世紀中頃）記載の説明，［ ］内は『山城名勝志』（正徳元年1711刊）記載の説明を示す．

Zen Temple *Jikkyo* 禅宗寺院の十境

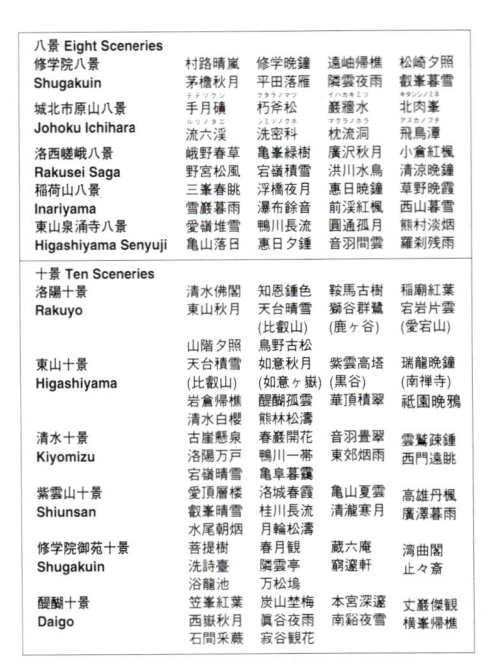

八景 Eight Sceneries				
修学院八景 Shugakuin	村路晴嵐 茅檐秋月	修檐晩鐘 平田落雁	遠岫帰樵 隣雲夜雨	松崎夕照 戴雪暮巌
城北市原山八景 Johoku Ichihara	手月磧 流六溪	朽斧松 (クラリノマツ) 洗密科 (ルリノタニ)	巌櫃水 (イハヒツミヅ) 枕流洞	北肉峯 (アカニクフチ) 飛鳥澤
洛西嵯峨八景 Rakusei Saga	嵯野春草 野宮松風	亀峯積雲 岩嶺晴雪	廣沢秋月 洪川水鳥	小倉紅楓 清凉晩鐘
稲荷山八景 Inariyama	三峯春個 雪巌暮月	浮嶺夜月 瀑布餘音	惠日映鐘 前溪紅葉	草野晩霞 西山淡烟
東山泉涌寺八景 Higashiyama Senyuji	亀山落日	惠日夕鐘	圓通孤月 音羽間雲	羅林残雨
十景 Ten Sceneries				
洛陽十景 Rakuyo	清水佛閣 東山晴雪 (比叡山)	知恩鐘色 天台晴雲 (比叡山)	鞍馬古樹 獅谷群松 (鹿ヶ谷)	稲庵紅葉 岩倉片雲 (愛宕山)
東山十景 Higashiyama	山階夕照 天台積雪 (比叡山) 岩倉帰樵 清水白櫻	鳥部古松 如意秋月 (如意ヶ嶽) 醍醐孤雲 熊林松濤	紫雲高塔 華頂積雲 (黒谷) 春巌開花	瑞雲晩鐘 (南禅寺) 祇園晩鴉
清水十景 Kiyomizu	古崖懸泉 陽陽万戸 岩嶺晴雲	春巌開花 鴨川一帯 亀阜碁翠	音羽疊雲 東郊烟雨	雲鷲疎鐘 西門遠眺
紫雲山十景 Shiunsan	愛頂層霞 叡峯飛嵐 水尾朝烟	洛城晴霞 桂川長流 月輪松濤	亀山夏雲 清麓寒月	高雄丹楓 廣澤暮雨
修学院御苑十景 Shugakuin	菩提樹 洗詩臺 浴龍池	春月観 隣雲亭 万松場	蔵六庵 窮翠軒	湾曲閣 止々斎
醍醐十景 Daigo	笠峯紅葉 西獄秋月 石間采蕨	炭山琺梅 眞谷夜雨 寂谷観杞	本宮深邃 南蹈夜雪	文巌傑観 横峯帰樵

Eight and Ten Scenes from *Kyo Habutae*, 1685
京羽二重（貞享二年）記載の 八景・十景

Oigawa River and Mt. Kameyama 大堰川と亀山

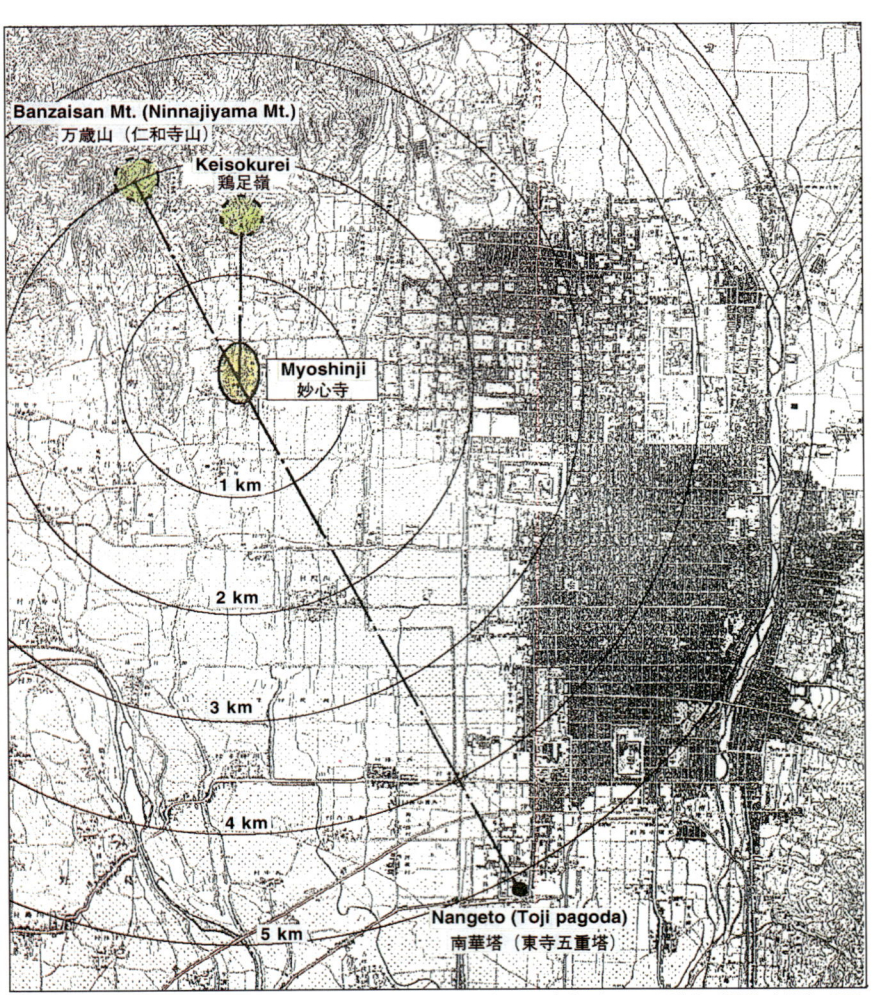

Relationship between Myoshinji Temple and its *jikkyo* 妙心寺とその十境に含まれる万歳山，鶏足嶺，南華塔の関係

Relationship between Kenninji Temple and its *Jikkyo*
建仁寺の東山十境に含まれていた鴨川，第五橋，清水山の位置関係

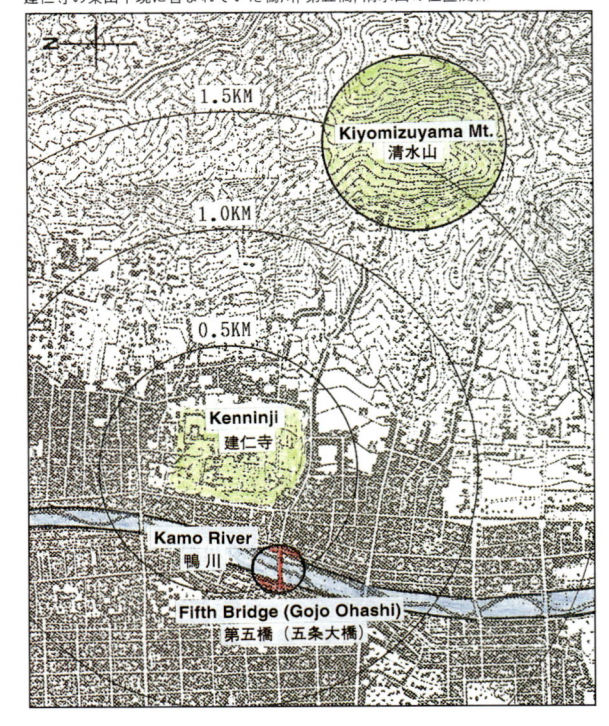

The view from Gohoro, the Main Gate of Nanzenji Temple　南禅寺．境致として五鳳楼と呼ばれた三門より望む

妙心寺では「当山に十境の風景あり」と記されている．このことは，十境とは「庭園」であり，また同時に「風景」でもあるという理解が，江戸時代中期にもなされていたというべきであろう．庭園としての風景，デザインされた風景，生み出された風景という概念がそこには存在したのである．

「十境」と呼んだのには「八景」の影響もあった．八景は中国の北宋末の画家宋迪が，平沙落雁，遠浦帰帆，山市晴嵐，江天暮雪，洞底秋月，瀟湘夜雨，烟寺晩鐘，漁村夕照からなる瀟湘八景図を描いたことから出た風景の見方で，風景を時間，天候，季節と結び付けて鑑賞する．『京羽二重』（貞享二年（1685）刊）が紹介する八景・十境によれば，京都では八景と十境の概念が混同されながら存在した．

ところで，何のために十境は作られたのか．なぜ，それは禅宗寺院で行われたのだろうか．

夢窓国師は「亀山十境」の選定をもって「教外別行之場」と為したとある（『夢窓国師年譜』）．禅宗とは「不立文字，教外別伝」をその根元的立場としてきた宗教であるといわれ，これは「経典・教説とは別に，釈迦以来，師の心から弟子の心へ直接，仏法そのものが受け伝えられた，という禅宗の主張」と説明される．「教外別伝」とは一字違い「教外別行」と写本されて伝わっているが，原書のない今日では誤写か否かは確かめようはない．また，亀山十境で嵐山を拈華嶺と呼びかえているのも，これと同じ意味を示唆する．「拈華微笑（ネンゲミショウ）」という語があり，禅宗ではこれも釈迦の故事にちなんで「教外別伝」と同じ意味を表すものとされている．拈華とは花をつまむことで，弟子たちを前に法を説かずただ一本の花を手にとって示し，弟子の摩訶迦葉ひとりが意を悟って微笑んだという故事を指す語である．これを考慮しても，夢窓国師が十境をもって「教外別伝」のための場，いいかえれば言葉を用いずして仏法を直接伝承する場とした，という意に解釈することが許されるだろう．とすれば，十境は禅宗寺院の存立基盤にほかならず，宗教の場，当時の学問の場としての禅寺が，今日いうところの境内とその建築施設のみから成るのでなく，周囲の環境とともにあってこそ成立するものであることがここに表明されている，といってよいだろう．

十境とは，禅宗寺院を成立させる文化的環境であり，それは周囲の自然環境，自然景観が混然として含まれる文化的環境であった．

京都の主だった禅寺にはおよそ全て十境があったし，江戸時代になっても京都の新たな禅寺には十境が定められた．その多くは境内からそとの風景を含んでいた．命名され，意味を与えられた環境は，美しくという表現は不適切かもしれないが，手を入れ育てられ，名所として，観光地として有名な存在になっていった．

紅葉で有名な東福寺の「通天橋」も，その下の「洗玉澗」という谷も十境の要素であった．幕末の頃には大阪方面からも多数の見物人が訪れる名所となっていた．そして，嵯峨嵐山は今では京都で最も多くの観光客が集まる名所である．京都郊外の代表的な名所が，十境の伝統をもって形成されたものでもあったことは，今後の景観整備を進めるにあたって示唆するところがあるはずであろう．

自然にたいするこうした態度から，永い歴史のうちに，やがて農耕あるいは林業といった生活のために自然に手を加えるだけでなく，また，文化的な美的な趣向に合うように景観を育てつくっていくようになったようである．じっさい，京都の周辺域では手入れをしないと育ちにくい桜や楓などが各所に植えられ季節を演出している．時代は現代にまで飛ぶが，京都府植生地図をみると，京都盆地の周辺部は特に多様な植生の細かい分布がみられ，この地域が自然といっても人工的な様相を色濃く示していることがわかる．古代・中世に端を発した態度が江戸時代を通じて広い意味で庭園的とも呼べるような郊外を形成し，現代に継承されているといってよいだろう．

Above, middle, bottom - Nanzenji Temple
上・中・下／南禅寺

Nanzenji Temple; *Miyako Meisho Zue* 南禅寺 『都名所図会』
十境のうちの「獨秀峰 Dokushuho」(1),「羊角嶺 Yokakurei」(2), 和漢禅刹次第 に境地として挙げられた
「神仙佳境 Shinsenkakyo」(3),「五鳳楼 Gohoro」(4), の名称を記している.

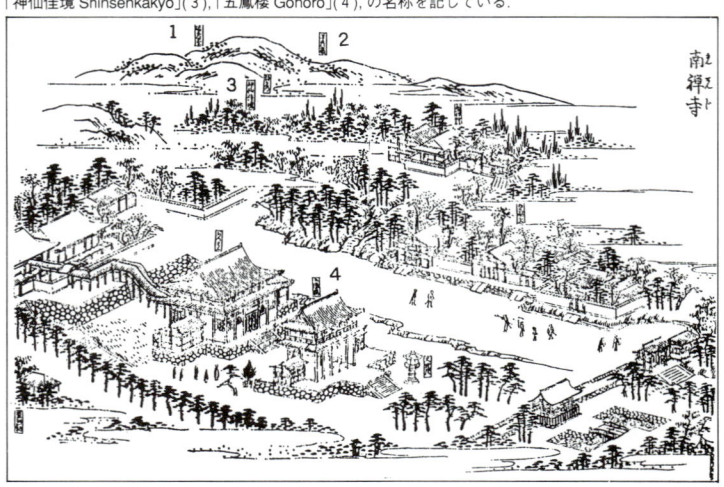

Buddha Hall, Tofukuji Temple　東福寺仏殿

Gaunkyo Bridge, Tofukuji Temple　東福寺臥雲橋

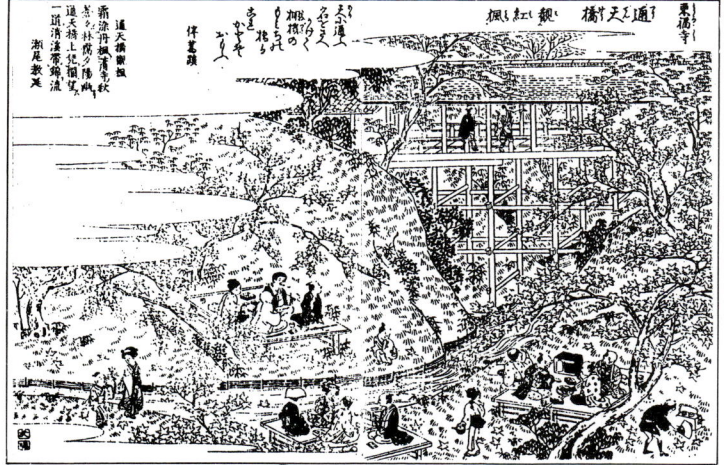

Tsutenkyo Bridge at Tofukuji Temple; *Miyako Rinsen Meishou Zue* 1799
18世紀末の東福寺通天橋　『都林泉名勝図会』　寛政十一年刊

Tsutenkyo Bridge, Tofukuji Temple　東福寺通天橋

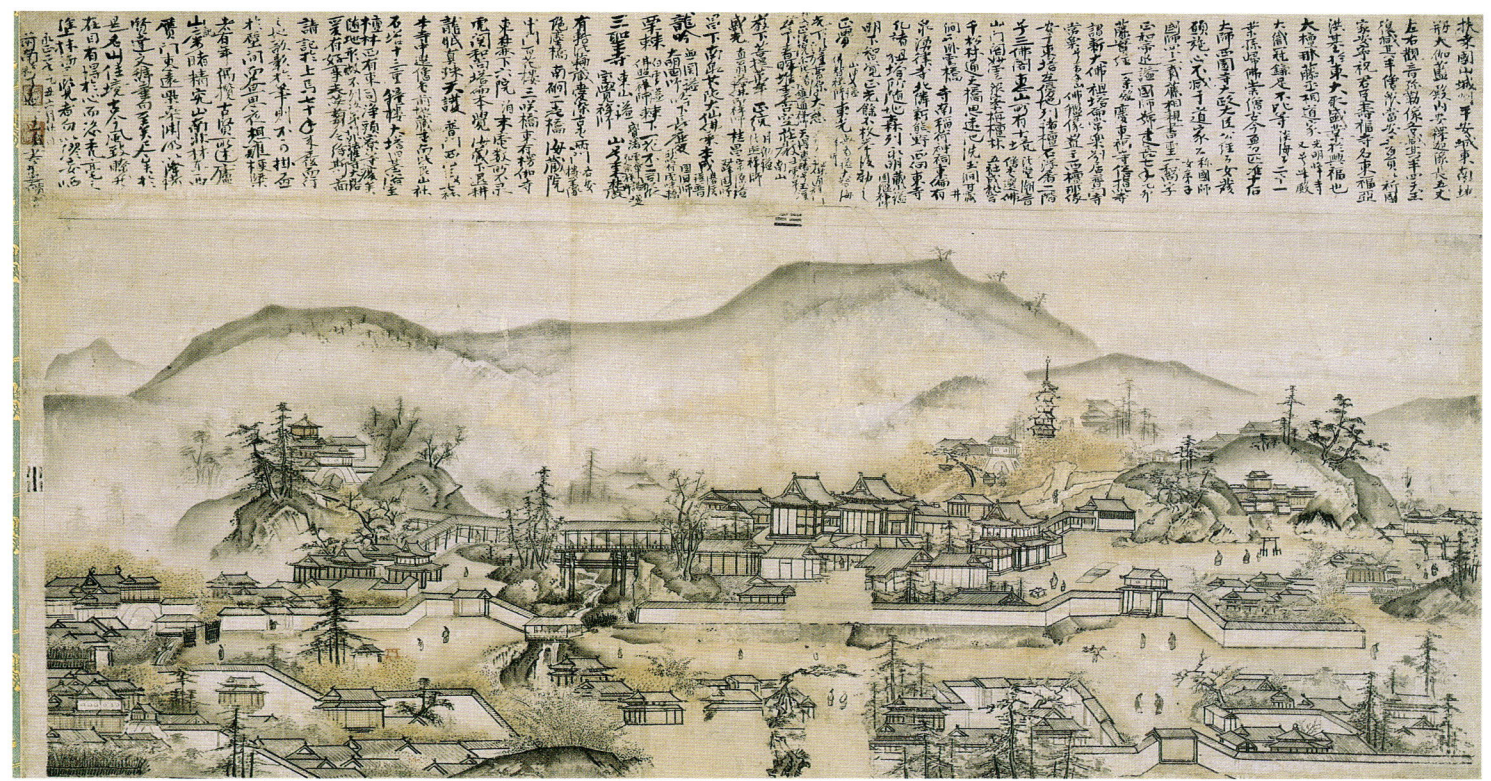

Site plan of Tofukuji Temple attributed to Sesshu, Muromachi period　東福寺伽藍図　伝雪舟筆　室町時代　京都国立博物館所蔵

Rakuchu Rakugai Relationships
Sagano - Symbolic Landscapes
嵯峨野

HamachouYusho from Saga Hakkei - "Eight Scenes of Saga" by Tomita Keisen
嵯峨八景より　浜町夕照
1919 冨田渓仙筆　個人蔵

Sagano is an expansive area located in the northwest of Kyoto. It is bounded on the east by Uzumasa, on the west by the foothills of Mount Ogurayama, and stretches from the foothills of Kami Sagano in the north to the waters of the Katsura River - the continuation of the Oigawa River - in the south.

It has attracted poets for centuries and while it is praised for its rural atmosphere in such works as Makura no Soshi, Sagano is perhaps most appealing for its landscapes which are modified and enhanced by the changing seasons.

It was the environmental psychologist, W. H. Ittelson, who said that up to a point, people all over the world use literature as a way of looking at the environment. We, too, should therefore consider the landscapes of Sagano and their symbolism, which will perhaps provide us with the key to understanding how to appreciate and maintain landscape rich in history and quality.

Symbolization of Landscapes in Sagano
According to historical documents, Sagano became an Imperial hunting ground from soon after the capital was moved to Kyoto. Seeing also that the area had already become much liked by the court, villas including Sagain of the Emperor Saga, and those originally built for Minamoto Toru and Prince Kenmei were also maintained in the area. It was these villas which later became temples in the true sense of the word and it is these which have come down to us today. But in addition to this, Sagano was also known as a place for those who wanted to retreat from the world. The calm and tranquility which Sagano offered such people was equally receptive to outcasts and this in turn fostered many legends and romantic fantasies in later years. In the A. D. 905 *Kokin Wakashu* collection of poems edited by Ki no Tsuryuki, and similarly in the *Sakaki* chapter of the *Genji Monogatari* dating from the eleventh century, references are made to Sagano, these being the first time that the area is mentioned in known literature. One example from the *Kokin Wakashu* gives us a good idea of how the landscape and atmosphere of Sagano were savored.

On a moonlit evening
The cry of the deer on Mount Ogurayama
Heralds the coming of Autumn

Yuzukiyo
Ogura no yama ni naku shika no
Koe no uchi niya Aki wa kuru ran

It is also a good example of how the expressions used by the writer provide us with a clear impression of Sagano.

References to this area can also be found in the *Shin-Kokin Wakashu*, another collection of poems edited by Fujiwara Teika, and in the *Heikei Monogatari*, both dating from the thirteenth century. But by now Sagano, is spoken of as somewhere with which the writers had a sense of affinity. The existence of the Adashino cemetery lent the area a sense of the transient and there are several poems in the *Shin-Kokin Wakashu* that refer to memories of the deceased, thus providing people with a chance to imagine various things in connection with the landscapes of Sagano. Furthermore, by writing a variation of an original poem by Ariwara no Yukihira, Fujiwara Teika achieves a layering of past time, referring to Sagano as a place of historical interest with admiration. The landscape, therefore, is already pregnant with references to other things and therefore also has a sense of symbolism.

References to Sagano made in Muromachi period Noh chants based on classical poems, take the impressions of the area created by past literature and handle them in a very calculated manner, and they are performed in a way peculiar to Noh theater. In the Noh play *Saigyo-Zakura*, the recluse and poet, Saigyo speaks of his doubt and confusion to a group of revelling cherry blossom viewers. The cherries take on meaning within Saigyo's literary world and then he expresses a very individual sense of mixed magnificences and solitude by making reference to an old, gnarled cherry tree. Sagano is, in other words, portrayed in this play as an area rich in literary symbolism by the impressions which are given of the cherries growing there and after this other places in Kyoto where there are cherries are enumerated. Thus the cherry trees are no longer simply trees but are natural elements invested with deep literary significance.

While the setting for *Saigyo-Zakura* takes place during the period in which Saigyo was alive, another Noh play entitled *Nonomiya* is a little different. Taking its title from the name of an area in Sagano, it is interesting as the setting for this play is an episode from the Tales of Genji. In this play, a travelling monk visits Nonomiya and while he is there he meets an old woman. At least that is what he thinks but actually she is the departed spirit of Rokujo no Miyasudokoro, one of the heroines from the Tales of Genji. The old woman then takes on the form of Rokujo no Miyasudokoro and performs

Nonomiya Shrine 野々宮

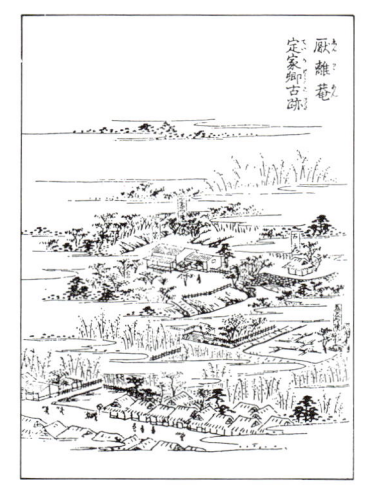

Scene from the Noh Play Nonomiya 能「野宮」京都新聞社提供
Left - Nonomiya Shrine; Right - Enrian; Miyako Meisho Zue
左／野宮神社, 右／厭離庵『都名所図会』

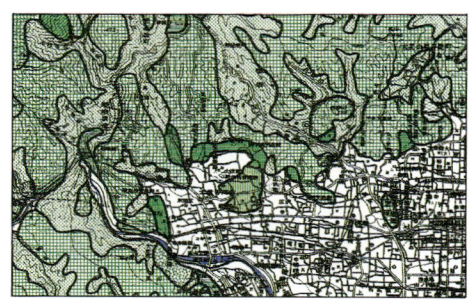

Trees and plant distribution map of Sagano 嵯峨野の植生分布図

Rakushisha 落柿舎

a dance, and thus reference is made to the Heian period in this play which is actually set in the Muromachi period. The monk had originally set-off on his travels in order to visit places of scenic beauty and historical interest which figured in literary works and it was the Noh actor Zeami who took this kind of trip as the setting for this drama. We might even say that he educated people through the medium of a Noh play, as to just how enjoyable it could be to visit such famous spots. The significance of the use of the spirit of Rokujo no Miyasudokoro was, therefore, in the way that it was used to personify the relationship between the landscape and its symbolic significance. And by employing past impressions of the area gained from a former literary work, the appreciation of nature was taken, in itself, as the main theme of the performance. We could also perhaps say that it is evidence an aspect of the medieval fascination with spirits and the occult, because of the way that a world with a strong sense of symbolism and history are portrayed in the one drama.

It would seem as though the way in which Zeami symbolized landscape by the use of literature in the plays he penned was actually an extreme eventuality. During the Edo period which followed, such places with inherent significance were enjoyed more simply as 'famous places'. In a poem composed by the poet Boncho at Rakushisha, the home of another poet, Mukai Kiyorai, Sagano becomes a place overflowing with the significance of the symbolism of its landscape in general and places of note.

Even the fields planted with beans
Wooden houses, too
Are places of beauty!

Mame ueru hatake mo
Kibeya mo
Meisho kana

In addition, it is a frank expression of the way that people understand the significance of something which is an integral, meaningful part of an area.

This particular poem appears in Basho's *Saga Nikki*, a dairy written while he was staying at Rakushisha. In it there are also factual or thoughtful references to three former sites of residences in the northern and southern parts of Sagano, once belonging to a woman know as Kogo. Basho, too, would visit such places of historical interest and, as if to satisfy the expectations of the visitor, he would do something in the way of bringing the location alive, to be consistent with the impressions of those people who had already been there. In the same dairy, he records the fact that he "planted a cherry tree to mark Kogo's tomb, which in the middle of a thicket near Sangenjaya". Later, in the *Miyako Meisho Zue*, a 'guidebook' with pictures to some of the more well know places in Kyoto published in 1780, it is recorded that the "Kogo cherry stands in the middle of a thicket, east of Sangenjaya, and to the north of Oigawa".

In this way, ancient literature influenced the way in which people in subsequent periods considered the elements of landscape and the environment as a whole, and landscape thus took on a symbolic significance due to the way it was recognized in a literary context. Zeami's plays were a direct expression of the symbolization of landscape. And today, this same phenomena offers us suggestions as to how to appreciate and maintain landscape. If, for example, buildings are to be put up in an environment with a rich historical background, simply trying to make them fit in with the surrounding historical townscape is not enough. Even if there were no surrounding townscape but if the location is one where there are views of areas with a rich cultural heritage, a design should be sought which is consistent with how such a landscape is appreciated, viewed and enjoyed.

嵯峨野は京都の西北部，東は太秦より西は小倉山々麓，北は上嵯峨の山麓より南は大堰川（桂川）に至る広い野である．

古来よりあまた歌人の心を強くひきつけ，『枕草子』の中で「野は嵯峨野，さらなり」と讃えられたこの地は，四季折々の情趣も加わってなにりも風景に心情を寄せられた地であった．

「どこの国でも，ある程度までは，文学を軸にして環境に対する見方ができている．」というW. H. イッテルソン（環境心理学者）の言葉は，これから嵯峨野とその風景と風景のもつ象徴性を考え，それによって我々がえられる質の高い歴史的な風景の維持と鑑賞のしかたを考える鍵となってくれる．

嵯峨野における風景の象徴化

京都に都が移されて間もなくの頃から嵯峨野は天皇の御狩場として史書にみえるが，その時すでに天下第一の景勝地として嵯峨院はじめ源融，兼明親王などが次々と別荘を営んだ．こうした別荘は主なきあと譲り受けられ寺院として今に残っている．また嵯峨野は同時に隠棲者の里でもあった．嵯峨野の静寂さはこうした世を捨てた人，世に入れられない人をも受けいれ，多くの伝説とロマンを後世に残した．次の10世紀初期に紀貫之の編纂した『古今和歌集』と11世紀はじめに完成した『源氏物語・賢木』では，歌に物語に嵯峨野が取り上げられた．嵯峨野が文学に取り上げられた最初期であった．「夕月夜　小倉の山に鳴く鹿の声のうちにや秋は来るらん（古今集　紀貫之）」この歌では文学は嵯峨野の風景を直接鑑賞し，作者の表現が鮮やかなイメージを嵯峨野に与えている．

13世紀に入ると『新古今和歌集』や『平家物語』に嵯峨野が登場するが，ここでは嵯峨野がすでに由縁のある地として描かれている．そうしてそれは嵯峨野に葬地化野があったことから無常感と結び付いて「有栖川おなじ流れはかはらねど見しや昔の影ぞわすれぬ」（新古今和歌集　中院右大臣）など風景に故人の昔を偲ぶという歌が数首あり，想像の契機としての風景が出現している．また，定家の「嵯峨の山　千代の古道のあととめてまた露分くる望月の駒」では，古跡としての嵯峨野が観賞されてあって，さらにこの歌は在原行平の歌を本歌とすることにより，二重に過去の時間を取り込んでいる．目の前にある風景は他との関係性すなわち象徴性をすでに示している．

室町時代の謡曲における嵯峨野の表現を見ると，過去の時代の文学がつくったイメージが極めて意識的に扱われ，能独特の雰囲気が演出されている．『西行桜』は賑やかな花見客の訪問に隠棲者西行が当惑する話であるが，桜を西行の文学的世界の中の桜として意味づけ，さらに老桜の精を登場させて寂しさと華やかさの混じった独特の趣を表現している．桜のそうしたイメージを嵯峨野という文学的象徴性に富んだ地によって演出した後に，その場所から京の他の桜の名所を列挙する．ここで桜は草木としての桜から文学的な深い意味をもった桜へと変わっていく．

『西行桜』の舞台は西行の生存時の時代設定であるのに対し，『野宮』は源氏物語の一節をとりながら舞台は能の演じられている同時代である点が注目される．

嵯峨野の野宮を訪れた旅僧が，そこで出会った老女と語らううちに，老女は実は他ならぬ六条御息所の亡霊であったことが明らかになり，姿を六条御息所に変えて舞いを舞う．室町時代の舞台に，平安時代の時間がこのとき一気に引き寄せられる．この旅僧は，早くも，文学の舞台となった古跡を訪ねる楽しみを求めて旅行をしていたし，世阿彌はこうした旅の仕方，名所の鑑賞のしかたを舞台の上で示した．名所の楽しみ方を教えたといってもよい．六条御息所の亡霊は，風景とその象徴的な意味の「関係」を体現するもので，過去の文学的イメージに導かれて自然を観賞するというそのこと自身を舞台状況として設定したわけであり，それによって象徴的な深みと時間的な奥行を併せもつ世界を表しているのも中世的「幽玄」の一面であろう．

世阿彌の謡曲において，文学による風景の象徴化という事象はひとつの究極に達したように思われる．江戸時代にはそうした意味を持つ場所が「名所」として好んで観賞された．凡兆の落柿舎に題すとした「豆植る畑も木部屋も名所哉」の句は，嵯峨野が由緒ある名跡すなわち風景の象徴的意味に溢れていたこと，また人々が何事にも意味を感じる見方がこの地で行われていたことの端的な表現であろう．この句を収めている芭蕉の嵯峨日記に，小督屋敷跡が上下の嵯峨野に三ヶ所ありいずれが真実かと思案する記述がある．芭蕉も文学的象徴としての古跡を訪ねようとしたのであり，そうした訪問者の期待に応えるべく，何人かが既にイメージに合わせて，今や風景の方を手直しし演出していたのであった．同日記に小督の「墓は三軒茶屋の隣，藪の中に有り．しるしに桜を植えたり．」

とあるが,『都名所図会』(1780年刊)にも「小督桜は大井川の北,三軒茶屋の東,薮の中にあり」と記されている.

古代の文学表現が,次の時代には風景の見方や鑑賞の仕方を方向付け,さらに風景が文学の古跡として象徴的な意味を持つに至った.世阿彌の謡曲は,実に,風景の象徴化の事象そのものを表現したのであった.さて,このことは現代の私たちに,風景の維持と鑑賞の仕方についても示唆を与えてくれる.歴史的環境で建築物を建てる場合,歴史的な町なみ景観に調和させるということだけでなく,たとえ周囲に町なみがなくとも,上で見たように,質の高い文化的な風景鑑賞の視線が作り上げられているような場所では,こうした風景の鑑賞の仕方,見方にふさわしい,イメージを支える意匠が求められるのである.

Osawa Pond　大沢池

The moon over Sagano　嵯峨野にかかる月

Deer on a moon lit light in Sagano　嵯峨野の月と鹿 『都名所図会』

Hirosawa Pond, *Miyako Meisho Zue*　広沢池 『都名所図会』

Rakuchu Rakugai Relationships
A Sense of Distance and Juxtaposition
洛中洛外の距離

In the vicinity of Ginkakuji depicted in *Nigatsu no koro* - February by Murakami Kagaku, 1911　銀閣寺付近　「二月乃頃」部分　村上華岳筆　1911　京都市立芸術大学資料館蔵

One day walking tour around Sagano from Keijo Shoran shown in red, and the route taken by Shiba Kokan shown in green.
『京城勝覧』の嵯峨野巡り一日観光コース(赤)と司馬江漢が一日で歩いたコース(緑)。ベースマップは明治20年測図仮製地形図.

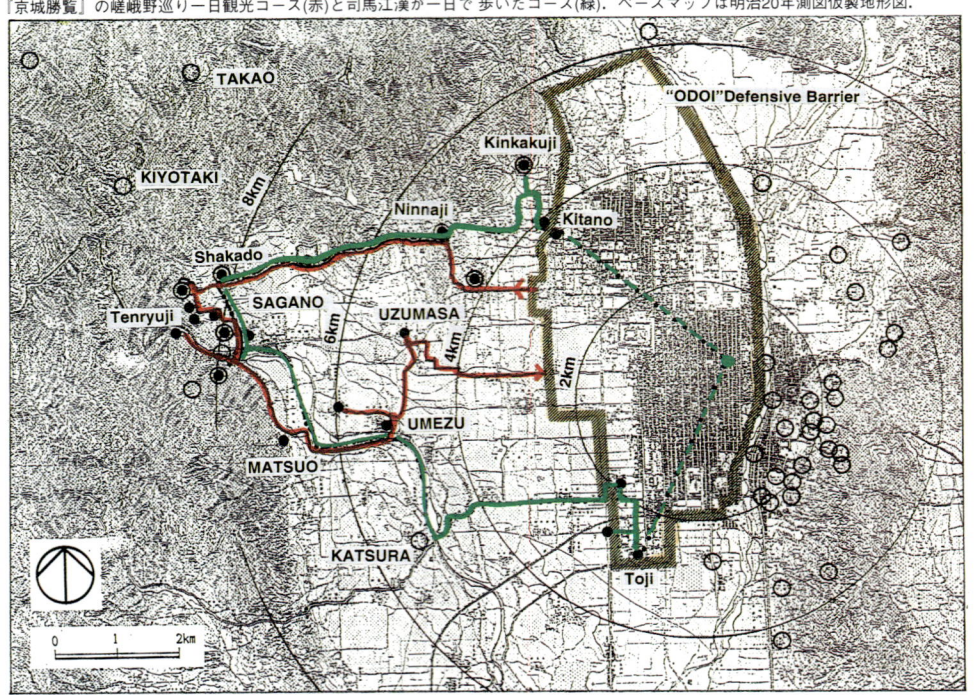

京名所案内記『京城勝覧』の一日観光順路

　江戸時代になると，早い時期から，京都の観光案内書が出版されるようになった.『都名所図会』のように当時のベストセラーになったものもあった.それらの中でいま『京城勝覧』が私たちの興味をひく，というのも，大方の書が町と名所旧跡を各々に紹介する形式によっているのにたいし，この案内書だけは，1日ごとに歩くべき観光順路を推奨する形式をとっているからである(36頁の表).

　私たちのように，自動車や鉄道といった機械的な交通手段の時代に生きる者は，近代以前の人々がどれほど歩くことができたかを，つい忘れがちである．ところで，『京城勝覧』は京都観光を17日間に設定し，それぞれの日に見るべき所を順に挙げて紹介し，1日で歩く経路を示している(35頁右の表)ので，昔の人の「歩く」という行為を再認識させるのである．この案内書の著者は学者としてよく知られている貝原益軒で，宝永三年(1706)の序があるが刊行されたのは享保三年(1718)であった．

One day walking tour route from Keijo Shoran by Kaibara Ekiken, 1718.
『京城勝覧』貝原益軒著,享保三年刊 一日観光コース. ベースマップは明治20年測図仮製地形図.

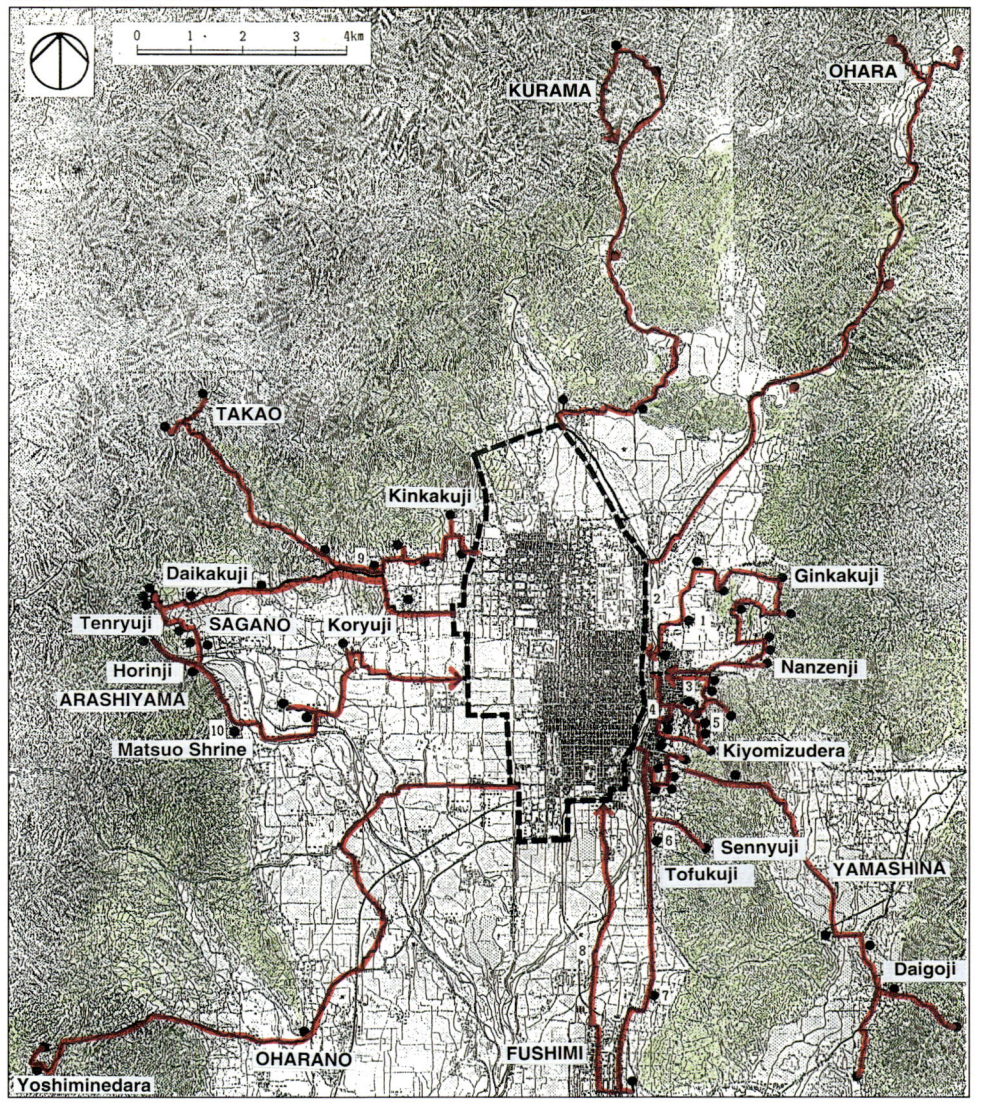

A Day in Kyoto

Sight-seeing guides to Kyoto began to be published from quite early on in the Edo period. In fact, the *Miyako Meisho Zue* was a 'best-seller' of its day. But from among these guides, the one known as the *Keijo Shoran* is of particular interest to us. This is because it was the only guidebook to recommend sight-seeing routes which could be covered in one day on foot, while most of the other guides simply introduced different areas of the city and places of historic interest and scenic beauty.

This guidebook was written by Kaibara Ekiken (1630-1714) who was a well known scholar. The Introduction is dated 1706, but the guide itself was not published until 1718. Ekiken was born in Fukuoka but he spent seven years studying in Kyoto when he was young and during his life-time, he visited the city more than twenty times. It would therefore seem as though he was particularly fond of Kyoto, especially considering the fact that travelling in those days was a great deal more difficult than it generally is today. The first thing which is particularly surprising about Ekiken's guide is the distances he expected people to be able to walk in one day. Several of the one-day walking tours he recommends have been marked up on a survey map dating from 1897 - *see page 33*. At the the end of last century, the population of Kyoto was in fact less than it had been during feudal times and the city had not grown much since then, except for the area which had developed to the east of the Kamo River. It is therefore quite easy to imagine from this map just what the routes Ekiken recommended were really like and what the actual relationship in terms of distance between the center of the city and its environs was like when Ekiken was alive.

The Odoi marked on this map was the defensive barrier constructed by Toyotomi Hideyoshi at the end of the sixteenth century. Although there were some variations in its size, it was generally three meters high and nine meters wide. It surrounded the main built-up area of the city and there is no doubting the fact that it was this barrier which made the people of Kyoto conscious of the relationship between the central part of the city and its immediate surroundings.

Let us now consider one of the walking tours in some detail, taking the one out to the Sagano area in the west of Kyoto as an example. This

益軒は京の人ではなかったが若い頃に7年間京で学んだことがあり，生涯に二十数回京都を訪れたというから，当時の旅の大変なことを考えるとよほど京が好きだったようである．私たちは郊外の美しい所へ行くのに車か電車を使うのがすっかり当たり前になっているので，益軒の推奨する1日観光の順路の長さ遠さにまず驚いてしまう．33頁の図で，明治二十年(1897)の実測地図上にその一日観光の順路のいくつかを描き込んでみた．明治二十年という時期には市街区域は鴨東の一部を除くと江戸時代からほとんど広がっておらず，人口は江戸時代より減少していたぐらいだから，この地図上で益軒の推奨した順路と洛中洛外の関係を想像してみることができるだろう．

地図上の太い破線の枠は「お土居」の位置を示している．これはいうまでもなく豊臣秀吉が16世紀末に建設したもので，所によってちがいはあったがおよそ高さ3m，幅は9mばかりの規模であった．これが市街地の周囲を取りまいて，京の人々に洛中と洛外の境界をはっきりと意識させることになったにちがいない．

いま，京の西方，嵯峨野見物の行程を例にとりあげてみよう．これは全体で17日間の観光日程のうちの第7日目に設定されている．道のりはおよそ五里半(約22km)あり，上下の嵯峨は見所が多いので朝早く出るのがよいと書いている．以下にこの案内書があげた見所を順に，また説明のうち興味深い点のあるものを適宜とりあげながらみてみよう．江戸時代の観光がどういうものだったか，また益軒が観光についてどういうセンスをもっていたのか，いくらか想像できるかもしれない．

まず，嵯峨にゆく道中で訪ねる所としてあげているのは，

内野．妙心寺．仁和寺：ここの八重ざくらは京随一，吉野の山桜に匹敵するもので，毎年花見の客多く，花の好きな人は始中終と三度見るのがよい（とすすめていて益軒自身相当桜好きだったことをうかがわせている）．

次に嵯峨の名所としてあげているのは，

大沢の池．名社の滝の跡．嵯峨釈迦堂．往生院：妓王妓女のこもった寺．三宝寺：滝口入道のこもった寺．二尊院．小倉山．野々宮．天竜寺．大堰川．嵐山．むかし吉野の桜の種を移した所で，花盛りの頃は人出がおびただしい．臨川寺：前に大堰川があり景色がよく，付近の薮の中に（平家物語の）小督の庵の跡がある．法輪寺：近年，十三参りといって三月十三日に13才になる都の男女が多数参詣する．櫟谷．大悲閣．松尾．梅津．梅宮．これから帰り道に太秦を見るとよく，広隆寺があり，太秦の東に木の島明神（蚕の社）がある．

司馬江漢の嵯峨野めぐりの道

『京城勝覧』の紹介した名所めぐりは，じっさいにそれだけ歩く人がなかったほど遠い行程を書いたのでは決してなかったようだ．西洋画の先駆者であった画家，司馬江漢が一人の旅行者として嵯峨野を訪ねた行程は，じっさい，益軒の行程より長

route was arranged for day seven of the whole 17 day sight-seeing schedule. In all it is about 22 km long and because there are many places to be visited in various parts of Sagano on the one day, an early start is recommended. Considering this guide in some detail may provide us with a better understanding of what 'tourism' amounted to in the Edo period and also something of what Ekiken's perception of this kind of behavior actually was.

First of all, there were a number of places to be visited on the way to Sagano, either because they were of historical interest or because of their natural beauty.

Next come the places of particular interest or scenic beauty in Sagano itself, starting with the pond, Osawa no Ike and followed by the site of the Nakoso Falls. Then there is the temple called Saga Shakado which is also known as Seiryoji. Next is Ojoin which was built in the Heian period but no longer exists. It was famous as being where Gio and Ginyo, two women of historical fame had hidden. Then there is Sanpoji Temple, another place of hiding, this time for Takiguchi Nyudo. He was an historical figure who assumed monk's clothing and appearance although he was not formally trained or ordained. This temple is followed by another, Nisonin and then Mount Ogurayama, the area of Nonomiya, another temple, Tenryuji, and the near-by river of Oigawa (Hozugawa). Then the route takes the traveller to the area of Arashiyama where the many cherries transplanted many years before from the mountains of Yoshino could be found. Arashiyama was therefore a place which attracted many visitors when the trees where in full bloom. Next is the temple Rinsenji from where there were good views of Oigawa River and the landscape beyond. In a thicket nearby, is to be found the site of the humble home of Kogo, one of the heroines from the Tales of Heike. The next place of interest is Horinji Temple, followed by Ichiitani, a valley of scenic beauty, followed by Daihikaku, a temple also known as Senkoji. Then comes the shrine Matsuo, the area of Umezu, and finally the most distance point, the Ume no Miya Shrine. On the way back to the city a visit to Uzumasa is recommended, as is the temple of Koryuji as well as the shrine to the east of Uzumasa, Konoshima Myojin, which is dedicated to sericulture.

Was the Guidebook Used?

The mere existence of such a walking-tour guidebook as *Keijo Shoran* does not necessarily mean that people were prepare to cover the distances suggest in it. However, there is proof that at least some people were willing and interested in doing so, in the form of an account of a trip to Sagano by one of Japan's pioneer Western-style painters, Shiba Kokan. It seems that he actually walked further than one of Ekiken's recommended tours, when he stayed for 20 days in Kyoto. According to Kokan's dairy, he made his tour on 21st March, 1789, and because the account of this day's walk is particularly long, it must be supposed that it was the high-light of his stay in the old capital. The date recorded was according to the old calender, so he would have taken the tour at the height of spring when the cherries were in full bloom.

Setting off in fine weather toward the northwest, he first went to the Kita no Jinja Shrine, and leaving by the north gate, he went on to the Hirano Jinja Shrine where the cherries were in full flower. Next he went to Kinkakuji and viewed the gardens and lake from the building. Next at Omuro Ninnaji Temple, he found large numbers of people enjoying the blossom in fine weather and he viewed the Imperial reception room there. Next he went to the Saga Shakado. At Arashiyama he found cherries blooming in the shadow of the pines and out in the shallow waters of Oigawa River, temporary decks had been set up by refreshment houses, where customers could enjoy a cup of saké, into which a "cherry petal might drift, blown on the breeze". After delighting in this scene, Kokan had a meal at the Dengaku Chaya restaurant in front of Horinji Temple. Seeing that he was in a spot far from the sea, he sipped at his saké lamenting the lack of fish on the menu. Going on past the Ume no Miya Shrine, he crossed Katsura River and went to Senbon-dori, a place in the west of Kyoto which had then be famous for its cherries for many years. Next he visited the area of Shimabara, and finally reached Toji Temple, which is in fact located in the south of Kyoto. Then passing in front of Honganji Temple and the site where the Rashomono gate once stood, he returned to his lodgings at around eight in the evening.

Comparing the kind of places which were visited or recommended by Ekiken and Kokan, some differences can be noticed. In the case of Ekiken, many of the places are associated with with historical literature and the Tales of Heikei in particular. Whereas Kokan, who was a painter and had an artist's eye, seems to have been most interested in seeing the blossom. Nevertheless, it is not difficult to imagine that people did walk from the center of the city in order to visit places of interest and beauty in the vicinity, in the way that these two individuals actually did.

The route around Sagano introduced in the *Keijo Shoran*, and the route over which Ekiken actually walked have been marked up together on the map - see page 32. In order to gain a better idea of the distances involved, the map has also been marked up with circles at 2 km intervals, with the junction between Shijo and Karasuma-dori as their center. This makes the distance to Sagano approximately 8 km. A person walking slowly will cover about 4 km in one hour, so at that pace it would take someone between two to three hours to reach Sagano. Perhaps I am alone in thinking how close Sagano seems but if, for example, there were a pleasantly arranged and safe cycle-track, it would even be possible to reach this culturally and naturally rich area in less than an hour.

Did the Citizens of Kyoto Visit the Environs?

However, the question is, were these places of interest and beauty in the environs of Kyoto only frequented by visitors, or did the citizens of Kyoto also go there? It is impossible to say just how frequently people went out to enjoy the surround areas of the city, but it is certain that they would go during particular seasons or on particular occasions. Compiled as a list of such locations, the chart - see page 35 - is an indication of those places which people visited for festivals or to go flower viewing, and were places visited by "many people from the capital", as is recorded in the *Miyako Meisho-guruma*, a guide to the city published in 1714. In addition, there are many festivals and events to which it must be supposed people would have been drawn. It is also natural to suppose that related places well

---

かった．このとき彼は富小路姉小路の宿に20日間滞在したが，その間嵯峨野方面を訪ねたことを日記にしるしている．日付は天明九年(1789)三月二一日，この日の文章はとりわけ長く，彼の京都滞在のハイライトだったにちがいない．日付は旧暦だから，季節は春，桜が満開だった．「天気，朝より西北の方へ行く」と歩き始めた江漢が訪ねた所は，

北野天神，北の門を出て，桜花さかりの平野神社へ．金閣寺は建物にあがって見物する．御室仁和寺では好天のもとで大勢の人が花見を楽しんでおり，御所の座敷を拝見する．嵯峨の釈迦堂．嵐山は桜が松の木陰に咲き，前は大堰川が流れ，出張の茶屋が流れの中に床机を出しており，「盃を持てば花びら飛来て酒にいる」．虚空蔵(法輪寺)の前の田楽茶屋へあがって，この地は海が遠いので魚がないなどとかこちながら，酒を飲む．梅の宮を過ぎ，桂の渡し，千本通(当時は京の西端で昔から桜で有名だった)，島原を見て，東寺に至る．羅生門の跡，本願寺の前を通り，日も暮れた五つ時(午後8時)前に宿に帰る．

益軒のあげた名所は昔の文学，ことに平家物語にまつわる由緒ある所が多いという傾向がうかがえるように思われるが，一方，画家であった江漢のほうはどうやら花見を楽しむのに夢中だったようだ．いずれにしても，都心から郊外のこうした場所へいかに人々が歩いて訪れていたか，想像できるのではないだろうか．

32頁下の図は『京城勝覧』の紹介するところの嵯峨野めぐりの順路と，益軒がじっさいに歩いた嵯峨野めぐりの行程を並列して地図に描きこんだものである．距離感をつかむため，いま仮に四条烏丸を中心にして2kmごとの間隔で円を描きくわえみた．四条烏丸から嵯峨野までおよそ8kmである．人はゆっくりめで歩いて1時間に約4km歩けるから，嵯峨野まで2〜3時間で行ける距離なのである．意外に近いと感心するのは私だけだろうか．もし安全で楽しいサイクリング道があったら，自転車なら1時間とかからずに行きつけるにちがいない．

京に住む人々も郊外の地を訪れていたのだろうか？

しかし，こうした郊外の美しい所も観光客だけの訪れる所で，京に住む人たちは行かなかったのではないのだろうか，と疑うのもしごく当然だろう．さて，実際どうだったのだろうか．どれほど頻繁に郊外へ出かけたかはわからないが，時折，特別なときに訪れていたことは確かである．35頁左の表はこうした場所の一例をあげたもので，正徳四年(1714)刊のやはり京案内書のひとつ『都名所車』の中で「多くの人が都から訪れる」と特に書いている場所と，祭事や花見などのそこへ訪れる目的との一覧である．他にも多数の人出を想像させる祭事・行事の記事は多い．郊外の社寺での祭事や行事，それに作られた花や紅葉の名所といったものは，都の人々が自然に富んだ郊外へ出かけ楽しむための，上手につくられた理由と機会を与える生活の知恵だったようにも思われる．

ここで注意しておきたいのは，これらの郊外の名所がすべて京の市街地の中心部から歩いて行ける所にあったということである．歴史的な京の街区には，たしかに多くのオープンスペースがない．町家は間に木を植える隙間もなく建てこんでいる．しかし，その気になって一歩足を郊外へ向ければ，その日のうちに本物の自然のある美しい所まで歩

名所	(km)	(1) 出来斎京土産 一六七七刊	(2) 京城勝覧 一七〇六刊	(3) 都名所車 一七一四刊	(4) 都名所図会 一七八〇刊	備考・訪問の目的
鴨川 Kamogawa					○	大文字送り火の観賞 (3)
四条河原 Shijo kawahara				○		6月7日より18日までの四条河原夕涼み (4)
観勝寺光明院 Kanshoji komyoin (東山安井)	1.0			○	○	藤の花見 (3)、中秋の名月 (4)
安井真性寺 Yasui Shinshoji			○			「藤有山吹つつじ桜もありて遊人多し」(2)
円山安養寺 Maruyama Anyoji	1.1	○	○		○	遊覧酒楽 (1・2)、集会遊筵 (4)
高台寺 Kodaiji	1.1				○	桜・萩の花見
双林寺 Sorinji	1.2				○	集会遊筵
東大谷 Higashiotani	1.3			○		桜の花見
正法寺 Shohoji (東山清閑寺町)					○	集会遊筵、眺望絶景
西大谷 Nishiotani			○			藤の花見
清水寺 Kiyomizudera	2.0	○			○	桜の花見 (1・4)
蓮華王院 Rengeoin (三十三間堂)					○	かきつばたの花見
東福寺 Tohukiji	2.8				○	10月16日開山忌の参詣、通天橋の紅葉見物
知恩院 Chionin	0.8				○	正月の大法会「御忌詣で」
青蓮院 Shorenin			○			かのへ申の日の参詣 (3)
聖護院 Shogoin					○	夏の夕涼み (3)
東岩倉真性院 Higashiiwakura Shinshoin (粟田口)			○			6月28日の千日詣で
真如堂 Shinnyodo	2.3		○			常の参詣「門前に茶屋多し遊人たえず」
吉田宮斎場所 Yoshida Shrine (神楽岡)	2.4				○	山躑躅・紅葉の観賞
下賀茂神社 Shimogamo Shrine	2.7	○	○		○	御手洗川の夏越しの祓 (1・2・4) 糺の森散策 (2) 葵祭り見物 (2)
上賀茂神社 Kamigamo Shrine	(5.5)	○				賀茂競馬の見物
舟岡山 Funaokayama			○			躑躅の花見
今宮のお旅所 Imamiya			○			5月7日から18日までの祭礼
千本寺閻魔堂 Senbonji Enmado			○			3月花の盛りの念仏参詣
北野天神社 Kitano Tenjin Shrine	4.8	○	○			縁日の参詣
御室御所 Ninnaji (仁和寺)	6.0	○	○		○	毎月21日の参詣 (1) 桜の花見 (2・4) 四国霊場遥拝八十八箇所の常時参詣 (4)
広沢池 Hirosawa Pond		○			○	月見 (1)、中秋の月見 (4)
松尾神社 Matsuo Shrine	7.9			○		8月朔日奉納相撲の見物 (3)
臨川寺 Rinsenji	8.2		○			桜の花見・月見
嵐山 Arashiyama	8.4		○			桜の花見
清凉寺 Seiryoji	8.8		○			3月5日から15日の大念仏参詣
愛宕神社 Atago Shrine	14.8					6月24日の千日参り・月毎の縁日
八瀬の里 Yase			○			四月の祭礼・神事の見物
西加茂神光院 Nishikamo Shinkoin						丑の年、丑の月、丑の日頃の参詣
鞍馬寺 Kuramadera	11.8	○			○	正月寅の日の参詣 (1・4)
岩屋山金峰寺 Iwayasan Kinbuji	17.4			○		7月16日の千日参り (3)
鵜の床 Uzura no Toko (伏見深草野)					○	鵜の声の観賞
藤の森神社 Fujinomori Shrine	(6.6)			○		5月5日の祭礼 (3)
竹田北向不動明王 Takeda Kitamuki Fudo				○		月例の参詣 (3)
城山 Site of Fushimi Castle (伏見城跡)					○	桃の花見
醍醐寺 Daigoji	8.8			○		桜の花見 (3)
上醍醐 Kamidaigo	11.8				○	7月5・6日の千日詣で
勝持寺 Shojiji	13.5				○	桜の花見
石清水八幡宮 Iwashimizu Hachimangu	18.5				○	正月15日から19日の厄難祓の参詣

注：○は各京都名所案内記に都人が多数訪れると記載のあることを示す。名所の後の数字は三条大橋からの距離．

Places visited by local people 京の人が多数訪れた名所

Takao Kanhuzu, Muromachi period 高尾観楓図(部分) 室町時代 東京国立博物館所蔵

	見物行程	Route of Sightseeing	(同書に記す概算距離を示す)
1日	・三条から清水へ	From Sanjo to Kiyomizu	4里 (16km)
	三条小橋―三条大橋―縄手町―大和大橋―建仁寺―愛宕寺―六波羅蜜寺―経書堂―子安塔―車宿馬駐―清水仁王門飾摩塚―田村堂―清水観音堂―地主権現―奥の院―音羽の滝―音羽山―音羽の滝―三年坂―下河原―霊山―八坂の塔―高台寺―安井真性寺―祇園感神院―双林寺―東本願寺墓所―長楽寺―丸山安養寺―将軍塚―知恩院―庚申堂―粟田口―白川橋―青蓮院		
2日	・南禅寺から吉田・聖護院へ	From Nanzenji to Yoshida, Shogoin	4里半 (18km)
	南禅寺―永観堂―若王子―非田院―黒谷―真如堂―鹿ヶ谷―無量寺―銀閣寺―吉田―百萬遍―聖護院の森―頂妙寺		
3日	・京より伏見へ	From Kyo to Fushimi	6里半 (24km)
	五条橋―大仏―三十三間堂―妙法院―智積院―大谷―今熊野―泉涌寺―東福寺―稲荷―深草―藤の森山―伏見―竹田		
4日	・上醍醐へ	To Kamidaigo	7里 (28km) 余
	清閑寺―歌の中山―山科―花山―勧修寺―小栗栖村―小野随心院―小栗栖―下醍醐―上醍醐―日野		
5日	・宇治へ	To Uji	8里 (32km)
	藤の森―矢島畔―仏国寺―六地蔵―黄檗山萬福寺―遠方町―大鳳寺町―御室戸寺―興聖寺―朝日山―谷の薬師―網代禁制の石碑―恵心院―宇治橋―宇治の里―平等院―扇の芝草―橘姫の社―橘の島		
6日	・大原野へ	To Oharano	5里 (20km) 余
	東寺―四ツ塚―吉祥院―唐橋―桂の里―桂川―久世―向日明神―大原野―小塩山―吉峰寺―三鈷寺		
7日	・嵯峨へ	To Saga	5里半 (22km) 余
	内野―妙心寺―仁和寺―大沢の池―名こその瀧の跡―釈迦堂―往生院―三寶寺―二尊院―小倉山―野々宮―天竜寺―大井川―嵐山―臨川寺―法輪寺―櫟谷―大悲閣―松尾―梅津―梅宮―太秦広隆寺―木の島明神		
8日	清滝川―愛宕山―月の輪	Kiyotaki - Atagoyama - Tsukinowa	8里 (32km)
9日	・高雄・槙尾・栂尾へ	To Takao	5里 (20km) 余
	北野―平野社―金閣寺―等持院―仁和寺―並の岡―光孝天皇陵―福王子村―鳴瀧―梅ケ畑―高雄寺―槙尾―栂尾―広沢の池		
10日	八幡―石清水八幡宮	Iwashimizuhachimangu	8里 (32km)
11日	雲母坂―比叡山―西塔―横川―八瀬	Hiei, Yase	8里 (32km)
12日	・鳥羽より山崎へ	From Toba to Yamazaki	8里 (32km)
	東寺―上鳥羽―秋の山―下鳥羽―納所町―淀町―淀姫明神―山崎		
13日	・鞍馬山へ	To Kuramayama	6里 (24km)
	鞍馬口―御菩薩池 (みどろ池) ―岩倉―市原―鞍馬町―僧正が谷―貴船		
14日	・大原（大原）へ	To Ohara	7里 (28km) 余
	大原口―八瀬―御陰の社―八瀬―小原―一梶井宮―証嵐の阿弥陀―音の瀧―おぼろの清水―寂光院		
15日	・江州東坂本へ	To Goshu Higashisakamoto	8里 (32km)
	賀茂川―白川村―山中―上坂本―東照宮―白髭社―下坂本―唐崎―三井寺―高麗―小関越		
16日	・石山へ	To Ishiyama	9里 (36km)
	三条大橋―白川橋―粟田口―蹴上―日の岡―二宮川原―十禅寺―追分―牛尾山―走井―逢坂山―関寺―大津―打出の浜―松本―膳所―粟津の原―瀬田川―石山		
17日	・ただすより上賀茂・千本へ	From Tadasu to Kamigamo, Senbon	4里 (10km)
	下鴨の社―上賀茂神社―西賀茂―今宮社―大徳寺―雲林院―船岡山―千本寺―鷹ヶ峰―常経堂		

Rakuchu Rakugai day-by-day guide from Keijo Shoran 『京城勝覧』の「洛中洛外名所毎日見物之案内」(一日観光コース)

Higashiyama Yurakuzu, Muromachi period　東山遊楽図　室町時代　高津古文化 会館所蔵

Pilgrims depicted at Horinji Temple at the end of 18th century from *Miyako Rinsen Meishou Zue*.
下嵯峨法輪寺の十三参りに詣でる人々　18世紀後期　『都林泉名勝図会』

know for their autumn tints or flowers as well as the festivals and events at the temples and shrines in the vicinity of Kyoto were cleverly arranged and orchestrated as a way of providing the citizens of the capital with a reason and an opportunity of going out to the environs to enjoy the wealth of nature that was to be found there.

It must be realized, however, that all of these places in the surrounding area were ones which could be walked to from the center of the city. In addition to this is should also be remembered that there were few open spaces within the central part of the city in the past and there was very little space between the buildings there for much vegetation of any kind but especially trees. Nevertheless, if the people were of a mind to do so and were prepared to make tracks to the areas surrounding the city proper, it was possible to reach areas on foot were there was a wealth of natural scenery and vegetation to enjoy before returning to their homes, all in the space of one day. It is this fact which perhaps suggest the reason why there was no real need for open space within the center of the city.

It will now perhaps be evident that Kyoto was a city full of appeal as a place in which to live, composed as it was of a built-up area surrounded by tracts of natural landscape. It was these surrounding areas which provided what the city itself could not offer and the two together were parts of an integrated whole. It is true, of course, that people had cultivated the land in these outlaying areas mainly to provide the essentials of life but, on the other hand, while occasionally adding to that cultural heritage for the sake of the enjoyment of the natural landscape, people were also contributing in a constructive way to that environment outside the city. The changing seasons could therefore be recognized and enjoyed all the more and it also led to the creation of an environment invested with an historical significance. The environs of Kyoto should therefore perhaps be recognized as an environment in which nature and culture have melded and, just in the same way that a house has a garden, it would surely be reasonable to call these areas around the old capital a "city garden" of a considerable scale. Put another way, the historical, central or *rakuchu* area of the city, had its own *rakugai* garden.

いて行って帰ってこれたのである．この事実がなぜ都心部にオープンスペースがあまりなくてもよかったのかを説明しているように思われる．

いまや，人が住むための魅力に富んだ都市，京都とは市街地と郊外の両者で構成されていたのだ，ということが理解できたように思う．郊外の美しい自然は都市の欠くことのできないペア（一対）の半分だったのである．人々は耕作し手を加えて郊外をつくってきた．もちろんそれは主には生活のためだっただろうが，一方では，自然景観そのものを楽しむために，しばしばそれに文化遺産を付け加えながら，街をとりまく郊外をつくってきたのでもあった．こうして，郊外の各所に四季折々に美しく，またさまざまな歴史的な意味を含んだ環境を形成してきたのである．京都の郊外は自然性と文化性が相半ばする環境というべきだろう．私たちはこのような性格をもつ郊外を，家々に庭があるように都市がもつ大きな庭園，「都市の庭園」と呼んでもよいのではないだろうか．京都の歴史的な市街地すなわち洛中は，洛外という庭園をもっていたのである．

II
Monuments – Urban Design Features
モニュメントの都市意匠

Higashi Honganji Temple within the cityscape 東本願寺と市街景観

Placement of Monumental Structures in the Cityscape

It is interesting to consider just what methods were used in the planning of the historic cities of Japan, but especially in the case of Kyoto. Here we will consider the overall changes in the urban framework of the city up until the turn of the century, paying particular attention to the way the city appeared at an urban scale, by looking at the placement of monumental structures which were built between the end of the Middle Ages and the beginning of modern times.

Jurakudai - Its Features and Palatial Qualities

Kyoto emerged as a castle town during the period between the end of the Middle Ages and the seventeenth century. But first, let us take a brief look at the situation before Jurakudai was constructed.

Nijo Castle, the residential castle of Yoshimitsu Ashikaga, was built by Nobunaga in 1569. However, it seems to have born very little resemblance to a castle as it lacked a tower and, in actual fact, it was destroyed by fire in a coup d'état at Honnoji temple in 1582. When Hashiba Hideyoshi made his triumphant return to Kyoto after his victory at the Battle of Yamazaki, he first made his seat of rule in Kyoto on the remains of Myokenji temple, now to the east of Nijo Castle. It is estimated that this seat of authority was completed in the fourth month of 1584. Surrounded by a moat and with its main turret soaring into the sky, it had every right to be called a castle and this was the first time that the people of Kyoto had been under subjugated to a samurai's rule.

Just two years after this castle was constructed on the site of Myokenji, Hideyoshi started building Jurakudai, in 1586. On completion, it was said to be "like a vast stone-walled mountain with 43,000 steps". The turrets were said to have steel pillars, the doors were made of copper and the many storied building rose high in the sky as if to "touch the stars". The roof tiles were magnificently finished with splendid tigers roaring to the wind and "dragons singing to the clouds", according to Oze Hoan in *Taikoki, a biography he wrote on the life of Hideyoshi, in 1625. We can therefor*e surmise that Jurakudai had palace-like qualities which were highly decorative as well as castle-like features and fortified defenses.

But just where was Jurakudai situated? There are many differences and discrepancies in the various topographical records drawn during the Edo period but Kenryo Ashikaga (Kyoto University), came to the conclusion that the main citadel of Jurakudai was situated in the area bounded by Ichijo-dori to the north, Demizu-dori to the south, Omiya-dori to the east, and Jofukuji-dori to the west.

Now let us consider some of the special features of the area built up around Jurakudai. It seems that it was situated on part of the former site of the old Heian palace called Uchino. It must be supposed that it was a matter of conceit on Hideyoshi's part, as supreme ruler of the times, that made him choose to build his court on the site of the old Heian palace. Higarashi-dori runs from about the middle of where Jurakudai once stood, in a southerly direction. The origin of its name comes from the beautiful gate at Jurakudai according to Edo period topographical records and as it is said that people lost all account of time when they caught sight of this gate, we can therefore deduce that the South Gate of Jurakudai must certainly have been a true spectacle.

Another point worth mentioning is the relationship between the palace and its location at that time. At the end of the Muromachi period, the palace was probably 120 meters along each side of its roughly square site, being bounded by Kamitachiuri-dori to the south, Takakura-dori to the east and Higashinotoin to the west. The northern boundary stretched slightly north of Ogimachi-dori, which is now called Nakatachiuri-dori. Ichijo-dori was one street to the north of Ogimachi-dori and Shimochojamachi-dori was one street to the south. In other words, Jurakudai was constructed due west of the palace and the central east-west axis of both buildings was roughly the same.

With its tower soaring up in front of the Imperial palace, Jurakudai must have been a vast palace-like, fortified structure which followed the orientation of the original palace and faced south on the site of the old Heian court. Arranging the buildings on the same axes and orientating it toward the south in this way, offers us a clue as to the logic behind the relationship between the Hokoji temple Daibutsuden and another temple, Nishi Honganji, both of which were monumental elements within the framework of the city.

Hokoji Daibutsuden and Nishi Honganji - Contrapositions of Landmarks

Hideyoshi started planning the construction of Hokoji Daibutsuden in 1587, the same year as building work began on Jurakudai, but two years later the site was changed to one north of Sanjusangendo. It was modelled after Todaiji Daibutsu-

近世京都のモニュメンタルな建築配置による都市景観構成

わが国の歴史的都市においてどのような景観形成手法がもちいられたことがあったのだろうか．他に抜きんでて巨大な建築物は，都市景観の中で特別な効果をもっている．都市を遠望したとき，或は都市内外の多くの視点から目立って見えるため，好むと好まざるにかかわらず，それは都市のシンボリックな代表的な存在となる．ここで言うモニュメンタルな建築とは，こういう性格をもつ巨大な建築物を指している．建築物の高さは色彩や形態などの他の性格に比べ，都市景観の公共性に強く関わるのであり，特別な配慮が求められる．巨大な建築は時に都市景観を支配しているような印象をも与える．歴史において，為政者たちは当然そのことに気付いていた．京都においても，巨大なモニュメンタルな建築物の歴史を紐解くと，その配置による景観形成手法とともに，特別な物語が浮かび上がってくる．ここでは，中世末から近世初頭の京都におけるモニュメンタルな建築物配置に見られる都市的規模の景観形成手法に注目し，あわせて江戸末期に至るまでの景観的影響について考察したい．

聚楽第の景観──その宮城的配置について

中世末から近世初頭にかけて，京都に城下町的景観が出現していった時期があった．戦国時代の覇者となった豊臣秀吉は京の町に聚楽第(ジュラクダイ)と呼ばれた城郭を築き，「御土居」(オドイ)と呼ばれた土塁で京の町を囲んだ．

まず，秀吉の聚楽第建設以前の動きを簡単に紹介しておこう．永禄十二年(1569)信長の手で将軍足利義昭の居城二条城が造営されたが，これには天守閣はなかったらしく，景観のなかで占めた性格は「城」というほどのものではなかった．これは天正十年(1582)本能寺の変に炎上した．山崎の合戦に勝利して，京へ凱旋した羽柴秀吉が最初に京都支配の拠点をつくったのは妙顕寺跡地，今の二条城の東の一角であった．天正十二年四月には完成していたと推定されている．これは堀をまわし，天主をあげていたから，「城」と呼ばれるべきものであった．京の都人が仰ぎ見たこれが最初の天守閣であった．

妙顕寺跡地に城を建設してからわずか2年後の天正十四年(1586)秀吉は聚楽第の造営に着手した．完成したそれは『太閤記』(小瀬甫庵著，寛永二年(1625)刊)に「四方三千歩の石のついがき山の如し．楼門のかためは鉄の柱，銅の扉，閣星を摘でたかく，(中略)瓦の縫ねには，玉虎風に嘯き，金竜雲に吟ず」と形容されている．防備を固めた城郭的性質とともに，華やかに飾られた宮殿的な相貌をもあわせもっていたことがうかがえる．

聚楽第の位置はどうであったか．江戸時代の地誌類の記述にはさまざまな不一致点がみられるが，歴史地理学者足利健亮氏は北は一条通，南は出水通，東は大宮通，西は浄福寺通に囲われた一角を聚楽第本丸跡と考定されている．

さて，この聚楽第の配置の都市景観的な特質に着目し検討してみよう．

聚楽第の場所は「内野」と呼ばれていた平安京の大内裏跡地の一角であった．秀吉が城郭建設の地を北へ北へと移し，遂に「内野」に地を選んだことは，覇者となった秀吉が都の本来の内裏のあるべき地に自らの居を構えるという自負心がはたらいていたはずである．聚楽第本丸跡地のほぼ中央から南に伸びて日暮通が現存している．その名の由来は江戸時代の地誌によれば聚楽第に美しい門があり，それを眺め入るうちに日を暮らしたことによるといい，華美な聚楽第南門があったことが知られる．江戸時代初期の「洛中絵図」を見ると，他の道にくらべ日暮通だけはまっすぐな直線であり，聚楽第建設時にその正面の通りとして，すなわち景観演出的な目的をもって，計画的にまっすぐに建設された通りであったことがうかがわれる．現京都大学蔵「洛中絵図　寛永後萬治前」を見ると，この通は余り太くはないが他の道にくらべこれだけが直線である．聚楽第建設時にその正面の通りとして，計画的にまっすぐに建設された通りであったかと想像される．

もうひとつ注目すべき点は，当時の内裏との位置関係である．室町時代末期，内裏は南辺を上長者町通，東辺を高倉通，西辺を東洞院，北辺は正親町通(オウマチドオリ)(現中立売通)より幾らか北に広げたあた

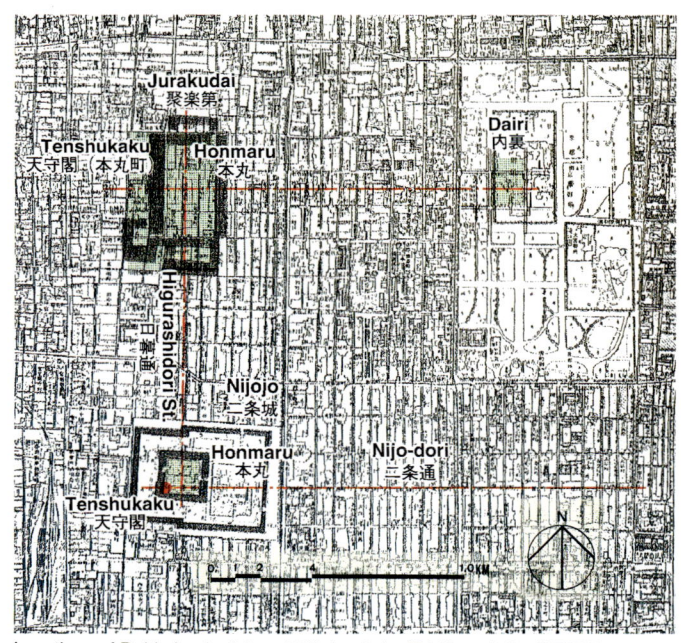

Locations of Dairi, Jurakudai, and Nijojo　内裏・聚楽第・二条城の位置関係

Drawing of Jurakudai, end of 16th century　聚楽第図　16世紀後期　三井文庫所蔵

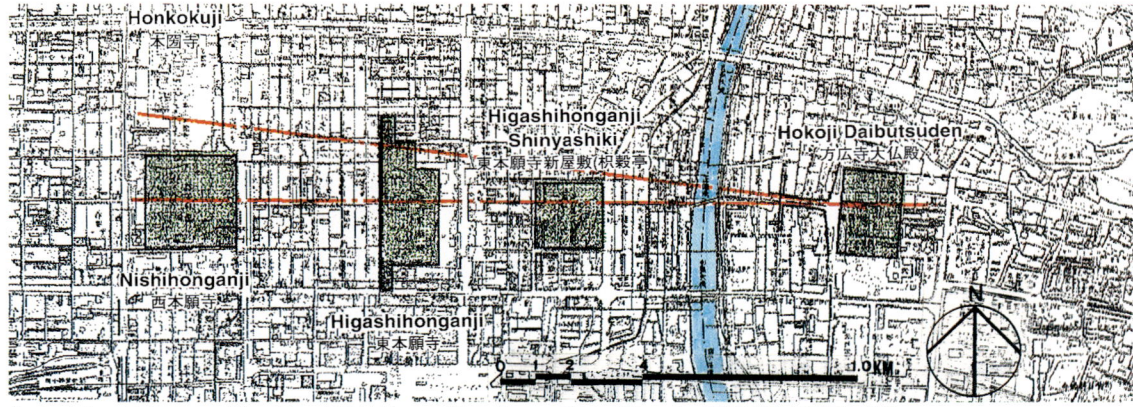

Axal relationship between Higashi and Nishi Honganji temples, and Hokoji Temple　東西本願寺と方広寺の軸線

Funaki Rakuchu Rakugai-zu – Townscape of Kyoto in early 17th century 舟木家旧蔵本洛中洛外図 景観年代17世紀前期 東京国立博物館所蔵

den, in Nara. But unlike Todaiji, which faces south, Hokoji was built overlooking the town of Kyoto and facing west from its site below Mount Higashiyama standing at its rear. It should perhaps be stated that the plan was along the lines of an enormous memorial edifice rather than the more traditional form of temple architecture. The fact that Hideyoshi was conscious of what kind of visual effect it would have, can be gathered by the way in which he arranged the long open space overlooking the Kamo River as depicted in paintings of Kyoto and its environs, dating back to the beginning of the seventeenth century. This open space between Fushimi-kaido and the site of Hokoji temple still remains to this day. A glance at the map will confirm the fact that the direction of this open space is slightly to the north of Kyoto's basic grid pattern of streets, but why was this so? Going back in time, to when Hideyoshi rode into the capital triumphant, he took up position at Honkokuji. According to an entry in Tamonin Diary, Hideyoshi tried to build a castle "in the south of Kyoto around Rokujo". In fact, around Honkokuji at the exact spot where he had first set up camp. However, Hideyoshi's castle was eventually built on a different site due west of the Imperial palace and north of Jurakudai on the remains of Myokenji temple. If a line is extended beyond the edge of the map in the direction in which the open space in front of the Daibutsuden faces, it meets Honkokuji at point where the site of the first castle was proposed.

Honganji, which had been moved to Osaka, was once again moved to Kyoto at the new year of 1591 at Hideyoshi's command. According to a book entitled *Tokitsunekyoki*, Hideyoshi had at one time appointed a place on the southern outskirts of the city. However, documentation of the Shinshu school of Buddhism, states that Hideyoshi changed his mind just one month later and chose Rokujo Horikawa instead. That site was located in the grounds of Honkokuji, the present site of Nishi Honganji. Thus the position at Honkokuji, where Hideyoshi had first planned to construct his castle, was once again adopted and plans went ahead to build Honganji on the site. However, it was just at the time that construction work on the Daibutsuden at Hokoji was in full swing. The site for Honganji was set directly in front of Hokoji and had its central axis along Shichijo-bomon-dori, a road built in the Heian period. Although Hokoji was situated some distance from the foot of Mount Higashiyama, the architect probably had a good idea that the vast Daibutsuden would be visible in the distance from around the position of Honganji at a time when there was nothing but low town houses to interrupt the view. This was just about the time that the rapid urban reconstruction, which had taken place in Kyoto from around 1587, began to slacken off. It seems as though this site was chosen for Honganji in order to defend the south of the capital, just as the sites for Teramachi in the east and Teranouchi in the north were supposed to be protective.

If we take into consideration the fact that the central citadel of Jurakudai was located due west of the Imperial palace, then it probably ought to be said that the composition of the streetscape was made consciously from the point of view of the contrapositions of the two buildings and the establishment of visual axis lines described. The central axis of the main building at Nishi Honganji was therefore turned to face Hokoji Daibutsuden in the east.

Relationship between Nijo Castle and Jurakudai - Planning Contradictions

Tokugawa Ieyasu, who ruled after Hashiba Hideyoshi, started constructing the castle at Nijo Horikawa in 1602 and extensions were made to it in 1626. But what we must consider now is the relationship between the locations of Nijo Castle and Jurakudai. As has been mentioned before, the southern face of the keep of Jurakudai faced down Higurashi-dori. If we extend the line of this street to the south it passes exactly through the middle of the keep of Nijo Castle, which was surrounded by an inner moat. The keep of Nijo Castle was therefore on the same line as that of Jurakudai and blocked the line of sight to the latter. However, the main façade of Nijo Castle was not facing south, but was turned 90° to the east.

Another extremely interesting point is the position of the castle tower at Nijo. It was built in the southwest corner of the bailey which is surrounded by the inner moat. This position lies exactly along the line of Nijo-dori. Having made this street the visual axis, the castle turret was then arranged so that it soared up directly at the end of that street. Nijo-dori was an especially wide street located to the south of the Heian period castle and was the dividing line between the districts of Kamigyo and Shimogyo, corresponding to the "upper" and "lower" section of the city, at the time Nijo Castle was built. Seven years before construction work began on Nijo Castle, Jurakudai was destroyed along with the downfall of Hidetsugu, Hideyoshi's adopted son, in 1595. Nevertheless, when Nijo Castle was planned, it completely blocked the previous position of Jurakudai. Furthermore, within the scheme for Kyoto drawn up by Hideyoshi, the new castle also blocked the axis on which the former building stood. Thus by changing the direction in which Nijo Castle faced and the axis of the new castle, he was able to sever the southward march of the axis extended from the site of Jurakudai.

In the same year as work begun on Nijo Castle, Ieyasu donated land for the building of Higashi Honganji, to Kyonyo, the 12th generation of Honganji retainers. It is now possible to ascertain that the way in which this site was chosen was similar to the way the site for Nijo Castle was singled out in relationship to the position of Jurakudai. The building erected on the donated site for Higashi Honganji stands directly in line with both Hokoji's Daibutsuden and Nishi Honganji, but facing the former and with its back to the latter. As a result, all three complexes describe a single east west axis.

The road running westwards from the front of the Daibutsuden was linked to the west bank of the Kamo River by a bridge which was built in the first half of the eighteenth century. The bridge curved from a corner of the square facing Honkokuji and linked up with the road leading to

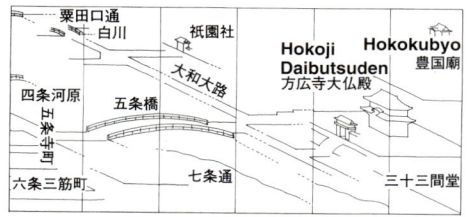

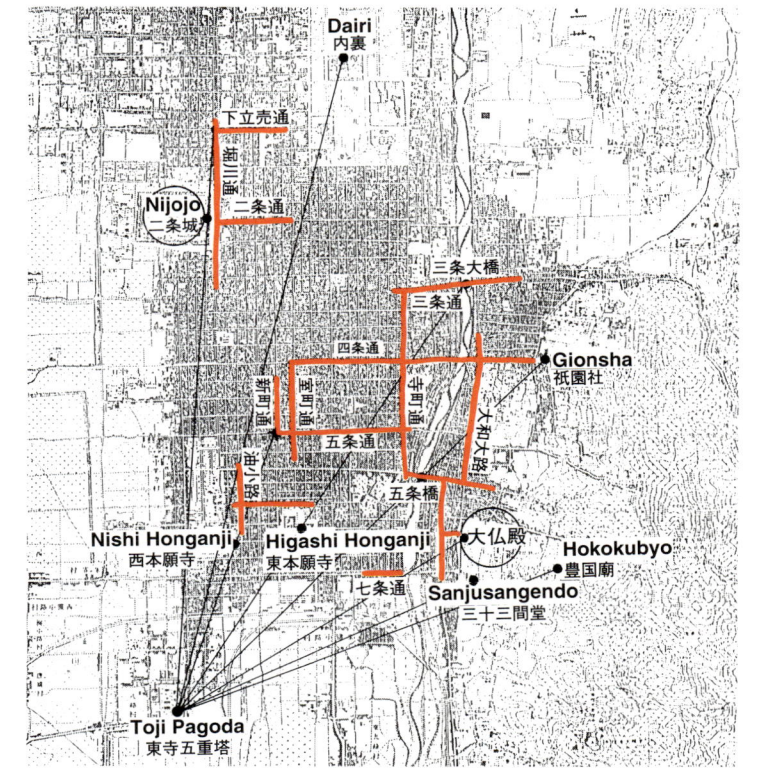

Actual surveied position of roads shown on *Funaki Rakuchu Rakunai-zu* and sight lines to principle buildings in the same illustration from the pagoda of Toji Temple.

舟木本に記載された通りの実測地図上の位置，および東寺五重の塔から舟木本記載のモニュメントを眺める視線

りで，およそ方一町の範囲にあった．正親通の一筋北は聚楽第本丸北辺の一条通，内裏の南辺より二筋南が聚楽第本丸南辺の出水通にあたる．

聚楽第は，禁裏の西正面に天守閣を聳えさせ，おおよそ平安京の内裏のあった場所に，元来の内裏の形式を踏んで南面する，城郭的にして宮殿的な大建築であったことになる．

方広寺大仏殿と西本願寺の位置について
——モニュメントの対置

秀吉は天正十四年，聚楽第建設開始と同じ年に，大仏殿を京に建設することを思い立った．寺院は方広寺と名づけられ，三十三間堂の北が敷地となった．東大寺大仏殿にならっての建設ではあったが，東大寺大仏殿が南面するのにたいし，方広寺は東山を背景に，西方すなわち京の町に向けて建てられた．伝統的配置形式より，巨大な記念的建造物の景観演出性を重んじた計画というべきであろう．景観的効果を意識していたことは，中井家蔵「洛外図屏風」にも描かれているように，大仏殿の前から鴨川へ向けて長い広場をとっていたことにもうかがえる．方広寺から伏見街道の間にあったこの広場は現在に伝えられている．広場の向きを地図上で確かめると，その方向が京都の碁盤状の町割よりわずかに北にふれている．なぜであろうか．時期は遡るが，山崎の合戦を終え京にはいった秀吉は本圀寺に陣をとっていた．「多聞院日記」天正十年(1582)七月七日条に，信長亡き後の勢力分担についての記事に，「(秀吉は)下京六条ヲ城ニ拵云々」とあり，ちょうど陣を張っていた本圀寺あたりに，秀吉は京における城を構えようとしたことがわかる．その後，秀吉の城は妙顕寺跡地，聚楽第と北上し，内裏の真西に位置したのであっ

た．さて，先ほどの大仏殿正面の広場の向く方向を地図上で延ばすと，その線は最初の城の候補地であった本圀寺敷地のちょうど下京六条の位置にゆきあたる．

天正十九年(1591)正月，当時大阪にあった本願寺は秀吉の命により京都へ移ることになった．秀吉は本願寺敷地を一度は「下鳥羽より下，淀より上の間」(『言経卿記』)と指定したが，1月後の閏正月，敷地は六条堀川に変更された．それは東西が大宮大路と堀川小路の間，南北は六条坊門小路(現五条通)と七条大路の間にあった本圀寺の寺域の一角であった．最初に城の建設を構想した本圀寺の場所がここで再びとりあげられ，本願寺が建設されることになったのである．ところで，この頃は方広寺大仏殿の建築工事たけなわの頃であった．

平安時代の七条坊門通の位置にあたる通を中心線とする本願寺の敷地は，あまりにも方広寺の真正面である．東山の麓の方広寺から離れているとはいえ，低い町家のほかに何といって視線をさえぎるもののなかった時代，建設中とはいえ，巨大な大仏殿は本願寺敷地の堀川通あたりからも望見されたであろう．この頃は，天正十四年から急速に進めていた京都の都市改造がほぼ一段落しかかっていた時期である．東に寺町，北に寺之内を配置したように，京の南を防御する場所として，本願寺の位置を決めたように思われる．しかし同時に，本願寺の方広寺大仏殿と相対する景観的な位置関係に秀吉が気づいていなかったとはかんがえにくい．同じ本圀寺の寺域内で，京の町の碁盤状の通の方向からすれば大仏殿を正面に見通す位置

both Nishi and Higashi Honganji. It was not until after the bridge over the river joined the two roads together that it became known as Shomen-dori over its whole length right out to the western outskirts of Kyoto. It was probably only natural then that the road running along the axis of the two Honganji temples and the Daibutsuden was so called because it literally means a "front facing road".

Hokoji Daibutsuden and Nijo Castle - Illustrated Planning Components

If we consider the relationship between the Daibutsuden at Hokoji and Nijo Castle, in the same way that people did at the time, by looking at the left and right hand portions of the *Ikeda Rakuchu Rakugai* illustration of Kyoto and its environs done in the seventeenth century, we find that these two buildings occupy positions more or less opposite each other. There was some discrepancy between the east-west axis of Tokugawa's residential castle, Nijo Castle and Hideyoshi's Daibutsuden at Hokoji in the townscape of Kyoto at the beginning of the Edo Period but people appear to have recognized them as governing landmarks which occupied mirrored positions.

Unlike many Rakuchu Rakugai paintings, which consist of two scenes set up on opposite sides of the room, each with a different viewpoint, the left and right parts of the one, originally owned by the Funaki family are continuous, making a single painting seen from a single view point. This rendering, which now belongs to Tokyo National Museum, provides us with a panoramic view of Kyoto and both the Daibutsuden and Nijo Castle are depicted facing each other on opposite sides of the picture. If we assume that the viewpoint was taken from the top of the pagoda at Toji temple then the general relationship between all the various facilities in the picture is very consistent with the actual townscape. Besides being an excellent position from which to view both the northern and southern parts of the city, it is possible to see the confronting forms of the two biggest structures in Kyoto, Nijo Castle and the Daibutsuden on either side of the city. However, the Funaki painting does not completely reveal the discrepancy in the east-west alignment of the two buildings. Looking at the picture, we find Gojobashi slightly to the left of the Daibutsuden at Hokoji and to the left of that again is Nijo-dori at the end of which stands Nijo Castle. If we cut the survey map of Kyoto at this point from Nishi Honganji through Shijo-Muramachi to Sanjo-Teramachi with a diagonal line and try to link the former Gojo-dori with Nijo-dori so that they are continuous, then the relationship of the other places is extremely consistent with the Funaki painting. The artist, who did this painting, divided the town diagonally between Kamigyo and Shimogyo and condensed it so that the Daibutsuden was exactly in line with Nijo Castle. The relationship between the location of the other roads, which are connected as shown here, is consistent on the whole with the relationship of opposite streets in many of the other Rakuchu Rakugai paintings that are set up opposite each other. In the case of the Funaki painting, Kamigyo and Shimogyo, the "upper" and "lower" sections of the city respectively, are viewed separately and the central parts of the city and its environs are depicted facing each other, the two sections being viewed from a south westerly position. However, the discrepancy of the view in the Funaki rendition is of no real consequence, because it is a representative example of one interpretation of the way the city was composed and therefore can be judged as an 'impression' of the appearance of the city as it was seen in those days. With Kamigyo and Shimogyo facing each other in this way, Nijo Castle and the Daibutsuden at Hokoji temple take up contrapositions and these two pieces of monumental architecture are shown as being fundamental to the composition of the appearance of the city.

Frontality to the East of the Kamo River

The five storey tower of Nijo Castle was struck by lightning and burnt to the ground in 1750. The Daibutsuden stood for nearly another 50 years before it was destroyed in 1798, when it too was struck by lightning. The composition of the cityscape, which had been dominated by these two vast structures, thus vanished in the middle of the Edo Period. I would like to take a look now at what kind of influence the production of the cityscape, whose visual axis was created by the location of magnificent buildings built at the beginning of the seventeenth century, actually has had on the appearance of Kyoto since then.

The Gion Shrine had its west gate at the end of Shijo-dori and the streetscape in front of the gate along Shijo-dori appeared in several renditions of the city and its environs soon after. However, the position of both the main shrine and the overall complex faced south. In contrast to this, the temple buildings of the Daibutsuden were built overlooking the town of Kyoto with Mount Higashiyama to the rear and a suitably

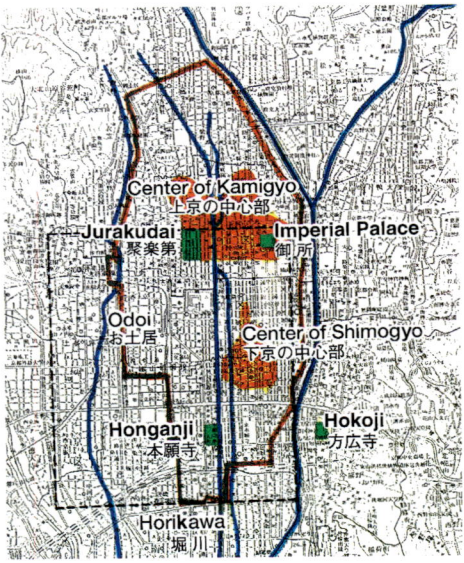

Rakugai-zu, mid-17th century
洛外図　中井家所蔵

近世初頭の京都
Kyoto in early 17th century

On the way up to Hokoji Temple　方広寺門前

View toward Higashi Honganji Temple and open space associated with Main Gate from in front of Hokoji Temple; *Yodogawa Ryogan Ichiran*, 1856
方広寺門前より正面の広場と東本願寺を眺める『淀川両岸一覧』
(安政三年刊)より

Miyako no Nanbanji taken from a fan shaped painting, end of 16th century
都の南蛮寺　狩野宗秀筆　16世紀末　京名所図扇面より　神戸市立美術館所蔵
室町通蛸薬師付近に在った。

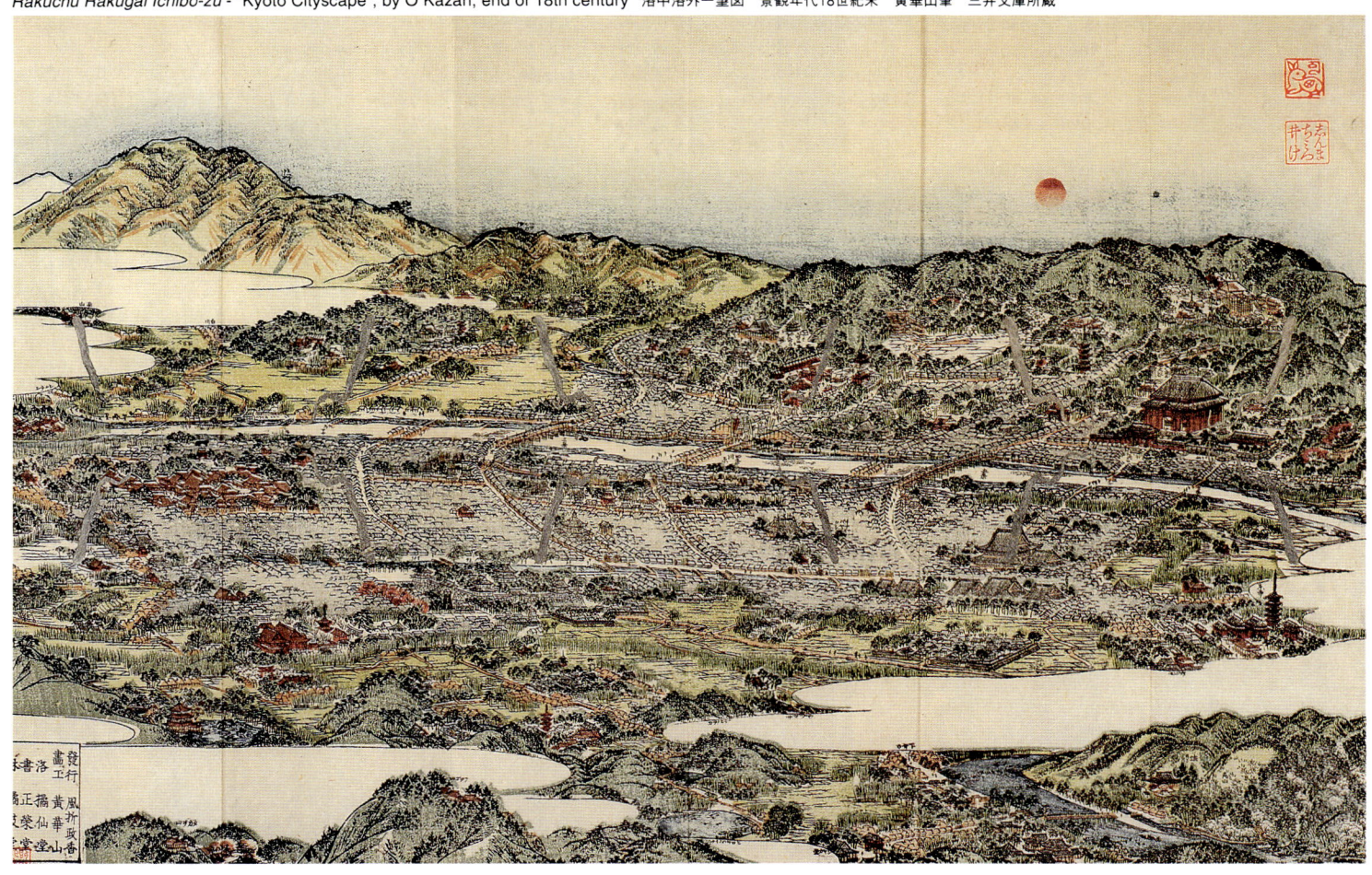

Rakuchu Rakugai Ichibo-zu - "Kyoto Cityscape", by O Kazan, end of 18th century　洛中洛外一望図　景観年代18世紀末　黄崋山筆　三井文庫所蔵

に本願寺を配置したものであろう．聚楽第本丸を御所の真西に位置させたことと考えあわせると，モニュメンタルな建築の対置という景観形成と，敷地の軸線を通すという配置計画が意識的になされたというべきであろう．西本願寺本堂の中心軸は方広寺大仏殿に向けられていたのである．

二条城と聚楽第の位置関係
——秀吉の都市意匠の否定

秀吉の次に天下を掌握した徳川家康は，慶長七年(1602)に新しく二条堀川に城郭の建設を始め，寛永三年(1626)に城の拡張を行った．ここに二条城と聚楽第の位置関係が注目される．先述のように聚楽第本丸の南正面に日暮通があった．日暮通の線を南に延ばすと，今度はちょうど内堀で囲まれた二条城本丸の中心を通る．二条城は聚楽第本丸の真正面に本丸を据え，聚楽第の正面を塞ぎ，その軸線の方向を90度回転させてしまったのである．聚楽第の方は二条城の建設が始まった七年(1602)より7年前に，その主であった秀次の失脚と同時に破却されていた．にもかかわらず，二条城は，南面した聚楽第の前方を正確に塞ぎ封じた配置計画をとっている．秀吉の構想した京の都市意匠を，その象徴的ともいえる軸線を塞ぎ，さらに新たな軸線の方向を回転させることによって，永遠にその実現を絶つものであったように推察される．

もうひとつ都市景観的に興味深い点は二条城天守閣の配置である．二条城天守閣は内堀で囲った本丸の西南隅に建設された．その位置は，ちょうど二条通の延長線上にあたる．二条通を景観的な軸とし，その真正面に天守閣を聳えさせたのであった．二条通は平安京では宮城の南端にあたり朱雀大路に次いで広い大路であったし，二条城建設の頃には上京と下京に分かれていた京の二つの町のちょうど中間でもあった．

二条城の建設開始と同じ年，家康は東本願寺の地を教如に寄進し，内紛のあった本願寺は二つの宗派に分裂した．その場所の選び方に，聚楽第に対する二条城の配置と同じ手法をいまや認めることができる．寄進された寺地は西本願寺の真正面をふさいだのであり，同時にそれは方広寺大仏殿の真正面でもあった．こうして，方広寺，西本願寺，東本願寺の三寺院は１本の軸線を形成して配置される結果となった．

大仏殿正面の広場から西へ延びる通りには18世紀前半に橋がかけられ，鴨川を越えて西岸と結ばれた．橋は北にずれていた広場の方角から屈曲して，両本願寺の中心に向かう通りに結びつけられた．洛中の西端まで通りの延長の全体を「正面通」と呼ぶようになったのは，鴨川を越えて通りが一本につながって後のことで，両本願寺と大仏殿の軸線にあたる通りとしてこう呼ばれるようになったのは自然ななりゆきだったであろう．

方広寺大仏殿と二条城
——洛中洛外図における京の支配的景観構成要素

17世紀になって描かれた洛中洛外図の右隻と左隻を当時の観賞の仕方にしたがって向き合わせて置くと，大仏殿と二条城が近い位置で向き合う．本書III章に池田家旧蔵本洛中洛外図を向き合う形で掲載したので参照していただきたい．江戸時代初期の京の景観では，秀吉の残した方広寺大仏殿と，徳川家の二条城とが，実際には南北にかなりのずれがあったのだが，支配的なランドマークとして対置するかたちで人々に意識されていたようである．「舟木家旧蔵本洛中洛外図」(現東京国立博物館蔵，以下「舟木本」と記載)は，他の洛中洛外図が左隻・右隻がそれぞれ別の視点を取った２図からなる構成であるのにたいし，この図では左右両隻の図が連続し，一つの視点から見た一枚の絵という構成をとっている．その左右両隻にまたがって京の町が長く横たわり，その両端に，大仏殿と二条城が両者向きあって描かれている．東寺五重塔の上に視点をとったものと想定すると，図中の諸施設の相互関係が現実の景観とよく一致する．この高さが上京・下京を一望するのに都合がよかったのと同時に，ここから見ると京の二大建造物，大仏殿と二条城がちょうど町を挟んで対峙するかたちで眺められたのである．しかし「舟木本」は両者の南北のずれを正確に描写してはいない．図上で方広寺大仏殿から左の方へ目を動かすと，五条橋があり，これを左へたどるといつの間にか二条通に変身し，そのまま二条城へ突き当たるのである．「舟木本」を描いた画家は上京と下京の間で斜めに町を切断し，これを圧縮して，大仏殿と二条城を真正面に対置させたのである．ここに現われた別の通りがつながる位置関係は，他の多くの洛中洛外図の左右両隻を向かい合わせに置いた時のちょうど向かい合う通りの関係とおおよそ一致する．「舟木本」の視点はまた，上京・下京を別々に描いた洛中洛外図を対面させて置き，その両隻を南手から眺めて描写したということもできる．「舟木本」の描写のずれは間違いというべきでなく，当時の「京の景観イメージ」すなわち京の都市景観構成にたいする把え方を代表的に表現しているともいえよう．都市域として上京と下京が対置し，また二条城と方広寺大仏殿のふたつのモニュメントが対置するのが江戸時代前中期の京の大きな景観構成なのであった．

wide street-like open space was provided leading up to the temple complex. The next building to adopt the same position as this was the Otani Mausoleum or Nishi Otani. If we look at its location, we can see that a small square was set up at the slight bend in Gojobashi-dori or the present day Gojo-dori and it was here that the gate was built as if it were the front entrance at the east end of Gojobashi-dori.

If we look at the *Rakuchu Rakugai Ichiboezu*, an illustration done by O. Kasan, giving a view over the city of Kyoto from the west at the turn of the nineteenth century, there is no doubt that the Otani Mausoleum is depicted at the end of Gojobashi-dori in line with the Daibutsuden. The roads running from east to west are shown to run at slightly different angles on the east and west banks of the Kamo River but the main road leading to the two Honganji temples from the Daibutsuden has been drawn as one continuous line. From this we are able to gather the fact that the cityscape axis, which had disappeared after Nijo Castle was burnt to the ground, reemerged in the form of the Honganji - Daibutsuden axis.

The Rakuchu Rakugai Ichiboezu illustration clearly shows the close connection the religious buildings at the foot of Mt. Higshiyama had with the center of Kyoto, in the way the shrines and temples have been drawn at the end of each of the streets running in an easterly direction. The reason why the line of the west facing shrines and temples was the main theme of this picture is because of pictures of Higashiyama which appeared in the *Karaku Meisho Zue* album. Here a combination of shrines and temples stand looking westwards at the eastern end of roads which cross over the Kamo River. Tofukuji is depicted looking down a street running in an easterly direction from Kamo River. Then moving northwards, Sanjusangendo is situated at the end of Shichijo-dori, the Otani Mausoleum is at the end of Gojo-dori, Kiyomizudera is at the end of the then Matsubara-dori, or the original Gojo-dori, and the shrine, Yasaka Jinja, is at the end of Shijo-dori. In some cases where the old existing buildings of the monasteries or shrines faced south, it was only the gate that looked out onto these roads. All of them were major constituents of the landscape in the environs of Kyoto. The picture of *Daibutsu Monsen-mimizuka* in the Yodogawa Ryog*an* Ichiran album, published in 1856, depicts the view looking westwards from Hokoji. Higashi Honganji and Honkokuji are drawn projecting above the townscape so disproportionately large that there is a feeling that we can almost reach out and touch them.

The existence of a psychologically adaptable way of looking at the world, in an age when there were neither photographs nor accurate survey maps, should always be remembered when trying to understand the formation of any historically appointed scene.

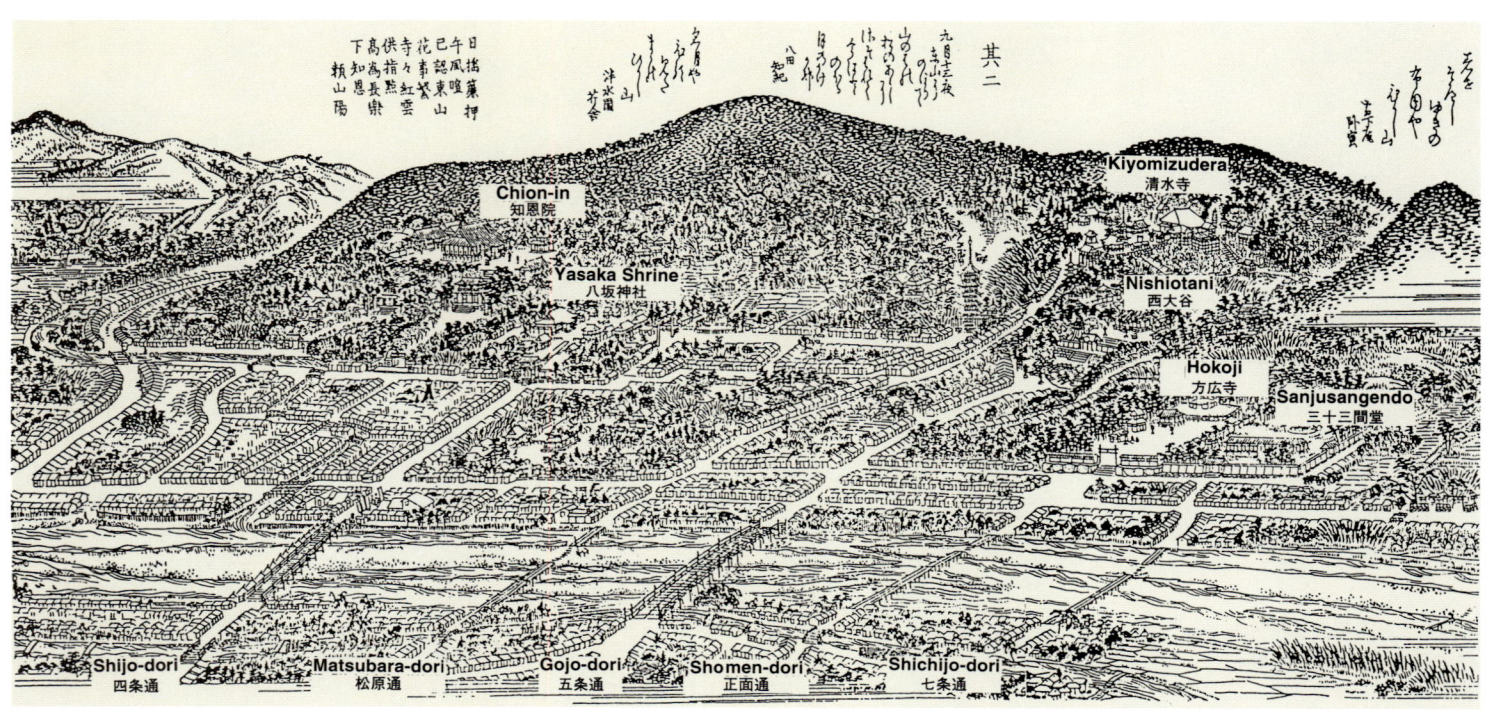

A section of an illustration showing the whole of Higashiyama, *Karaku Meishou Zue*, 1864　各々の通の正面に社寺が位置する東山の景観　江戸時代後期『花洛名勝図会』(元治元年刊)より

鴨東における正面型景観の形成

寛延三年(1750)二条城の５層の天守閣は雷火によって焼失した．その後約50年間大仏殿は存続した後，寛政十年(1798)やはり落雷で焼失した．巨大なモニュメントが対置する景観構成はこうして江戸時代中期には消えていった．しかし，近世初頭に華々しく現われたモニュメントの配置によって景観の軸をつくりだす景観演出は，その後の京の景観に影響を残したように思われる．

古代以来の歴史をもつ祇園社は，四条通の鴨川を越えた突き当りに西楼門を構えていたが，本殿はじめ全体の配置は南向きであった．これに対し，方広寺大仏殿は東山を背景に，伽藍全体が京の町に向けて建てられ，それを仰ぐに適当な広い道のような広場を正面に用意したのであった．大仏殿につづいてこれと同様な配置をとったのが，大谷本廟(西大谷)であった．大谷本廟は慶長年間に今の東山五条の地に移転し，17世紀後半から18世紀始めにかけて諸施設が整備された．その配置を見ると，当時の五条橋通のゆるい屈曲部に小広場を設け，そこに門を配して，あたかも五条橋通の東の正面に位置するかのように見せている．19世紀初頭頃の京を西の上空から見おろした黄華山筆「洛中洛外一望絵図」を見ると，大仏殿に並んで，五条橋通の突き当りに大谷本廟が描写されている．この図では東西方向の通を鴨川の東と西で屈曲させる構図をとっているが，大仏殿から両本願寺を結ぶ正面通は直線で描かれている．二条城天主閣の焼失によって大仏殿—本願寺という景観の軸線が再び浮かび上がっていたことがうかがえよう．

「洛中洛外一望絵図」でもうひとつ注目すべき点は，東山山麓の社寺が京の町から東へのびる道で町と結ばれた景観が描かれていることである．洛中洛外図では，祇園社と大仏殿を除いて，これらの社寺と町とは金雲で隔てられ，両者の関係はあいまいであった．それが鴨東に人家がひろがったこととあいまって，いまや町との明快な関係のもとに描写されるに至ったのである．その明快な関係とは，東へ向かうそれぞれの通の突き当りの正面に社寺が位置するという図式である．このように通りの突き当り正面にモニュメントが位置する景観図式を「正面型景観」と呼ぶこととしておきたい．さて，鴨東の正面型景観の並列するさまを図の主題としたかのように描いたのが，幕末に出版された『花洛名勝図会』所収の「東山全図」である．鴨川を越えて東へ延びる通と正面の社寺の組合せとして，四条通—八坂神社(祇園社)，松原通(元の五条通)—清水寺，五条通—大谷本廟，七条通—三十三間堂，さらに東福寺が鴨川から東へ延びる通の正面に描写されている．伽藍が古来南向きの社寺は門だけを通の正面に向けたものであったが，すべては東山山麓に正面型景観を並列するものとして，京の景観の大きな構成を形成していった．安政三年(1856)刊行の『淀川両岸一覧』所収の「大仏門前　耳塚」図は方広寺から西方を眺めた景観を描写しているが，広場の向こうに東本願寺と本圀寺が町なみの上に突出する様子を手に取るほど近く大きく描いている．写真や正確な実測図のなかった時代の，融通性のある心理的な視線を忘れては，歴史的な景観構成を理解することはできない．

III
Streetscape – Their Development and Buildings
町屋と町並み景観の発展

Historical Development of Streetscape Styles

Historical Development of Streetscape Styles
When considering the transformation which the town houses of Kyoto have gone through, we are faced with the problem that very few really old examples still remain, which is certainly not the case with shrines and temples. Although there were a number of fires down through the ages, one of the principle reasons for this lack of historical town houses is the result of one particular fire, which started during the 1864 Hamaguri Gomon coup d'état, and destroyed many buildings over a wide area. In fact, almost all of the town houses, or *machiya* of a traditional design which remain in Kyoto today were either built after this incident or during the early part of the twentieth century. This means that although the city itself is extremely old, its town houses are relatively new. In order to consider the development of the streetscapes and their buildings over the centuries, we must therefore resort to an investigation of historical depictions of the streets and town houses of Kyoto.

Simplicity of Pre-medieval Machiya

Heian period streets can be found depicted in the *Nenchu Gyoji Emaki*, a scroll painting which was commissioned by the Emperor Goshirakawa in the second half of the twelfth century, and shows a whole year of the events and festivals of the city. In the portion illustrated - see page 46 - we see the *Gion Goryoe*, which is thought to show the streetscape along Shijo-dori. While the buildings are somewhat roughly built, they are orderly lined up with their ridges parallel to the street and the entrances are at the side of the buildings. They all follow a basic, existing pattern and it can be assumed that this style of building had been followed for a thousand years. The roofs are of large, roughly laid wooden boards with a grid of poles laid on top. The walls are boarded, each board being 'woven' into a wickerwork pattern. However, there is an absence of daub walling as yet. Compared to subsequent periods, the windows are small and, although there is not one in the section illustrated, in other parts of the scroll there are buildings with hinged shutters called *shitomido*, which were lifted up and caught or propped open with a stick.

Moving on to the end of the Muromachi period (1568-1600), the *Rakuchu Rakugai* illustrations of the city and its environs show a great deal of detail and a large number of town houses. The oldest of these is the *Machida Rakuchu Rakugai* painting, which probably dates from the first half of the sixteenth century. Similar paintings in the possession of the Uesugi and Takahashi families were done after it but show the same tendencies. The roofs are the same as those of the Heian period but narrow bamboo

Shijo-dori in the Heian period; *Nenchu Gyoji Emaki*
平安時代の四条通の町並み 12世紀後期 『年中行事絵巻』（部分） 田中家所蔵

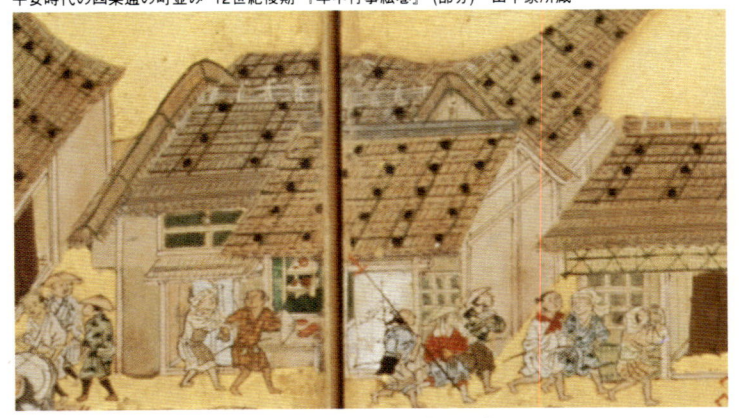

Machiya along Muromachi-dori, *Uesugi Rakuchu Rakugai-zu*
室町通の町家 上杉家旧蔵本洛中洛外図より 米沢市所蔵

An example of a machiya with a *kabuki*, or lintel and an *udatsu* firebreak device, *Machida Rakuchu Rakugai-zu*
卯立と冠木のある町家 町田家旧蔵本洛中洛外図より 国立歴史民俗博物館所蔵

町並みの様式発展史

京の町家の意匠について，その変遷をたどろうとするとき，寺社の場合とは違って古い遺構が残っていないという問題がある．幾度かの大火があった上に，幕末の元治元年(1864)蛤御門の変のため八百十一町が消失してしまった．そのため，京都に残る伝統的な町家は，殆どがその復興の後，明治時代以降に建てられたものである．意外に歴史都市京都の町家は新しい．そこで，私たちは絵画に描写された京の町家や町並みをたどり，その発展を見てゆくことにしたい．

中世以前――素朴な町家

平安時代の京の町並みが「年中行事絵巻」に描写されている．「年中行事絵巻」は12世紀後半に，後白河天皇の命で一年の行事を絵に描きとどめている．46頁左上の図はその中の祇園御霊会を描いた部分で，町並みは四条通と思われる．町家を見ると，粗末なものではあるけれど，軒を接して並び，棟を通りと並行にした「平入り」形式であるという基本的な枠組みは既にあり，この形式はおよそ千年にわたって踏襲されたことになる．屋根は板葺で，丸太を縦横に置いて重しにしている．壁は板張りと，板か草を網代に組んでおり，土壁は見られない．窓は後世と比較すれば小さく，この図の部分にはないが別の部分では板戸を上に押し開ける蔀戸になっている．

それから時代が飛ぶが，室町時代末期になると洛中洛外図が出現したので，それに詳しく，また多数描写された町家を見ることができる．町田家旧蔵本洛中洛外図は描写された景観の年代が最も古く，16世紀前半と推定されている．景観年代が幾らか下る上杉家本や高橋家本でも，描写された町並みはおよそ似かよっている．屋根は平安時代と同じく板葺だが，細い棒か竹を2本ずつ対にして縦横に格子状に並べ，交差部分に重し石を載せている．卯立を上げている家もかなりあり，卯立につけた屋根は板葺より草葺が多い．当初の機能は隣家の屋根との間の雨漏り対策であったようだ．変わった例では，卯立を通り側の壁面にまで回しているものがある．これはかえって雨仕舞が悪かったのだろうか，後の時代には見られなくなる．壁面は年中行事絵巻からかなり変化して，土壁になっている．窓は大きくなり，上端は鴨居位置よ

poles in pairs have been laid in a grid, with a rock placed where they intersect. Some buildings have an *udatsu* - later to become a kind of raised fire-break - but in many cases the roofs are of grass rather than wooden boards. Originally, the function of the *udatsu* seems to have been to prevent rain from going down the gap between the buildings, but there are examples where it is extended round to the street side of the roof. However, this subsequently seems to have disappeared, probably because of its failure to deal with rain. There is considerable development in wall treatments from those seen in the *Nenchu Gyoji Emaki* scrolls, the daub wall having made its appearance. Windows are also larger with their tops being positioned below the wall plate and their bottoms at the same height as the floors. There are examples of these large openings with a vertical and horizontal mesh of thick members over them as well as examples with no such grill at all. In the case of houses which are selling goods there is a display shelf fixed at the foot of such openings. But because there are examples of these 'shops' with grills, it must be supposed that they were either provided as a form of protection in troubled times, or that they were actually providing structural support for such a large openings. The entrances fall into three basic types. The first is one flanked by two columns joined by a wall plate; and the second is similar, but two poles are joined below the wall plate by a lintel. Simply speaking the latter is a 'hole' opened in a daub wall. The third type is a combination of these two. It goes without saying that the older lintel type, or *kabuki* type of entrance disappeared during the Edo period which followed.

Although there does not seem to have been many of them, a number of diverse two-storey buildings made their appearance at the end of the medieval period. In fact, the first two-storey buildings with boarded floors upstairs were the bell-towers which were introduced from the Chinese mainland for use in Zen temples. Despite the fact, however, that both Kinkakuji and Ginkakuji had already been built with two floors some years before, it seems that two-storey town houses were not generally built until the end of the Muromachi period. The walls of the first and second floors of town houses depicted in late-medieval illustrations of Kyoto and its environs are on the same line, with a shingled canopy roof fitted between the two floors. Supporting such a projecting canopy roof must have been a problem and there are no stones on them to weigh down the shingles. In fact, in the copy of a Rakuchu Rakugai painting held by the National Museum in Tokyo, there are examples of two-storey buildings with no such canopies. There are some much more unusual examples in fan painting of the sights of Kyoto done by Kano Munehide and dating from the end of 16th century. Of more than 60 of such paintings which are said to have existed, two show town houses in the Kamigyo area of the city. In one of these there is a building with what appears to be a balcony rather than a canopy roof. In the other there is an example of a building with what is like a tower perched on the roof of the lower floor. It would seem, therefore, that such buildings were enough of a novelty to be included in these paintings showing the sights of Kyoto.

Streetscapes and Buildings in the 17th Century

As if to make amends for the sadness and strife of the Sengoku period (1482-1558) of civil war, the town buildings of Kyoto developed markedly afterwards. In point of fact, the large number of paintings done of the city and its environs throughout the seventeenth century would seem almost to be evidence of the admiration there ap-

Commercial properties along Ogawa-dori, *Rakuchu Rakugai-zu*, Heian period 小川通の商家　同左

An example of a two storey building; *Rakuchu Rakugai-zu*, Heian period　二階屋　同左

り低いが，下端は床と同じ高さにまで下がっている．この大きな開口部全体に太い縦横の格子をはめている例と，格子なしで開口している例がある．物を売る家は開口部の外に店棚を出して商品を並べている．物売りの町家でも，格子のある場合とない場合があるから，格子は物騒な時代ゆえの用心か，あるいは大きな開口部の補強の意味もあったかもしれない．出入口には3つの形式がある．2本の柱の間に鴨居を渡したものと，桁まで届かない2本の棒の上に横棒(冠木)を乗せたもので，いわば土壁に穴を開けた形式とが見られる．また，柱を立ててはいるが鴨居で結合せず，柱より外にはみだした冠木を打ち付けているものがある．先の2形式の混合型といってよい．言うまでもなく，冠木形式は江戸時代には消えていった古い形式である．

中世末の町家では，数は少ないが，二階建ての建設が多様に試みられた．ちなみに，二階に床を張って使用する二階建て建築というものは，わが国では禅宗寺院が中国から取り入れた楼閣から始まっている．金閣・銀閣も既にあったが，町家の二階建ては室町時代末に試みだしたようだ．中世末の洛中洛外図では，1階と2階の壁面は同じ位置で，1・2階の間には板葺の通り庇がついている．迫り出した庇を支えるのは難しかったとみえ，重し石は乗せていないし，東京国立博物館所蔵洛中洛外図模本では庇のない二階屋が描かれている．もっと変わった例が，狩野宗秀筆「京名所図扇面」に見られる．60余面あったといわれる中に，上京の町並みの描写が2面あり，その一つには庇はなくバルコニーらしきものを回しているものがあり，他の一つには櫓のように小さな二階を一階の屋根に乗せた例が描写されている．こうした町家のある町並みは京名所に挙げられるほどに都らしく珍しい景観であったのだろう．

江戸時代初期の町家と町並み景観

戦国時代が終わると，戦火の愁いがなくなったからだろうか，京の町家は急に立派なものに発展した．そうした新しい都市景観の出現を賛美するかのように，江戸時代初期には17世紀の間を通じて多数の洛中洛外図が描かれたのであった．

この時代の洛中洛外図に描写された町並みを見れば，平屋の町並みの中に，二階建ての町家が連続する町並みが出現したことに先ず目を引かれる．少し注意して二階屋を見ると，その骨格が現存す

parently was for the new guise which the old capital had taken on.

Looking at such paintings, the first thing which is noticeable is that the streetscapes are composed of single storey buildings interspersed with two-storey ones. Paying particular attention to these two-storey buildings we find that they are of two types. Firstly there are those in which the walls of the upper and lower storeies are set one above the other like existing types, with a canopy roof between the two floors. Whereas with the other type, the upper wall stands proud of the lower wall and there is no canopy roof. This latter type is called *dashigeta-zukuri*, or more colloquially *segai-zukuri*, but is more or less equivalent to buildings with jetties found in Europe. If we now concentrate on looking to see which type of two-storey town houses are depicted along the streets during the seventeenth century, we find that it is possible to classify the depictions of Kyoto and its environs done during this century into three types. In the earlier paintings we find that the streetscapes are composed almost exclusively of two-storey buildings with jetties, and there are either very few or no two-storey buildings with canopy roofs at all. In the second type, the streetscapes are composed of a mixture of both two-storey buildings with jetties, and those with canopied bays. In paintings dating from nearer the end of the seventeenth century, however, there are no buildings with jetties and the streetscapes are composed exclusively of two-storey town houses with canopied bays. It would seem, therefore, that the buildings and streetscapes of Kyoto went through this progressive pattern of transformation during the seventeenth century.

The most representative painting of the first type described above is the *Fanaki Rakuchu Rakugai* painting now retained by the National Museum in Tokyo. It shows something of the new developments which occurred along the streets of Kyoto right at the beginning of the seventeenth century. Not only are there shingle roofs with stones to weigh them down, but there are also some more finely finished roofs of shingles as well as a few tiled roofs, too. These tiled roofs are not done with the interlocking type of pan tile which came along later but are of a simpler, classical type using a flat tile and a round tile like those used on the roofs of temples. But what is of particular interest is the use of grills for the second floor of the jettied town houses. The grills are either composed of narrow vertical rails or of a slanting type, and there are even some which are curved producing a wave pattern. At street level, on the other hand, the rails are widely spaced and differ very little from those used during the Muromachi period. This change in the handling of the second floor marked the beginning of a move toward the establishment of a more settled design for such town houses.

Moving on to look at the *Ikeda Rakuchu Rakugai* illustration now at the Hayashibara Museum in Okayama, we find that the design of

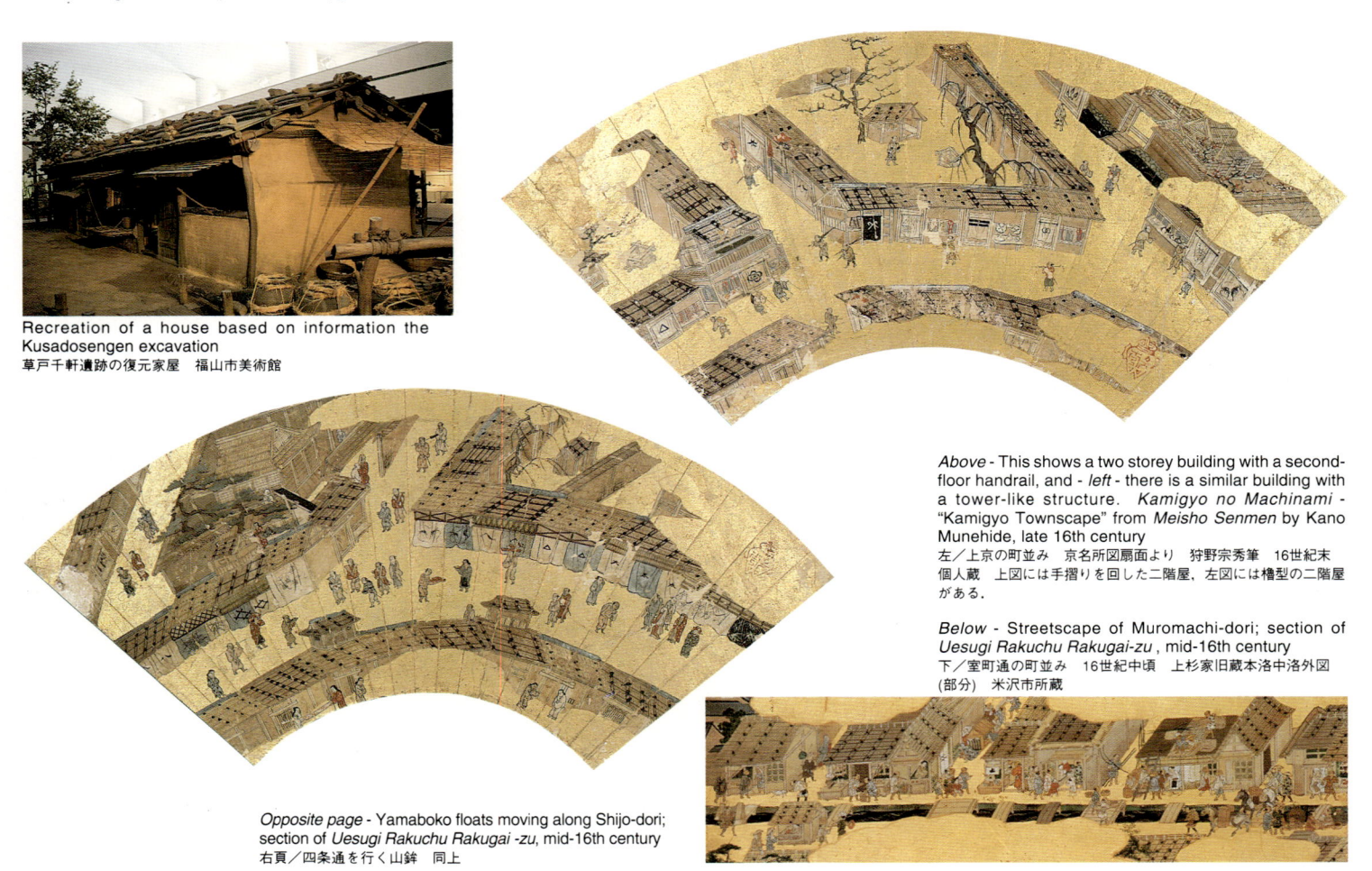

Recreation of a house based on information the Kusadosengen excavation
草戸千軒遺跡の復元家屋　福山市美術館

Above - This shows a two storey building with a second-floor handrail, and - *left* - there is a similar building with a tower-like structure. *Kamigyo no Machinami* - "Kamigyo Townscape" from *Meisho Senmen* by Kano Munehide, late 16th century
左／上京の町並み　京名所図扇面より　狩野宗秀筆　16世紀末　個人蔵　上図には手摺りを回した二階屋、左図には櫓型の二階屋がある．

Below - Streetscape of Muromachi-dori; section of *Uesugi Rakuchu Rakugai-zu*, mid-16th century
下／室町通の町並み　16世紀中頃　上杉家旧蔵本洛中洛外図（部分）　米沢市所蔵

Opposite page - Yamaboko floats moving along Shijo-dori; section of *Uesugi Rakuchu Rakugai -zu*, mid-16th century
右頁／四条通を行く山鉾　同上

る二階建て町家とほぼ同じように2階壁面が1階壁面の上にあり1・2階の間に庇のある形式と，それとは違って2階壁面が1階壁面より迫り出し，1・2階の間に庇のない二階屋の2つの形式がある．後者を「出梁造り」と呼ぶことにしておこう．さて，どちらの形式の二階屋の町並みが描写されているかに注目すると，江戸時代初期の洛中洛外図はおよそ次の3群に分類することができる．I群＝出梁造りの二階屋の町並みが描写され，庇付の二階屋は全くないか殆どない．II群＝出梁造りの町並みと，庇付の二階屋の町並みの両者が混在しているもの．III群＝庇付の二階屋の町並みのみが描写され，出梁造りは見られないもの．江戸時代初期の町並みはこの順序で変遷をたどったようである．

I群を代表する舟木家旧蔵本洛中洛外図（現東京国立博物館蔵）で，江戸時代に入ってからの新しい京の町並みの展開を見てみよう．屋根は石置き板葺屋根だけでなく，板を密に重ねた柿葺や，まだ少数だが瓦葺も見られる．当時の瓦葺はまだ桟瓦ではなく，寺院と同じ平瓦と丸瓦を交互に並べる本瓦葺であった．それより目を引くのは出梁造りの二階屋で，その二階壁面には細い縦格子や，斜めに矢来型に組んだ格子，中には波形の曲線の格子もある．いっぽう，1階壁面は相変わらず粗い格子があって室町時代と余り変化がない．町家は二階から意匠に凝り始めたのだった．

池田家旧蔵本洛中洛外図（現林原美術館蔵）になると，町家の意匠は多様を極める．土壁の色も茶系色，赤っぽい色，白，青色などがあり，それも1棟の壁面を多色に塗分ける例も多々見られる．これはII群に属す図で，出梁造りの町並みと，庇のある二階屋の町並みの両者がある．格子のパターンが多様な他に，中には茶室のような下地窓があったり，半円形の窓さえ見られる．2階の屋根の上に櫓を乗せているものもある．これは大きさからいえば人が登れる3階のようだが，煙出しだったかもしれない．蔵の建物には背の高い三階蔵があり，町の各所に突出している．井原西鶴の『日本永代蔵』（元禄元年1688刊）に都の富裕な商人を「一に

town houses has become extremely diverse. The color of the daub walls range from brown to a reddish color and even to white and a bluish green. There are even examples where various wall surfaces of the same building are painted different colors. This particular illustration corresponds to the second of our classifications above and the streetscapes are therefore composed of buildings with jetties, or are composed of buildings with a projecting canopied bay. The grills at the openings are of various patterns. There are other interesting examples such as those where the framework of bamboo for the daub wall is exposed in the window opening (*shitaji-mado*) as seen on commercial tea houses and there are hemispherical windows, too. There are also examples of two-storey buildings with low towers perched on their roofs. Such towers could be called a third floor for one person as they are not much more than a smoke outlet. Some storehouses are of three-storeies in height and can be seen all over town. The writer Ihara Saikaku wrote in his *Nihon Eitaigura* - "The Eternal Storehouse of Japan" (1688), that the rich merchants of the old capital were those who had bails of rice at their door, a two-storey building and a three-storey storehouse, and it is indeed possible to gain some idea of what Kyoto was like when such wealthy people were in business from this particular depiction.

The styles of buildings depicted in this colorful and diverse streetscape reminds us of a number of famous seventeenth century pieces of Japanese architecture. Dating from about the same period and both in Kyoto, such things as the freely composed shapes of the *tsuke-shoin*, or alcove windows of the Katsura Detached Palace and the decorative windows of Hiunkaku, are reminiscent of the hemispherical windows found on town houses. The same is true of the dyed curtains, or *noren* at the entrances and hanging in front of the buildings. The design of Sumiya, a house of lordly entertainment now mostly dating from the eighteenth century, is highly representative of its type. A variety of colors are used for the walls including a rich red-ocher as well as cooler hues and it has a number of grills of various patterns, too. The bold design of umbrellas on the room-dividing screens at Wachigaiya located in the same area is another example of the diversity and freedom exercised in architectural and interior design which, although existing in a modified and refined form, must surely be indicative of the aesthetics of the period when the *Ikeda Rakuchu Rakugai* illustration was done. The core of the Sumiya complex goes back to a seventeenth-century building and the kind of design and decorative features it displays as well as the obvious enjoy-

俵，二階造り，三階蔵」を持つ人々と表現しているが，この洛中洛外図からはそういう分限者のいた頃の京の景観がうかがえる．

　こうした多彩，多様な町並みの意匠は，江戸時代初期の有名な建築の幾つかを想いおこさせる．およそ同じ時代の桂離宮の付書院の窓，飛雲閣の花頭窓の自由な形と用い方と，町家の半円形の窓，あるいは壁を覆う暖簾に染め抜いた文様の自由な大胆さ．角屋の意匠は花街独特とされてきたが，赤色や青色の壁の色，波形や斜線の多様な格子，或は同じ島原の輪違屋の襖の大胆な傘のデザイン，これらの自由で多様な意匠は，変形され洗練された形になってはいるが，旧池田家本の時代の美的

ment there seems to have been gained from mixing new flamboyant design features with a variety of other motifs, suggests that this kind of aesthetic was common to all echelons of society up until the middle of the seventeenth century. If Katsura and Hiunkaku are indicative of the highly refined sukiya-style, then it could also be said that the same style of architecture was evident in the streetscapes of the period, too.

Concerning the illustrations of Kyoto in which there are no two-storey buildings with jetties, the streetscapes display a overall air of consistency. There is no obsession with individuality in the designs but the grills at street level are now of a much more delicate type. Attempts to create finer and more refined designs with verticality are also much more evident.

A New View of the World

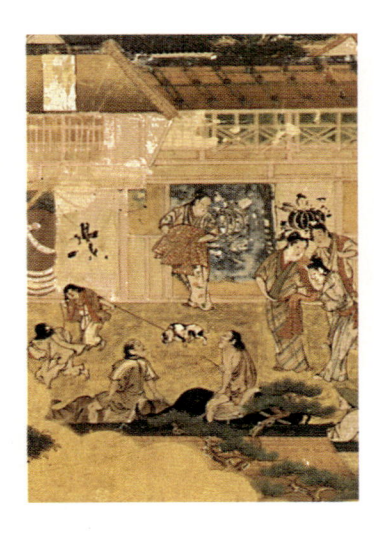

Maruyama Okyo who was the founder of the Maruyama school of artists, was in Kyoto as a young man and did what were called *megane-e* utilizing a form of linear perspective. It seems, in fact, that he made his mark more as a draughtsman than as an artist because of them. This technique of representation which is said to have been introduced from the West along with the required equipment, involved looking at a picture reflected in a mirror through a lens. By viewing the virtual image in the mirror through the lens it became possible to enjoy the reality of the illusionary image as if it were the real thing. The feeling of depth which was brought out by the use of linear perspective was the key to the success of this technique and street scenes and street–scapes were therefore some of the most appropriate subjects. It was a little after the middle of the eighteenth century, therefore, that the first true linear perspective drawings were made in Japan.

Apart from being a new method of drawing as far as Japan was concerned, it also opened up a new way of looking at the city. Such works as *Shijo Shibai* and *Shijo Otabisho*, both streetscapes attributed to Maruyama Okyo and dating from mid-18th century, were done at a time when the Japanese people were first able to consciously appreciate depictions of streetscapes and to view street scenes from the eye-level of a person standing on a street, in the same way that we have now become used to looking at such scenes in a photograph. Up until then, a streetscape was always seen from above and was depicted using a system of parallel lines, and this was true of any representation including the Rakuchu Rakugai pictures. However, these new perspective drawings brought the viewpoint down to ground level.

Above - Jetted two-storey buildings in Muromachi Gojo; section of *Funaki Rakuchu Rakugai-zu*, early-17th century
上／出梁造り二階屋の並ぶ室町五条付近　17世紀前期　舟木家旧蔵本　洛中洛外図(部分)　東京国立博物館所蔵

Left - above and below, Two-storey buildings with jetting
左／出梁造り二階屋　同上

趣味を伝えてはいないだろうか．角屋は17世紀の建物を母体としている．これらの例を並べてみると，多彩な新しい意匠の創出と，多様な意匠の並存混在を楽しむ美的趣味が，17世紀初期から中頃の社会に貴賎を越えて広く嗜好されたものとして浮かび上がってくる．桂や飛雲閣を「数寄」の意匠と呼ぶとすれば，その数寄は町並みにもあったといえるだろう．

出梁造りの二階屋が見られない洛中洛外図の一群では，町並み全体に静かな調子が広がってくる．個々に変わった意匠が見られず，その分，1階壁面にも千本格子が用いられたり，繊細化と洗練への兆しを漂わせている．

江戸時代中期――眼鏡絵が開いた街路景観の視点

写生を重んじる円山四条派を開いた円山応挙は，若い頃京都にあって線遠近画法を導入した眼鏡絵を描き，芸術家というよりは画工的なその仕事で世に出たと伝えられる．西洋からその器具とともに伝わったという眼鏡絵とは，一度鏡に写し，それをレンズを通して見るというもので，鏡の中の虚像をさらにレンズを通すことで，実際の風物を見ているような錯覚にも似たリアリティが楽しまれた．線遠近画法を駆使した奥行きの表現が眼目であり，その格好のテーマとして街路景観，町並み景観が取り上げられた．日本人がかなり正確な線遠近画法で描きはじめたのはこの時期，18世紀中頃を少し過ぎた頃であった．

さて，この出来事は画法の導入ということの他に，都市への新しい眼差しを開いたのでもあった．

応挙筆と伝えられる「四条芝居」や「四条御旅所」の町並みを描いた図を見てみよう．私たちが写真で見慣れた町並みの構図，街路に立つ人の目の高さで見た街路景観，それを日本人が明確に意識的に見ることができるようになったのがこの時期だった．洛中洛外図をはじめこれまでの絵画では，町並みは常に空中から見た姿であり，平行透視図として描写されていた．眼鏡絵とともに，都市を見る視点が地上に降り立ったわけである．

眼鏡絵に描写された町並みは，いまや洛中洛外図の町並みとは異なり，格子は縦格子に統一された互いに似た意匠の町家が軒を連続させている．奥行きの表現のために連続性が強調されているかもしれない．洛中洛外図では約500m離れた三条・四条間で町家を5軒程選んで描くという省略法に

(54頁につづく)

Unlike the earlier representations of Kyoto and its environs, the streetscapes depicted in the *megane-e* are composed of buildings of a consistent design with vertical grill-work, all standing in strict lines along the streets. It is of course possible that the continuity of these streetscapes is being emphasized by the sense of depth these pictures have. The actual distance of approximately 500 meters between Shijo-dori and Sanjo-dori is considerably abbreviated in Rakuchu Rakugai illustrations with only five buildings being shown in this distance. However, this serves to create an overall impression of the city while still bringing individual buildings to the attention of the viewer. Compared to this, Western perspective drawing did not only provided the artist with a new method of expression but it also gave the viewer a new viewpoint, while also drawing people's attention to street scenes per se. The sense of surprise and wonderment created, therefore, focused the eyes of the people on these scenes. Artists, in other words, were able to focus the sense of aesthetic appreciation of the people on an overall impression of a streetscape.

Subsequently, there were no great changes in the design of the buildings along the streets of Kyoto, but there were signs of a process of refinement and the channeling of energies into the job of standardizing town house forms.

Standardization and Refinement

Streetscapes are depicted in illustration of the Sanjo Ohashi and Gojo Ohashi bridges included in the best selling guide to Kyoto, the *Miyako Meisho Zue*, published in 1780. Functioning both as illustrations and as guide maps, the bridges and surrounding areas are seen in a bird's-eye view. Nevertheless, the number of buildings show was probably more or less correct. The roofs are all tiled and all the canopied bays are linked in a continuous line and in fact the exteriors of the town houses are depicted as being almost entirely consistent with each other.

The truth of the impression which can be gained from these illustrations is backed up by a detailed colored depiction of the streetscape between Sanjo-dori and Rokkaku-dori along Aburanokoji-dori. This picture done in 1820 and is now in the Kyoto Museum of Local History - *Kyoto-fu Sogo Shiryo-kan*. For many years it was in the possession of the Omiya, a shop actually shown in the work. What is immediately noticeable is the degree of standardization in the design details of the exteriors of the buildings. Firstly, all the roofs are now tiled with pan tiles. Secondly, adding up the number

(Continued on page 54)

Above - Jetted two-storey buildings along Shijo-dori above, and below those with *hisashi* standing along Sanjo-dori; section of *Goin Sairei-zu*, mid 17th century
出梁造り二階屋の四条通(上)と庇のある二階屋の並ぶ三条通(下)17世紀中頃　祇園祭礼図(部分)　海北友雪　八幡山保存会所蔵

Interior of Hiunkaku 飛雲閣内部

Hiunkaku 飛雲閣

Ikeda Rakuchu Rakugai-zu
The two sections were set up on either side of a room like this. The left-hand section shows Kamigyo while the other shows Shimogyo and Nijojo and the Daibutsuden face each other in close proximity.

Hieizan 比叡山	Maruyama 円山	Yasakano-to 八坂ノ塔	Kiyomizudera 清水寺
吉田	黒谷		
Shimogamo Shrine 下鴨神社	Nanzenji 南禅寺	Chion-in 知恩院	Yasaka Shrine 八坂神社	Hokokubyo 豊国廟
Kamigamo Shrine 上賀茂神社	Kamogawa 鴨川	Sanjo Bridge 三条橋	Kenninji 建仁寺	Fushimijo 伏見城
百万遍		本能寺		
Shokokuji 相国寺	紫宸殿 Imperial Palace	Teramachi-dori 寺町通	Shijo-dori 四条河原	Sanjusangendo 三十三間堂	Tofukuji 東福寺
	内裏殿	二条殿	Hokojidaibutsuden 方広寺大仏殿	
		六角堂		Gojo Bridge 五条橋	
	室町通	Higashinotoin-tori 東洞院通	Karasuma-dori 烏丸通	Higashi Honganji 東本願寺
			竹田	

池田家旧蔵本洛中洛外図 景観年代17世紀中期 林原美術館所蔵
洛中洛外図はこのように座敷の左右に向い合わせに置いて観賞された．左隻は上京，右隻は下京の町を描写しており，二条城と大仏殿が近い位置で向き合う．町並みが最も多様で華やかであった状況を描いている．

of buildings shown along the eastern and western sides of the street comes to 39 buildings of which only two have an *udatsu*, and only about one-quarter of the canopied roofs are tiled with wooden boards. Most of the second floor walls of the façades have heavily mullioned windows - *mushiko-mado* - and generally speaking columns are visible at both ends of these walls. This means that these windows are long rectangular openings unbroken by structural columns. There would also seem to be a conscious effort to expose the columns in the design of the façades. In seventeenth-century depictions of Kyoto and its environs, there are a few examples of the plastered type of town house known as a *nuriya*, in which the columns are completely plastered over. It would therefore seem that such buildings made a relatively early appearance on the streets of Kyoto. It should be noted, however, that despite the fire-resistant qualities of such buildings, subsequently the people of Kyoto seemed to prefer the *shinkabe* or 'half-timber' style, in which structural columns and beams were exposed. Some of the grills at second-floor openings were also probably of wood. In fact, judging from other illustrations of people watching the Gion Matsuri from second-floor windows, it would be very difficult to say that all the streets were lined with buildings which had second-floor opening with heavy mullions.

Turning our attention to the first floor of these buildings there are both projecting screened bays with a transom and those without one. However, the degree to which the height between the eaves and the bottom sill is standardized and the proportion of the framing of these projecting screened bays is also standardized, is particularly surprising. It is often said that one of the special features of the town houses of Kyoto is the fineness of the individual members but that is not really the point. In contrast to the narrow rails of the grills there is always a framework of a standard width on all houses and it is therefore the proportion of the members that is important. This kind of standardization clearly shows that the people of Kyoto were more interested in 'marrying' the details of the designs of town houses than they were in exteriors with individuality.

The trend of standardization and refinement continued during the rest of the eighteenth century, a fact which is born out by the streetscapes depicted in the *Karaku Meishou Zue*. In these illustrations the streets are composed of buildings which are even more similar to each other than the one shown in the Omiya illustration of Aburanokoji-dori. Furthermore, the way the il-

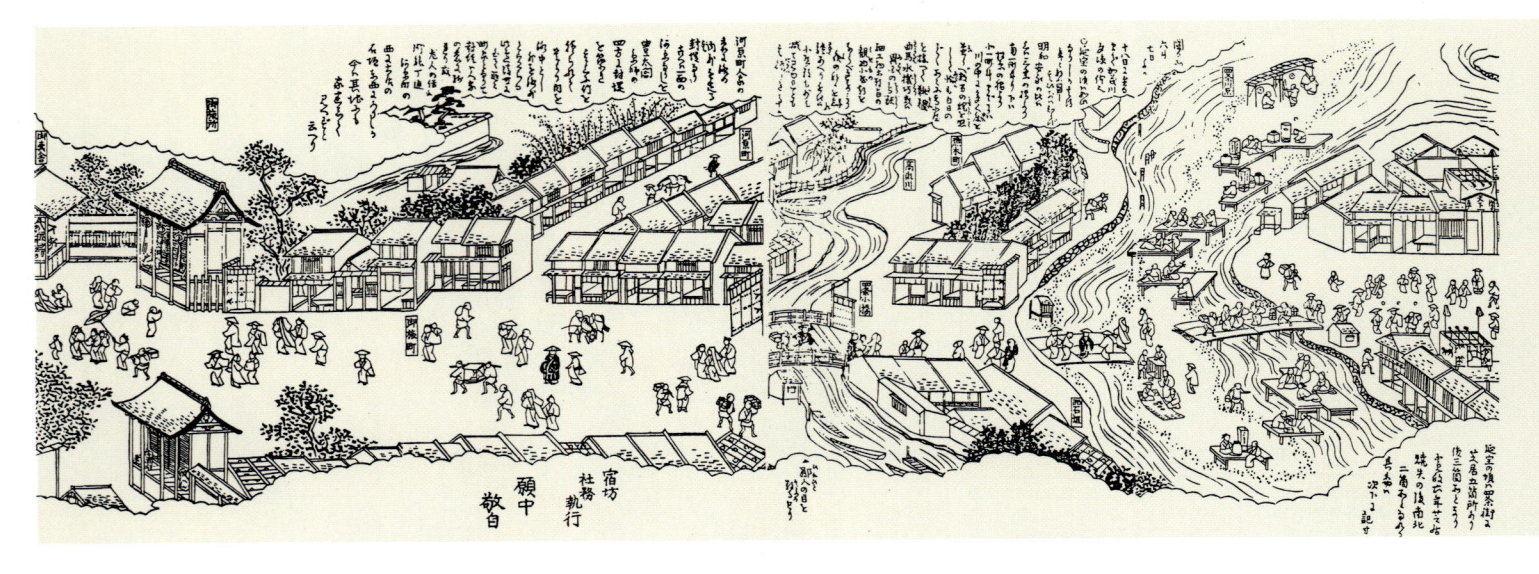

Above - Streetscape of Shijo-dori from section of Gionsha and Otabisho-zu; Hengakukihan, 1676
上／四条通の町並み　祇園社併御旅所図(部分)『扁額軌範』(延宝四年)より

Left - A three-storey storehouse and a two-storey sukiya-style building are visible here. *Ikeda Rakuchu Rakugai-zu*
左２点／三階蔵や数寄屋風二階屋が見える　17世紀中期　池田家旧蔵本洛中洛外図(部分)　林原美術館所蔵

Opposite page, right - a plastered machiya
右頁の右／塗屋造りの町家　同上

lustrations have been drawn is also more precise with very straight lines being used and the fineness of the rails of the screen-work and the proportions of the frames and rails themselves is also very well expressed. Even at the end of the eighteenth century, the streets of buildings put up after the great fire of 1864 also displayed evidence of the continued trend of 'marrying' details, standardization and refinement, a fact which can be verified from contemporary photographs. Perhaps the only noticeable development was the appearance of a long, thick chamfered beam running under the canopied bay or lean-to roof. This *maku-kake* beam clearly defined and emphasized the horizontal of the façades and there were even those which were left completely exposed, and were thus devoid of any cosmetic boarding. However, because most of the *maku-kake* of town houses that existed in the late nineteen-twenties were uncovered, it must be supposed that the use of this beam was further refined during modern times.

The degree to which the streetscapes of Kyoto had become standardized was noted by Kitagawa Morisada, who moved to the city from Edo (Tokyo), about the middle of the nineteenth century. He thought that compared to Edo the streetscapes of the old capital were not at all muddled and presented what he termed an "unbroken view of natural orderliness". There is no doubting the fact that compared to other cities in Japan, the degree to which even the fine details of the distinctive town houses of Kyoto have been standardized is surprising. It would be wrong to supposed that this is simply due to the strict rules which existed during feudal times. Nevertheless, not all of the town houses are exactly the same, because on occasions there are variations from the norm and the widths of the windows with heavy mullions and the projecting screened bays are of various widths according to the size of the frontages. Such variations provide rhythm and an acceptable degree of variety to the overall feeling of unity these streetscapes have. It would seem, in other words, as if the people of Kyoto had chosen to follow regular shapes and to refine existing forms, rather than to allow streetscapes to be jumbled and confused by simply using something which may have been new but was vulgar to the eye. Such an attitude may very well have much in common with the Classicism found in Western architecture and there is evidence to suggest that these tendencies continued on through the latter half of the nineteenth century and into the early part of the twentieth century, too.

The type of jetted buildings with projecting second floors which can still be seen at the post-towns of Tsumago and Narai along the former Nakasendo were soon disappeared from the streets of Kyoto.
妻籠の出梁造りの町家．迫り出し型の二階屋は京都では早い時期になくなったが、旧中山道の妻籠や奈良井などの宿場町では出梁造町家が現存している．

い．京の町家は部材の細さが特徴のようにも言われるがそうではない．細い格子に対し，一定の太さの框をどの家でも用い，比例にこだわっている．こうした定型化は明らかに，京の人々の町家建築にたいする嗜好が，デザインの個性より外観の定型化へ向かったことを示している．

幕末から明治へと，この定型化と洗練の傾向は続いた．『花洛名勝図会』に描写された町なみは，近江屋油小路絵図よりいっそう類似した家々の並びを示している．また，その描写方法も定規を用いて正確な直線を引き，千本格子の細やかさや，框や格子の比例をよく表現している．明治時代に入っても，幕末の大火の後に復興された町並みは定型化と洗練を示すものであった．その様子は，当時の写真によって知ることができる．意匠の変化と言えば，幕掛けが太い長い角材になり，それが1階庇の下で直線を見せ，すっきりした水平感を強調するようになっている．板を張らず，角材だけの幕掛けも見られる．ところで，昭和に存在した町家の幕掛けは板を張らないものが大半であったから，幕掛けの洗練は近代になっても行われたと考えられる．

19世紀中頃に江戸から京を訪れた喜多川守貞は，江戸に比べ町並み景観に乱れがなく「一望自ら整然たり」と評している．確かに，京の町並みは他都市に比較して細部に至る定型化が著しいところがある．封建時代の厳しい規制の結果とのみはかんがえられない所以である．ただ，全く同一の外観を示すのではなく，時に変化型が入り，また間口の変化に応じて，虫篭窓も出格子も横幅は家によりまちまちである．こうして町並み全体としては統一感のうちに穏やかな変化とリズムを持ちあわせている．目新しくその分だけ粗野な形を採用したり，それによる町並みの混乱を選ぶより，既存の形態を洗練し一定の姿へと収斂していくのが，京の人々の選んだ好みであった．その態度には，西欧建築における古典主義（クラシシズム）とも共通するものがあるといえるだろう．こうした傾向は幕末から，さらに明治時代にかけても進んでいったのであった．

Gion Otabisho by Maruyama Okyo; a *megane-e*, mid-18th century, looking east from the vicinity of Shijo-dori Tera-machi
祇園御旅所　伝円山応挙筆　眼鏡絵　18世紀中期　神戸市立博物館所蔵　四条通寺町付近から東を見ている．

Ryogokubashi Yusuzumi Ukie Kongen by Okumura Masanobu, 18th century. This is an early example of the use of perspective in Japan.
両国橋夕涼見浮絵根元　奥村政信筆　18世紀　神戸市立博物館所蔵　日本における初期の線遠近法

Megane-e, Sanjusangendo Toshiya by Maruyama Okyo, mid-18th century
眼鏡絵　三十三間堂大矢数　伝円山応挙筆　眼鏡絵　18世紀中期　神戸市立博物館所蔵

Megane-e, Shijo Shibai by Maruyama Okyo
四条芝居　伝円山応挙筆　眼鏡絵　神戸市立博物館所蔵

Two women looking at a *megane-e* by Suzuki Harunobu
眼鏡絵を見る女性　鈴木春信筆　神戸市立博物館所蔵

A tool to look at *megane-e*
のぞき眼鏡(反射式)　神戸市立博物館所蔵

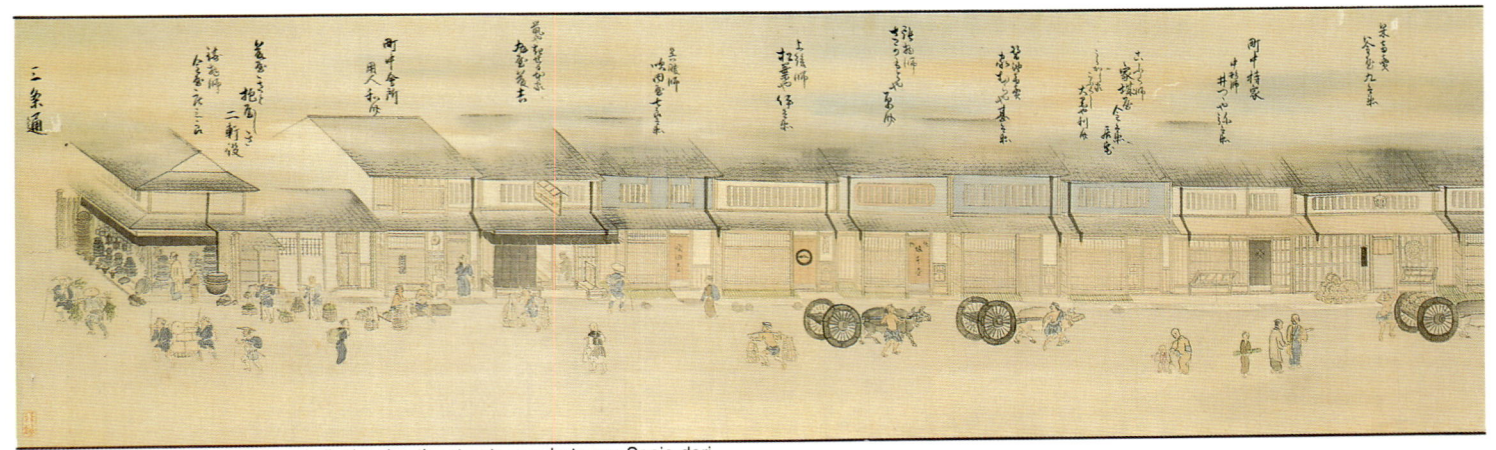

Above and below - Omiya Aburanokoji, showing the streetscape between Sanjo-dori and Rokkaku-dori. *Omiya Kichizaemon Monjo*, 1820
上・下／近江屋油小路絵図　三条通と六角通の間の町並みを描いている．『近江屋吉左衛門文書』
(文政三年)　京都府総合資料館所蔵

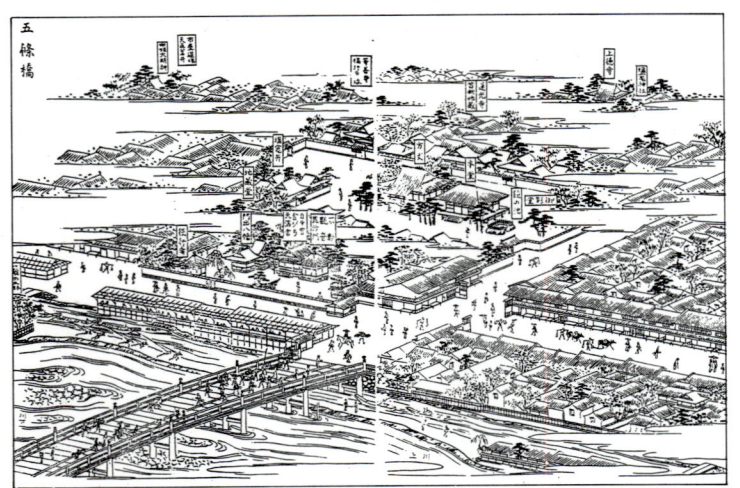

Gojobashi Bridge, *Miyako Meisho Zue*, 1780　五条大橋　『都名所図会』(安永 九年刊)より

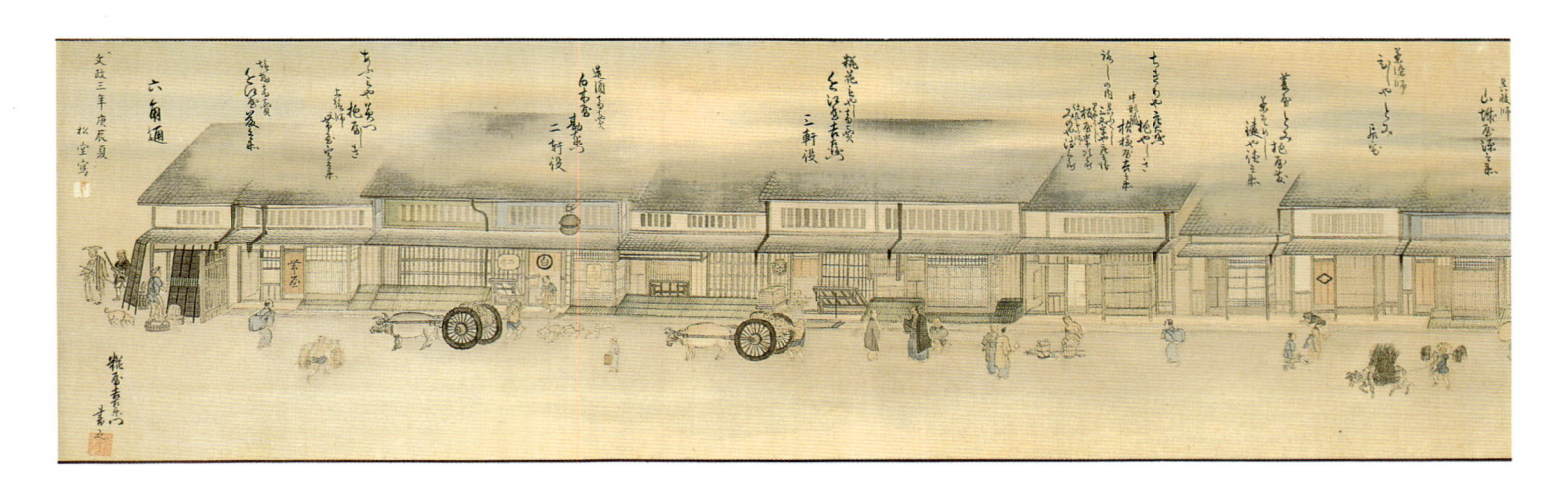

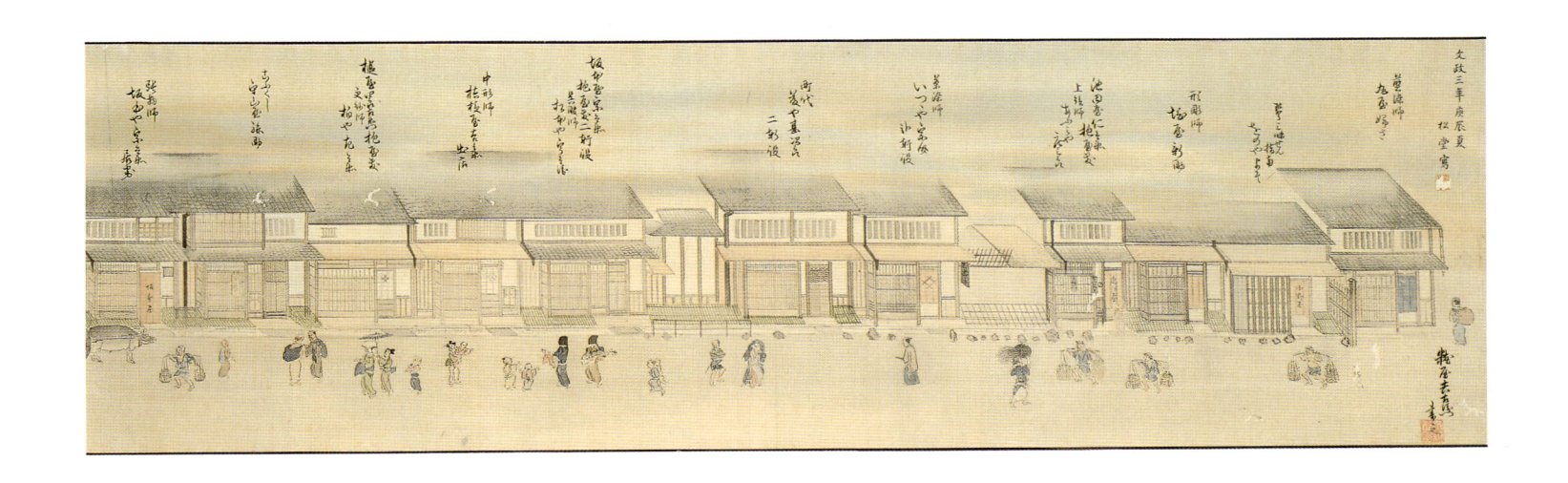

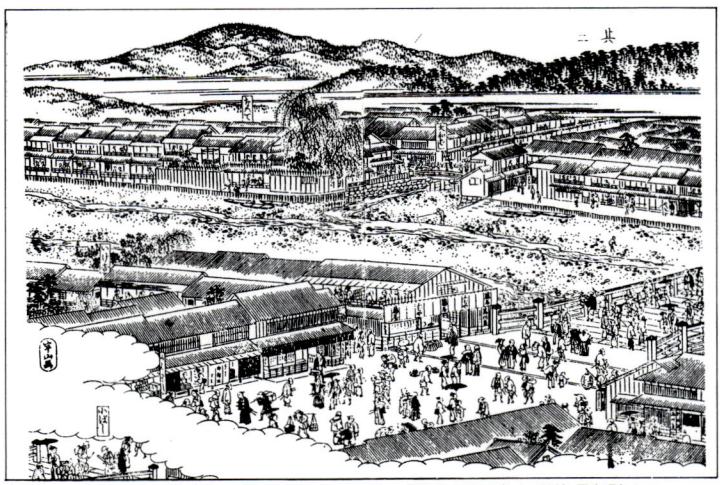

Shijobashi, *Karaku Meishou Zue*, 1864 四条橋 『花洛名勝図会』(元治 元年刊)より

North side of Gioncho 祇園町北側　井筒の茶店　同左

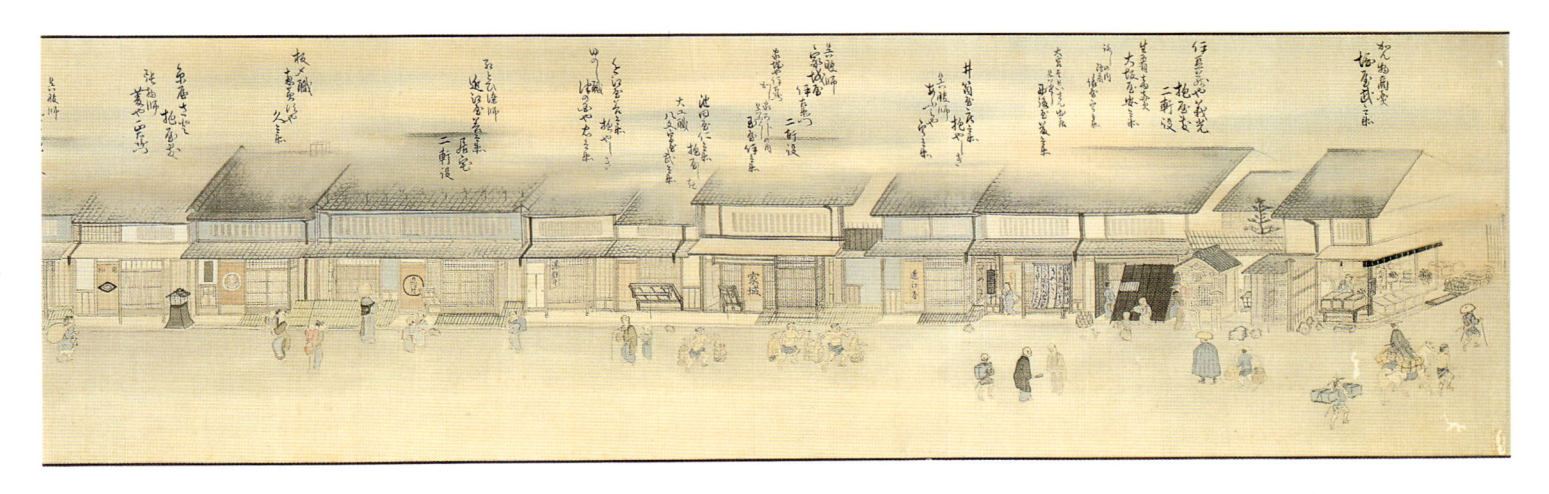

Shijo-dori in the vicinity of the west gate of Yasaka Shrine, Meiji period　四条通　八坂神社西楼門付近　明治時代　横浜開港資料館所蔵

Looking north from the Uodana crossing, high-fronted two-storey shops have appeared along Karasuma-dori, early 20th century
背の高い二階建て町家が出現した烏丸通　魚棚交差点から北を見る　明治末　京都市水道局所蔵

Sakaicho Sanjo Sagaru district, at the turn of the century
堺町三条下ル　明治中頃　京を語る会提供

Dozo-zukuri, or plastered shops in the vicintiy of Shijo Tera-machi, about 1915
土蔵造りの町家　四条寺町付近　大正初期　京都府総合資料館所蔵（石井行昌撮影写真）

Kyoto Machiya Now
京の町家

Almost all of the machiya standing in Kyoto today, were built a little before the turn of the century or since then. The fire which spread over a large area of the city from Hamaguri Gomon coup d'état in the middle of the nineteenth century wiped out many buildings. Nevertheless, the machiya which were put up afterwards mostly followed the traditions established since the beginning of the Edo period, although the designs were further refined. During the early part of the twentieth century, some of the almost completely fire resistant *dozo-zukuri*, or thickly plastered storehouse-style shops also began to appear in Kyoto. Apart from their fire-proof qualities, their introduction may have had something to do with the massiveness of this style of building which became favored, possibly as a result of the influences exerted by Western architecture on people's sense of beauty. In addition to this, machiya built since the early part of this century generally have a higher second floor than those that were built before them. By about the 1920s, even the older styles of machiya were given higher second floors, the wooden grills at the windows were replaced by metal ones, and it became fashionable in the center of the city to fit a skirt of slabs of real or artificial stone to visible exterior walls of shops. During the 1950s many people boarded over the internal passageways which traditionally had beaten earth floors and the fitting of new kitchen equipment became quite popular.

It is now therefore almost a century since most of the machiya in Kyoto were built and in many cases, these buildings are in need of rebuilding or major repair. But that does not apply to all of them, because if they were built well in the first place they still stand as true as ever, even after one hundred years. Many of the timbers and especially the columns of such building glow with a patina acquired over the years and will no doubt go on standing for some time to come yet.

現存する京の町家は，その殆どが明治時代以後の近代になって建てられている．幕末，蛤御門の変から出た火が京中に広がり，町の大半が消失したからである．とはいえ，その後の復興で出来た町家は江戸時代以来の伝統を継承し，それをさらに洗練させるものであった．明治時代の中頃以後には，京都でも土蔵造りの店舗が建てられることもあった．西洋建築の影響で，土蔵造りのマッシヴな構成が好まれたのであろう．明治時代末期頃から後に建てられた町家では2階の背を以前より格段と高くするのが一般的になる．昭和10年頃には，古い形式の町家も二階を高くし，木造の千本格子を取りはらって鉄の格子にし，腰壁に石板や人造石を貼る改造が都心部の店舗で流行した．戦後の昭和30年代には通庭の土間を板張りの床にし，新しい台所設備を設ける改造が広く行われた．

現存する京の町家の多くは建設からおよそ100年を経ており，一般的には建て替えの時期を迎えつつある．しかし全ての町家が老朽化しているわけではなく，造りの良い町家は100年を経ても殆ど狂いもなく，柱などの木部も艶光して未だ健在している．

Wachigaiya 輪違屋

Exterior 外観

Main Reception Room 座敷

Wachigaiya, 1857
Shimogyo Word, Nishi-shinyashiki Nakanocho

輪違屋
安政四年建造　京都市指定文化財　下京区西新屋敷中之町

Verandah 縁

Kasa no Ma 傘の間

Sugimoto House 杉本家

Exterior 外観

Small stone garden 石庭の坪庭

High-ceilinged section above internal passageway 通り庭の吹抜け

View of the garden from the main reception room　座敷から内庭を見る

Sugimoto House, 1870
Shimogyo Ward, Ayakoji Shinmachi Nishiiru
The shop building faces the street with the dwelling parallel to it behind - an arrangement known as *omoteya-zukuri*.
It was the home and commercial premises of a cloth and kimono merchant.

杉本家
明治3年建造　下京区綾小路新町西入ル
通り沿いの店棟と，背後の居住棟が平行する表屋造り．
呉服店であった豪商の商家である．

Axonometric, *Shin, Miyako no Sakigaki*
アクソノメトリック図『新・都の魁』より

The entrance stands between the shop and dwelling
店棟と居住棟の間にある玄関

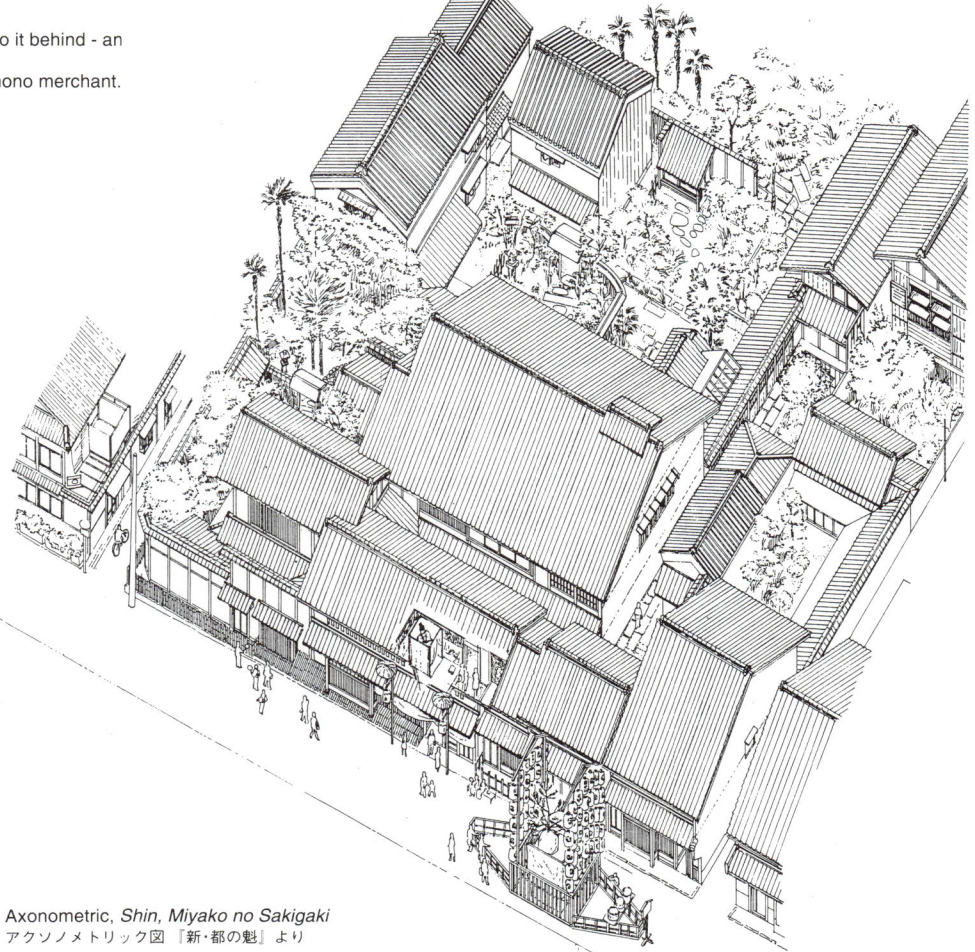

並河家 Namikawa House

Exterior 外観

Main Reception Room 椅子席の座敷

Namikawa House, 1893
Higashi Yama Ward, Sanjokita Urashirakawa-suji

An omoteya-zukuri merchant house where a cloisonné was made and sold. The dimensions of the main reception room were adapted to accommodate foreign guests and chairs were also used. Arranged so that the pond continues on under the building, the garden flanking two sides of this room is an example of the early work of the famous landscape gardener, Ogawa Jihei, who lived next door. Standing on the other side of Shirakawa River from the Namikawa house, these buildings create a delightful streetscape.

並河家
明治26年建造
東山区三条北裏白川筋

七宝を製造し商った表屋造の商家．座敷は外国人の客のため鴨居や棚を高くし，椅子席用に造っている．座敷の二方を囲む庭園は隣家に住んだ名庭師小川治平の若い時期の作庭で，池水が座敷の下へ入り込む意匠となっている．小川治平旧宅は白川沿いにあり，並河家へと続く家並みが美しい．

Namikawa House 並河家

Exterior of main reception room from the garden designed by Ogawa Jihei
小川治平作の庭園から座敷を見る．

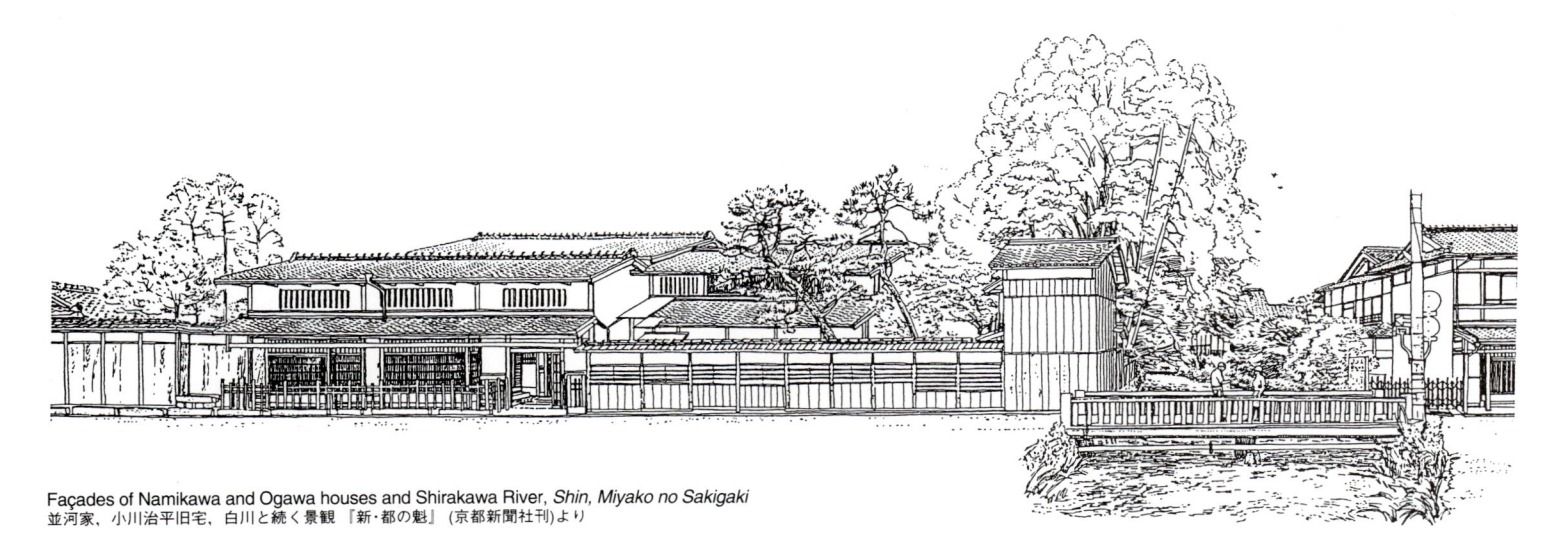

Façades of Namikawa and Ogawa houses and Shirakawa River, *Shin, Miyako no Sakigaki*
並河家、小川治平旧宅、白川と続く景観 『新・都の魁』（京都新聞社刊）より

Exterior from the garden　庭園側外観

Court garden　坪庭

Seifuso

Seifuso was the former residence of Saionji Kinmochi and although not a machiya, it has some things in common with the design of the garden side of such machiya as the Namikawa house. The high quality of the design of this sukiya-style building gives us some idea of the very high standards of timber building which still existed in the Meiji period (1868-1912). The garden was laid out by Ogawa Jihei and it is nationally designated as a Place of Scenic Beauty.

清風荘

これは町家ではなく、西園寺公望旧邸宅であるが、意匠的には並河家などの町家の裏側と共通するところがある。上品な数寄屋的意匠が明治時代の木造文化の質の高さを伝えている。庭園は小川治平作で国指定名勝。

Verandah of main reception room　座敷土庇

Sukiya　数寄屋

View of the garden from the main reception room　座敷より庭園を見る

Exterior from Hanamikoji 花見小路の外観

Ichiriki

This *chaya*, or house of refined refreshment and entertainment, is an example of the height of architectural elegance at the turn of the century.

お茶屋　一力
明治時代の洗練の頂点を伝える建築の一つ．

Tea Room 茶室

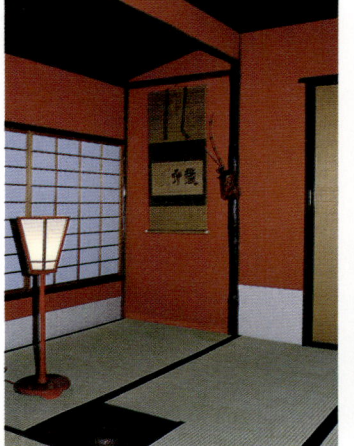

Entrance 玄関

Main Reception Room 座敷

Tokonoma of main reception room 座敷床の間

Above - An example of a large machiya, Tanakacho; Middle left - A modern sukiya-style house; Middle center - A plastered merchant house on Sanjo-dori; Below - Omoteya-zukuri merchant house in the Anekoji Higashinotoin Nishiiru district

上／大規模な町家　田中長
中・左／近代の数寄屋風住宅
中・右／三条通りの土蔵造りの商家
下／表屋造りの商家　姉小路東洞院西入ル

Nishikikoji 錦小路

Maruyata fish-store in Nishikikoji 錦小路の魚屋「丸弥太」

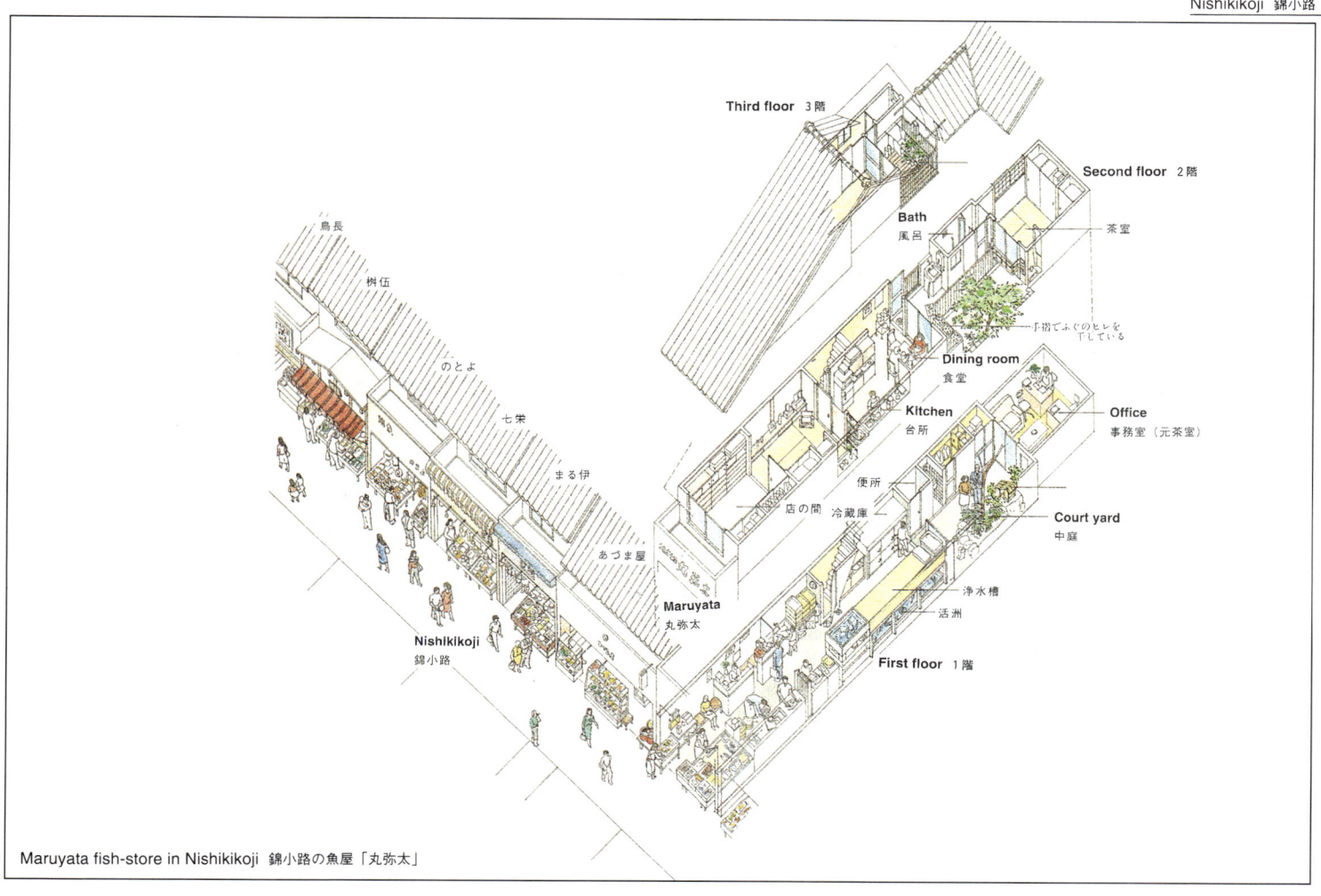

Nishikikoji 錦小路

Interior of the Maruyata fish-store 丸弥太の店内

Court gardens behind the stores of Nishikikoji 錦小路の裏側に連続する坪庭空間

69

通り

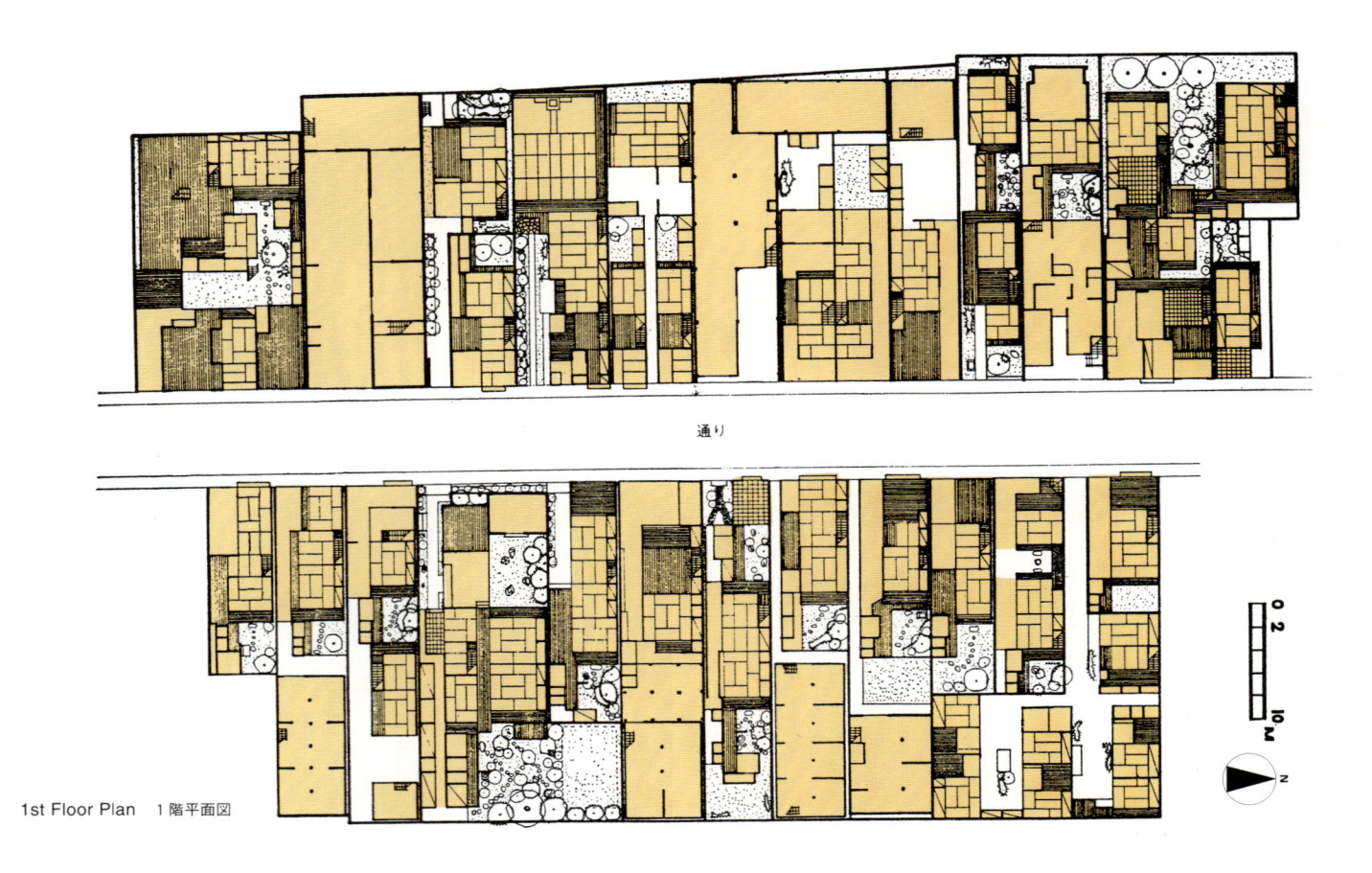

2nd Floor Plan　2階平面図

通り

1st Floor Plan　1階平面図

Plan of town house block in Nakagyo Ward, from *Kyo no Machiya* by Shimamura Noboru and others, 1971
町家街区平面図　中京区夷町　島村 昇・鈴鹿幸雄他著『京の町家』より　鹿島出版会刊　1971年

IV
Traditional Streetscapes – Design Features
伝統的町並みの意匠

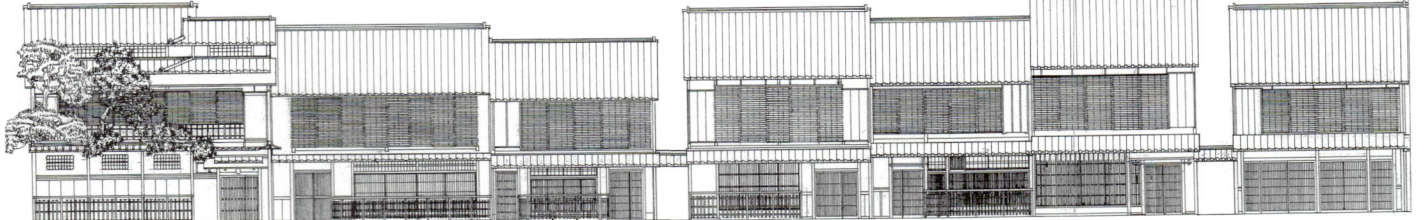

Gion Shinbashi 祇園新橋

Traditional Neighborhood - Commercial and Domestic
伝統的町並み

The area at night 祇園新橋夜景

Gion Shinbashi 祇園新橋

Streets of Gion Shinbashi

Growing into a suburb of Kyoto during the Edo period, the refined splendor, consistency and sublimeness that has slowly emerged in the vistas along the streets of Gion Shinbashi, fully convey in their present form the heritage from which they herald.

The area which begins at the Mizujaya teahouse in front of the west gate to the Gionsha (Yasaka Shrine), developed as a public entertainment area associated with the artisans of the arts and crafts workshops to be found in Shijogawara before they were moved to Kabukigoya on the east bank of the Kamo River, to facilitate maintenance work to the embankment at the beginning of the Edo period. Following the fire toward the end of the Edo period, the area betrays its Meiji period restorations, the design of the buildings here still reflecting the patterns of the Edo period. The highly refined Kyogoshi, or screens so indicative of the city that stretch along the streets at street level, can be said to be a refinement largely seen in the very heart of Kyoto. The height of the upper storey, a particular feature of this area, stems from the fact that guests of the teahouses were entertained upstairs, hence a height over and above that of the normal house. The *sudare*, a type of horizontal reed blind, found hanging outside the upper windows, flutter in the wind and are a typical attraction of Gion. In the old days, the guest rooms of the houses formed a continuous line along both sides of the Shirakawa River but the war saw the demise of property on one side, owing to people leaving for the interior to escape the war, and all that remains to be seen now is a roadway paved with stones.

As far as those who remained, the subsequent erection of modern buildings and an associated increase in land prices profited them very little and there was a general outcry for the conservation of the area. As a result, based on a local city planning act in Kyoto in 1974, the area was listed as a special conservation area. As of 1976, following the Cultural Heritage Protection Act it has become an architectural heritage conservation area of special merit.

祇園新橋の町並み

京の町で江戸時代を通じて形成され，洗練と統一と穏やかな変化の妙を見せる町並みが，街路景観としてまとまった形で今日に伝えられているのがこの祇園新橋地区である．

祇園社（八坂神社）西楼門の門前の水茶屋から始まった町並みは，四条河原で行われていた芸能興業が江戸時代初期の堤の整備にともなって東岸の歌舞伎小屋に移ると，この芸能とも結びついて庶民の遊興の場として発展した．幕末に火事で焼けたため明治時代の再興後の町なみを伝えるが，その意匠は江戸時代の姿をよく継承している．その一階に連続する洗練された京格子の町並みは，かつての京の都心に広く見られた洗練を伝えるものといってよい．二階の背が高いのはこの地域の特徴で，お茶屋は客を二階でもてなすため一般の町家より二階が高い．どの家も簾を垂らしそれが風に揺れるのも祇園ならではの風情である．かつては白川の両側に家々の座敷が接して並んでいたが，戦争疎開で片側の家屋が取り払われ，今は石畳の道になっている．

住み続けようとする者にとってはビル化も地価上昇も利益をもたらさないと，地域住民自らが町並み保全を市へ要望し，1974年に京都市条例に基づく特別保全修景地区に指定された．1976年以降は文化財保護法による重要伝統的建造物群保存地区となっている．

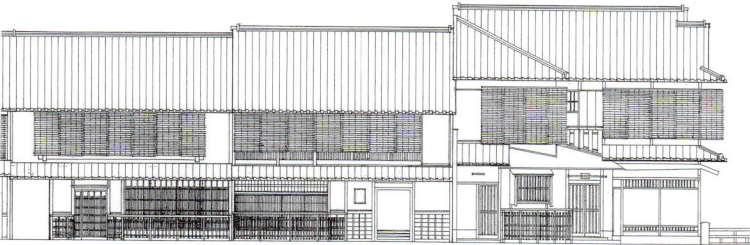

Elevation of north side of Shinbashi-dori, 1993　新橋通り北側連続立面図 1993年

Gion Shinbashi 祇園新橋

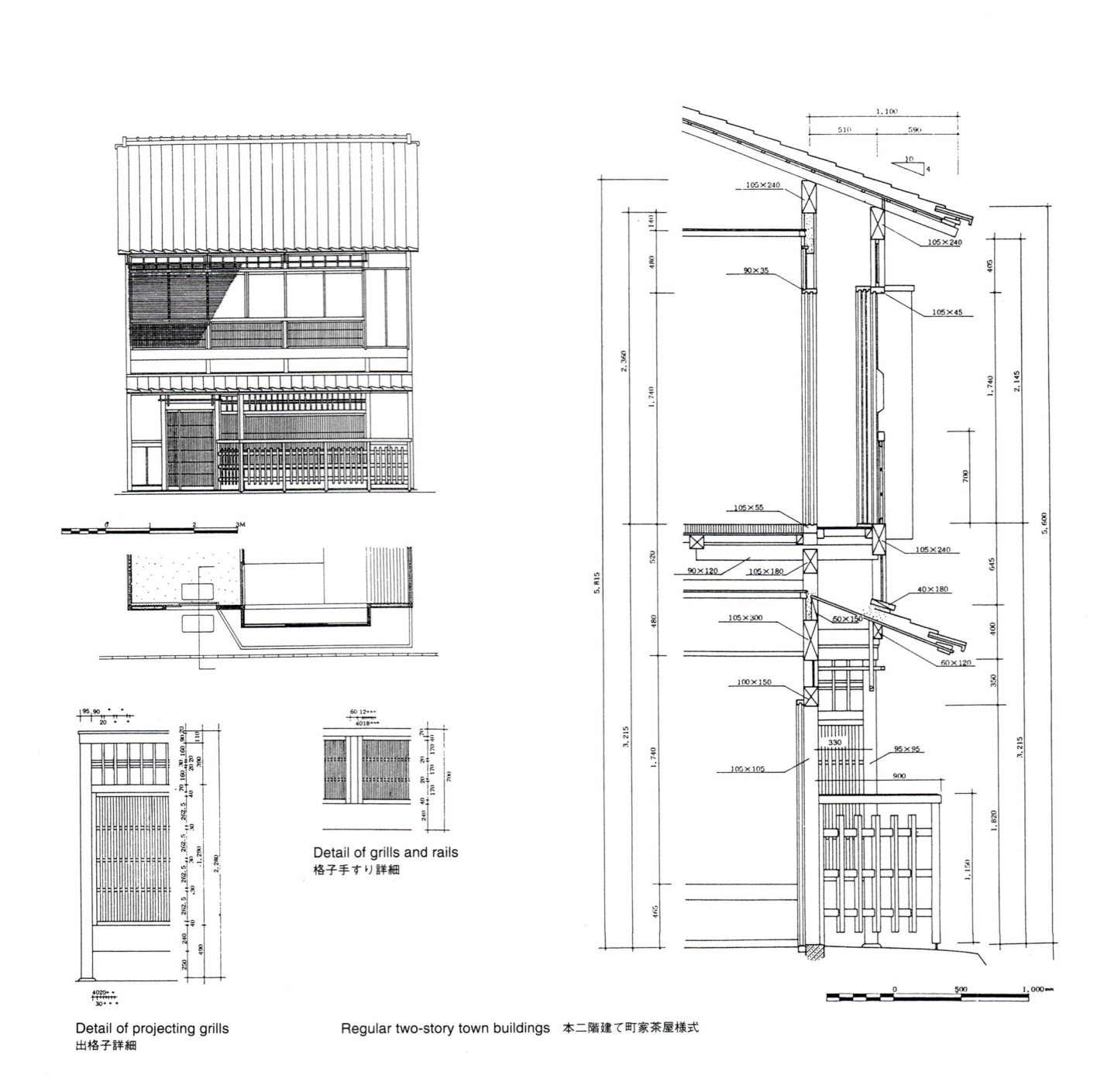

Detail of projecting grills
出格子詳細

Detail of grills and rails
格子手すり詳細

Regular two-story town buildings 本二階建て町家茶屋様式

Shimosato House - connecting corridor
下里家渡り廊下

Tea room 同 茶室

Second-floor reception room 同 二階座敷

Gion Shinbashi 祇園新橋

Shimosato House - shop　下里家店の間

Exterior　同　外観

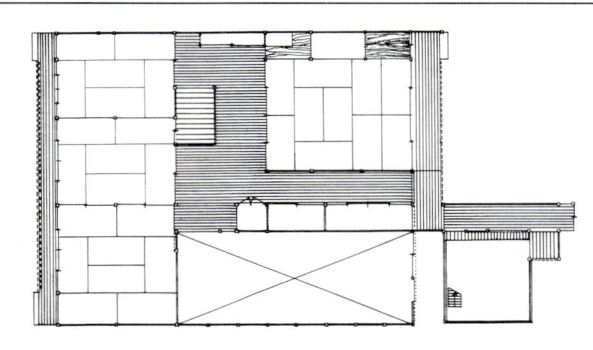

This is a typical example of a chaya, or tea house. The guest rooms are on the second floor and the use of a landing characterizes the plan of this type of establishment. The Shirakawa River runs at the back of the premises.
典型的なお茶屋建築．客間は二階にあり、階段上に「踊り場」のあるのがお茶屋の平面を特徴づける．離れ座敷の裏には白川が流れる．

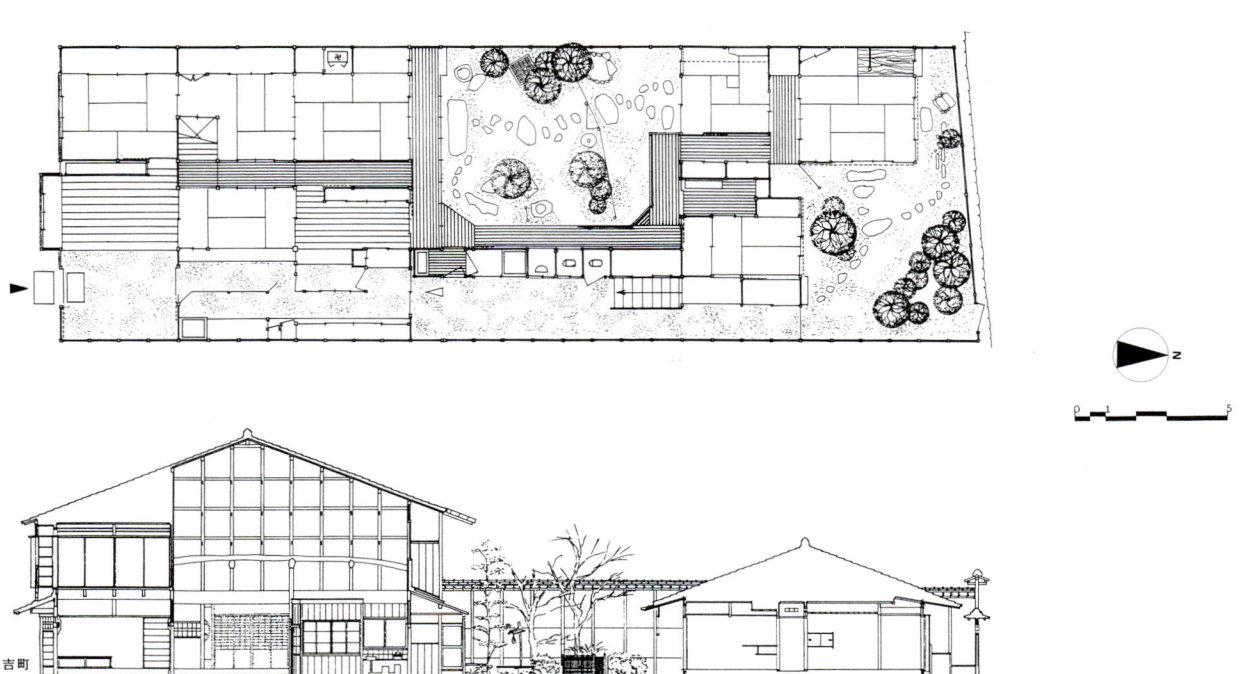

Plan and section　下里家平面図・断面図

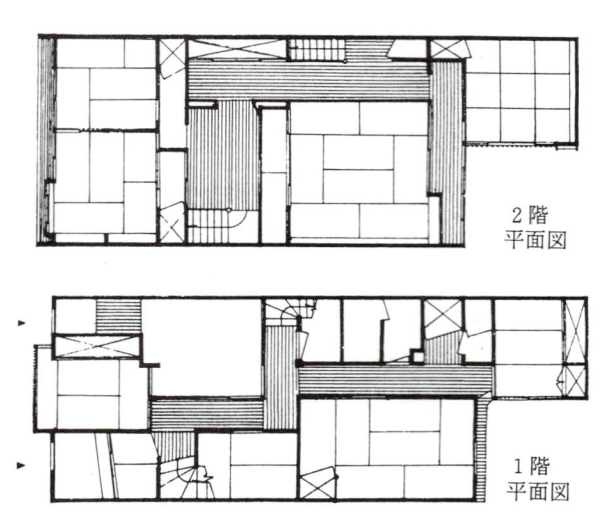

Gion Shinbashi 祇園新橋

2階平面図
1階平面図
立面図 

Because such establishments as this have guest rooms upstairs, the height of the building is somewhat higher than other town houses, more open in character, and there is alsoasllow verandah.
お茶屋の建物は二階を客用座敷とするため、町家外観としては二階の背が高く開放的で、浅い縁が張り出している特徴を持つ.

Survey drawing of a chaya　お茶屋実測図

Second floor guest room at the Yamazaki house　お茶屋の内部(山崎家)二階座敷

Guest room at the front of the building　同　二階表側の座敷

Second floor guest room　同　二階座敷

Court garden　同　坪庭

Gion Shinbashi 祇園新橋

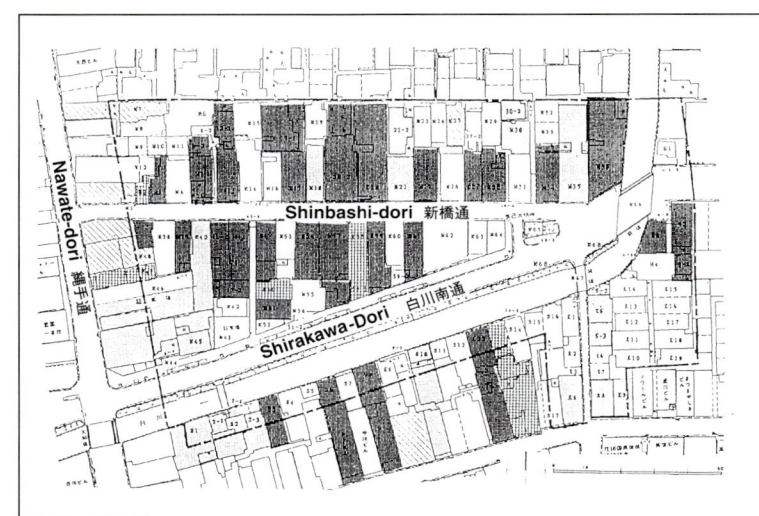

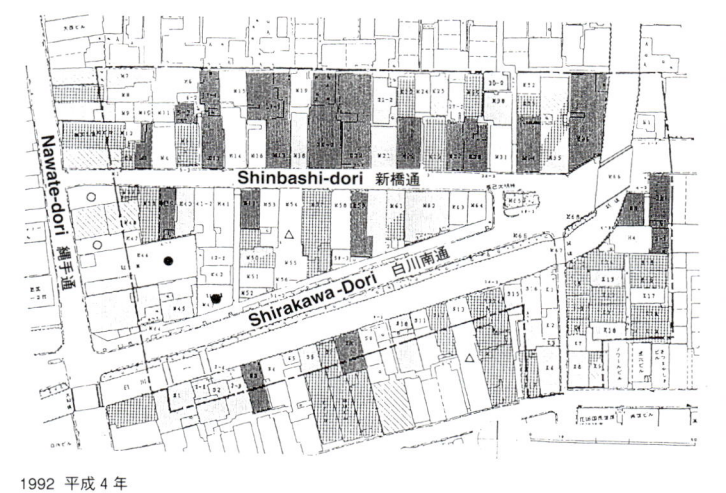

1973 昭和48年

1992 平成4年

Land Use Plan for Gion Shinbashi　祇園新橋地区土地利用状況図

Legend 凡例

- Ochaya　お茶屋
- Restaurant, Hotel　料亭・旅館・料理店
- Snack bar, Bar　スナック・バー等
- Shop　販売店
- House, etc.　住宅,その他
- △ Under construction　工事中
- ○ Empty lot　空地
- ● Parking　駐車場

Gion Shinbashi Traditional Structures
Concervation Area - Roof Plan, 1993
祇園新橋伝統的建造物群保存地区　屋根伏図　1993年

77

Gion Shinbashi 祇園新橋

Houses lining the banks of Shirakawa River; *Kyoko Minkahu*, 1949
白川両岸の家並み 『京郊民家譜』 昭和24年

Shirkawa River 白川

The alley known at "Kiritoshi" 「切り通し」と呼ばれる路地

Shinbashi-dori 新橋通

Gion Shinbashi 祇園新橋

Above - The Join Nexus building has a reinforced concrete construction but it was given a traditional exterior.
Bellow - Gion Shinbashi in evening light

上／JOIN NEXUS. 鉄筋コンクリート造建築に伝統的外観を復元している.
下／祇園新橋夕景

Gioncho Minamigawa 祇園町南側

This shows Shijo-dori during the Meiji period before the road was widened, from the foot of the Gion Ishidan steps
道路拡幅前の明治時代の四条通り，祇園石段下　大日本スクリーン提供 (撮影:石田明)

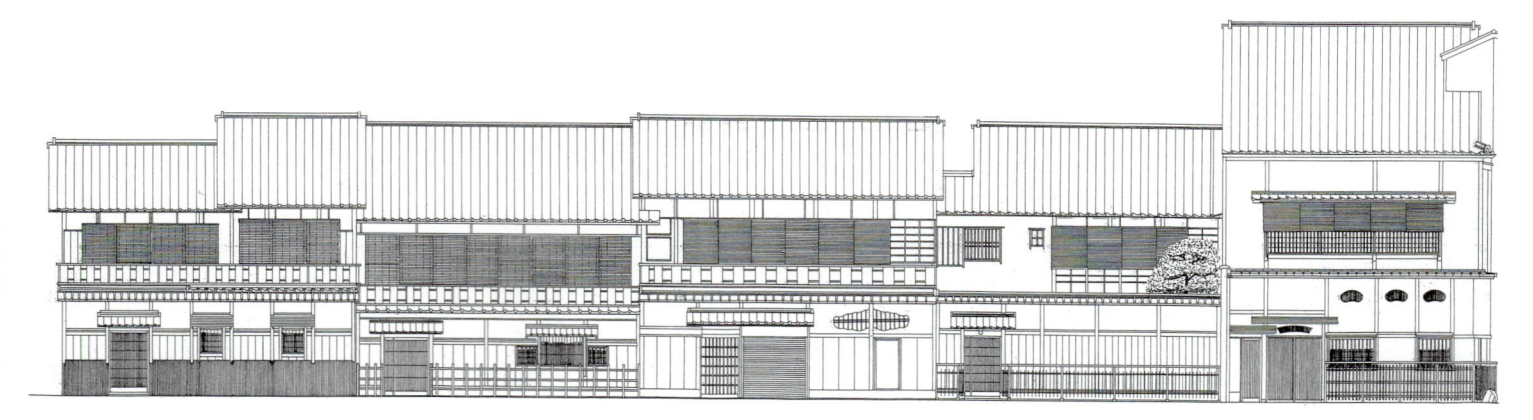

Gioncho Minamigawa　祇園町南側

祇園町南側

四条通りと建仁寺の間に広がるこの地域はかつての祇園情緒をもっとも広い範囲で色濃く伝えている．街区が形成されたのは明治以後である．有名なお茶屋一力の角で四条通りと交わるのが花見小路で，町家ながら粋な塀が連続し，いくらか郊外的で数寄屋的な柔らかい風情が祇園の中でもこの通りを特別にしている．家々は壁を塀の意匠にして風情の演出にこだわりを見せている．芸伎を教える八坂女紅場学園が付近一帯の土地を所有し，学園を運営するお茶屋の女将や主人たちが自らの努力で町なみ景観と情緒の保全に努めてきた．

Gioncho South (Gioncho Minamigawa)

This area, which extends between Shijo-dori and Kenniji Temple, strongly conveys in a variety of ways, the character associated with the Gion of old. This quarter came into being after the Meiji period. At the corner where the legendary Ichiriki stands and the Shijo-dori intersects with Hanamikoji, the buildings, despite being simple town houses, are distinguished by splendid continuous fencing which, even within the relaxed atmosphere generated by the suburban teahouse like architecture to be found within Gion, makes this street particularly outstanding. The walls of the houses have been designed as fencing which clearly illustrates, more than anything else, the distinctive characteristics of the area. The individual mistresses and masters who administer the Yasaka Nyoko Gakuen, a school which teaches the courtesan arts and owns a large plot of land within the area, have endeavored to ensure the preservation of the character and singular charm of the area.

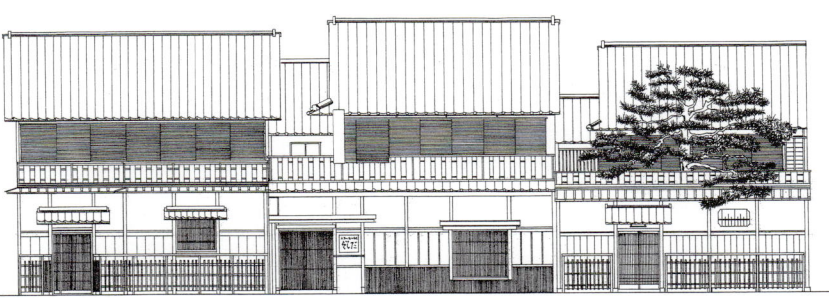

Elevation along Hanamikoji　花見小路連続立面図　1993年

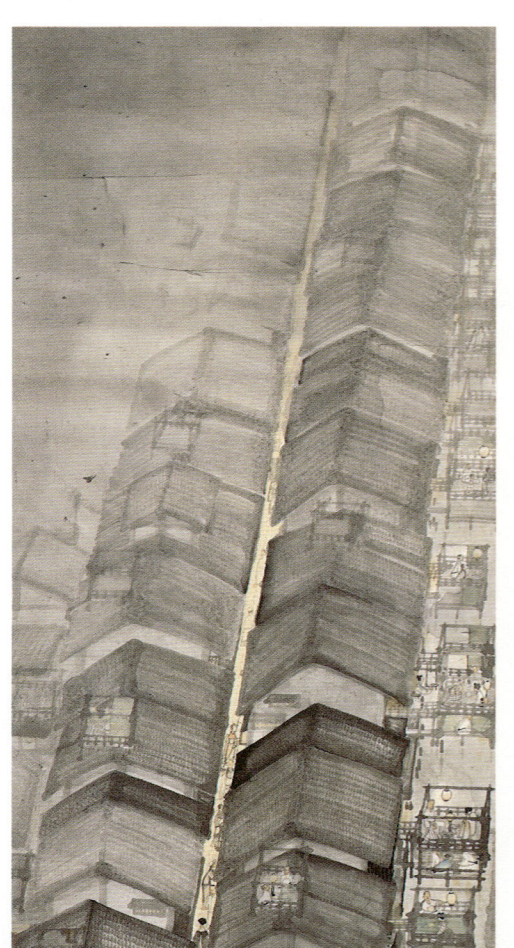

Pontocho

In summer, the inhabitants of Pontocho sit outside to take advantage of the cool evening breeze coming off the Kamo River. Just as the Gion district once was, Pontocho was also originally a teahouse quarter, and the narrow streets are lined with traditional teahouse architecture and eating houses giving rise to a distinctive, intimate atmosphere. The inhabitants, however, are faced with a number of problems as the very existence of these narrow streets contravenes present-day building regulations.

先斗町

先斗町の町並みは夏には鴨川に納涼の床を出す。元来は祇園同様にお茶屋街で，狭い路地に並ぶ伝統的なお茶屋建築や料亭が独特の親密な風情を醸している。法律では路地の存続が認められないため町並みは困難に直面している。

Pontocho, one of eight scenes of Kyoto attributed to Maeda Seison
京名所八題のうち　先斗町　前田青邨筆　東京国立博物館所蔵

Teranouchi, Kamishichiken　寺の内，上七軒

Ogawa-dori, in the vicinity of Urasenke　小川通　裏千家付近

Teranouchi
Toyotomi Hideyoshi, the sixteenth century warlord, erected a sumptuous residence in a corner of Jiincho for the teachers of the three main schools of Japanese tea ceremony, and shops for the purveyors of its accouterments in a highly elegant style.

寺の内
秀吉が開いた寺院町の一隅に，三千家の茶匠の屋敷と茶道具店などの町並みが品のよい佇まいを見せる．

Kamishichiken
The street up to Kitano Tenmangu Shrine is lined with commercial teahouses, or *chaya*, houses of refined refreshment and entertainment.

上七軒
北野天満宮の参道に形成されたお茶屋街．

Facade of Omotesenke　表千家の表構え

Streetscape of Kamishichiken　上七軒の町並み

83

Nishijin

This area of the city developed and blossomed owing to the textile mills which thrived in the town houses built in this quarter. The area still conveys its strong manufacturing Edo period roots.

西陣

西陣織りを家ごとの分業体制で支えてきた町なみ景観．江戸時代の逞しい生産都市の面影を伝える．

Sanneizaka 産寧坂

産寧坂の町並み

清水寺へ参詣するには古来二つの経路がある．一つは松原通(元の五条通)から鴨川を渡って清水道を上る．もう一つは八坂神社の南門から法観寺五重塔(八坂ノ塔)の前を通り，産寧坂を上がって清水道に出るもので，江戸時代初期の地図にもこの参詣路が描かれている．何時しか円山公園から高台寺の下を通り二年坂を経て産寧坂に至る経路も，その一種鄙びた風情が人々に好まれるようになった．与謝野晶子が「清水へ祇園をよぎる桜月夜こよいみる人みな美しき」と詠んだのもこういう道の何処かであったのだろう．

京都市は国の制度に先駆けて，昭和47年に特別保全修景地区という町並み保全制度をつくり，最初の指定地区として円山公園から産寧坂に至る道沿いの町並みを「産寧坂地区」として指定した．生きている町の景観をどう保存すればよいのか，試案の末に，木造家屋は何時かは建て替えるものと考えて，建築物そのものを保存する方法を取らず，建物外観の伝統的な意匠・様式を継承するという方法が選ばれた．昭和51年には国の制度による重要伝統的建造物群保存地区に選定された．産寧坂は三年坂とも呼ばれ，坂の下には江戸時代から家並があった．低い二階に虫籠窓(ムシコ)のある町家が江戸時代以来の古い様式を伝えている．二年坂の下は大正時代に建てられた家並で，各々に数寄屋風の意匠が加えられている．大正という新しい時代の町並みを保全地区に取り上げたのも画期的なことであった．

Sanneizaka in the snow 雪の産寧坂

Looking toward Sanneizaka. The low two-story machiya on the right dates from the late Edo period (1600-1868). 産寧坂を望む．右の低い二階屋は江戸時代の町家．

Sanneizaka 産寧坂

Sanneizaka 産寧坂　　Ninenzaka 二年坂

Sanneizaka

Visitors to Kiyomizudera have a choice of two routes up to the temple, both trodden since ancient times. One is Kiyomizumichi which leads up from Matsubara-dori (formerly Gojo-dori) and across the Kamo River. The other, which also leads up on to Kiyomizumichi, begins at the southern gate of the Yasaka Shrine and passes in front of the tower of Hokanji pagoda (Yasaka pagoda). This particular street is to be found even on maps dating from the beginning of the Edo period (1600-1868). The former street, began life at sometime as a route from the park of Maruyama. Passing below Kodaiji Temple and traversing the length of Ninenzaka before reaching Sanneizaka, the provincial scenery afforded by this route has become very popular. It is perhaps somewhere along this street that Yosano Akiko paused to reflect and write a *waka*, or five line poem, the gist of which may be poorly expressed as:

Strolling toward Kiyomizu
Along the Gion street
Cherry blossoms glimpsed in the moonlight
Enchant, and for a moment
Lend their beauty to the upturned faces of the passersby

Kyoto was the forerunner with respect to legislation aimed at conserving areas of outstanding natural beauty, historical and architectural merit. The city instituted a system of special conservations areas in 1973, the first of which was the area stretching along the road from Maruyama Park to Sanneizaka. With regard to preserving the character and essence that constitute such areas, it was decided, after protracted deliberations, that when a house needs rebuilding, as wooden houses by nature do, then rather than just preserve the exiting fabric it would be better to replace it with something that supersedes it in terms of traditional design and appearance. Four years later, in 1977, in accordance with national legislation, it was selected for conservation as an area of outstanding architectural merit. Sanneizaka is also called Sannenzaka. At the foot of its slope is an area that has been in existence since the Edo period. The second stories here with their low ceilings and windows with closely spaced mullions convey a style synonymous with town houses dating from the Edo period. The house at the foot of Ninenzaka dates back to the nineteen-twenties and has the added attraction of being designed in a teahouse style. The move to conserve buildings from this relatively recent period is an event of particular note in the history of conservation in Japan.

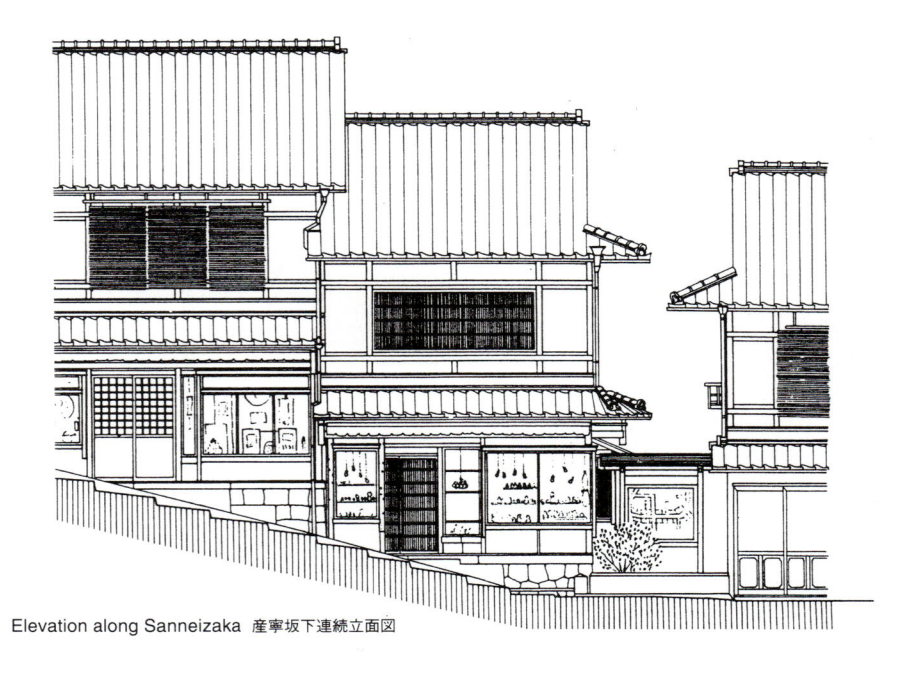

Elevation along Sanneizaka 産寧坂下連続立面図

Sanneizaka 産寧坂

Kyoyamato Rinsen designed by Yoshinobu Ashihara　京大和林泉　芦原義信設計

Present conditions in the vicinity of Ninenzaka　二年坂付近　現況

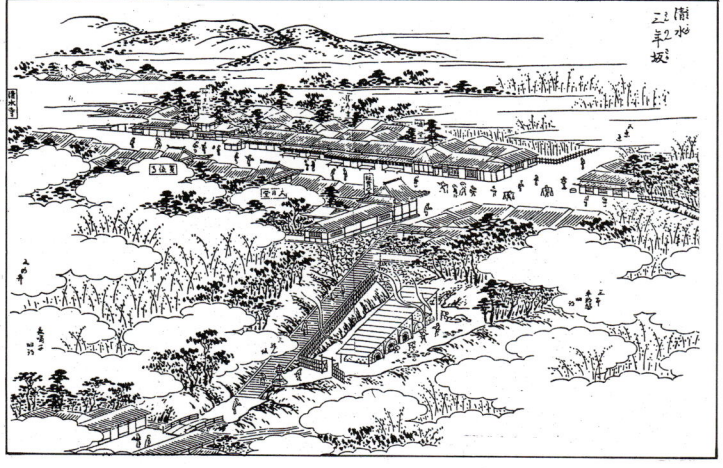

Sanneizaka in the Edo period; *Miyako Meisho Zue*　江戸時代の産寧坂　『都名所図会』

Before adjustments were made in the vicinity of Ninenzaka
二年坂付近　修景前の状況

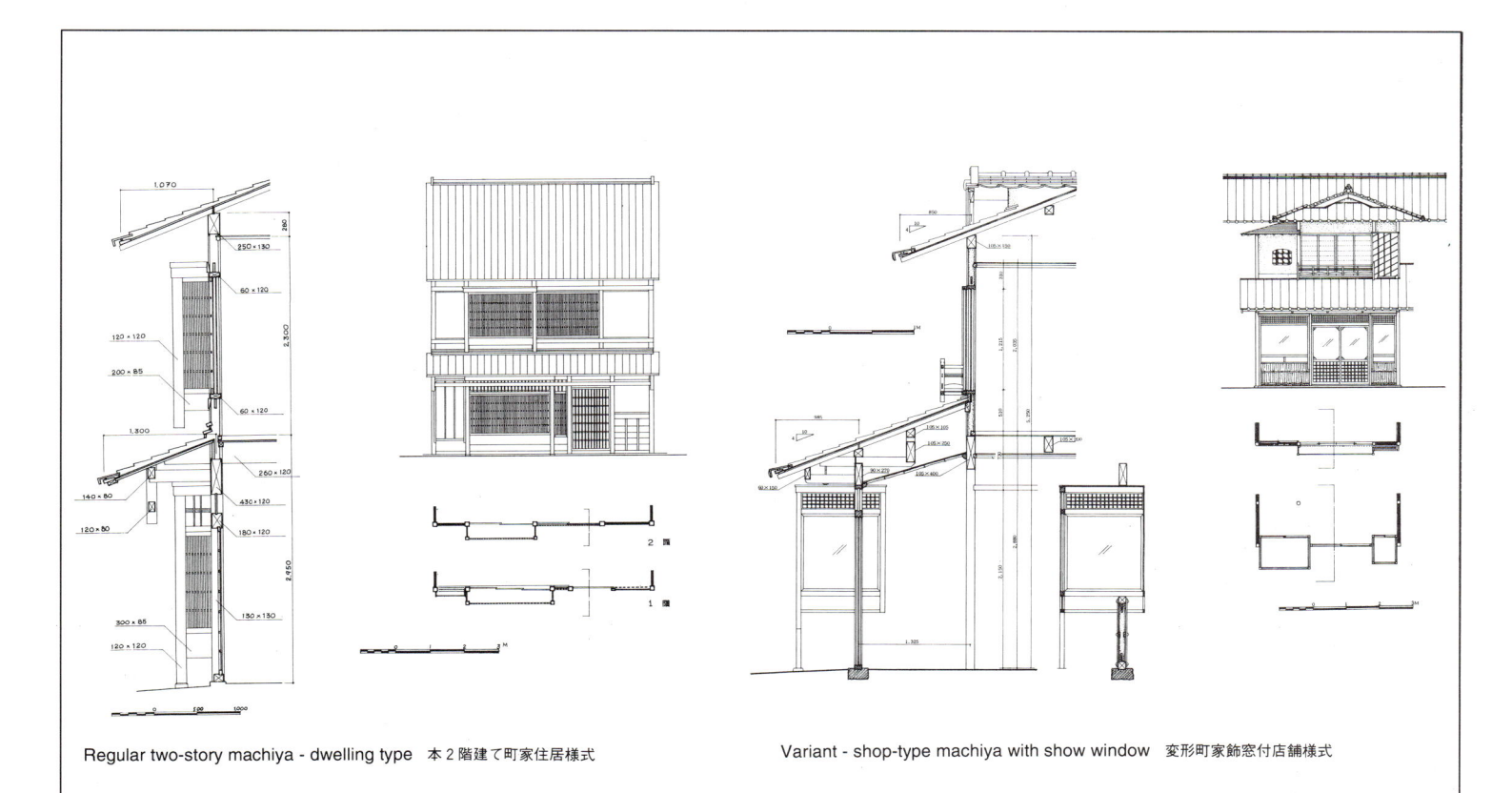

Regular two-story machiya - dwelling type　本2階建て町家住居様式

Variant - shop-type machiya with show window　変形町家飾窓付店舗様式

Sanneizaka 産寧坂

In front of Yasaka Pagoda - before adjustments
八坂ノ塔正面　修景前

Near Yasaka Pagoda - before adjustments
八坂ノ塔付近　修景前

Near Yasaka Pagoda - after adjustments　同上　修景後

In front of Yasaka Pagoda - present condition　八坂ノ塔正面　現況

Gojozaka

While Gojo-dori follows the course of a smaller thoroughfare known in the Heian period as Rokujobomonkoji, the original Gojo-dori has become Matsubara-dori. Toyotomi Hideyoshi rebuilt the Ogojo Bridge in its present position and so the name accordingly also moved with the rebuilding of the bridge. Along the sloping road that leads from the bridge to Otanihoncho (Nishiotani), a village engaged in the production and sale of pottery sprung up in the Edo period. This became known as Gojozaka (*saka*/*zaka* meaning slope), an area which prospered and gave birth to many famous potters. At present along this road, famous potters such as Rokube Shimizu and Michiya Takahashi are still active. Otanihoncho has a small open space at a bend in the road, which in a rather clever way unveils a delightful view, as though it were deliberately positioned so as to face one to the road in the fashion.

Toward the end of the Pacific War, the houses to the south of Gojozaka were cleared away, owing to evacuation and abandonment by the inhabitants. This resulted in an intensive open swathe some 50 meters in width. Only the buildings to the north still remain. After the war, this evacuated area was preserved and maintained as a very wide road. Its proximity and relationship are completely out of keeping with the low-rise buildings to the north which face on to it. The building of anything in wood has been forbidden in area along the road. This, in turn, has started a move toward high-rise buildings and as this trend continues apace, the area is faced with losing is quaint atmosphere of pottery and potters. Conversely, near the Otowagawa River, which winds its way through the central part of this area, a largely unchanged portion of housing lies exposed to the road and there is little to relieve the eye with regard to the confused scene it surveys. Today, an overhead interchange blocks off the entrance to Otanihoncho and the monuments that adorned the former view are similarly lost to sight.

五条坂

現在の五条通は平安京の六条坊門小路にあたり、元の五条通は今は松原通と呼ばれている。豊臣秀吉が五条大橋を今の位置に架け替えたため、やがて通りの名称も移ったのである。五条橋から大谷本廟（西大谷）にかけての緩い坂道沿いに、江戸時代に陶器の製造と販売を営む町なみが発達し五条坂と呼ばれるようになり、多くの名陶工を生み出して繁栄した。沿道には清水六兵衛や高橋道八ら名工の窯が現在も営まれている。大谷本廟は通りの屈曲点に小広場を設け、巧妙に通りの正面に位置するかのような景観を演出していた。

太平洋戦争末期の疎開で五条坂の南側が幅約50メートルにわたって家並みが取り壊され、北側の町並みだけが残った。疎開地は戦後広幅員の道路として整備され、北側には道路と不釣合いな低層の町並みが面することになった。沿道は防火地域に指定され、木造での建て替えは禁止され、高層化の誘因が働いて陶器の街の町並み継承は困難に直面している。いっぽう南側は疎開で街区の中央を蛇行する音羽川付近の狭く不整形な宅地割が大通りに露出し、混乱した景観から脱する見通しのない状況が続いている。立体交差路が大谷本廟の正面を塞ぎ、通りの正面をモニュメントが飾る景観も失われた。

Nishiotani is at the end of Gojozaka
五条坂の正面突当りに位置していた西大谷　京を語る会提供

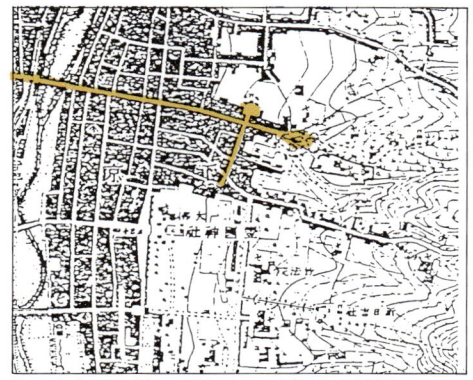

Rough Survey Map of Kyoto and Osaka, 1887
京阪地方仮製地図　明治20年

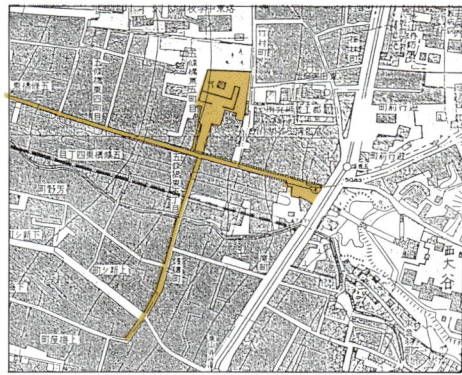

Gojozaka before it was widened　五条通拡幅以前の状況

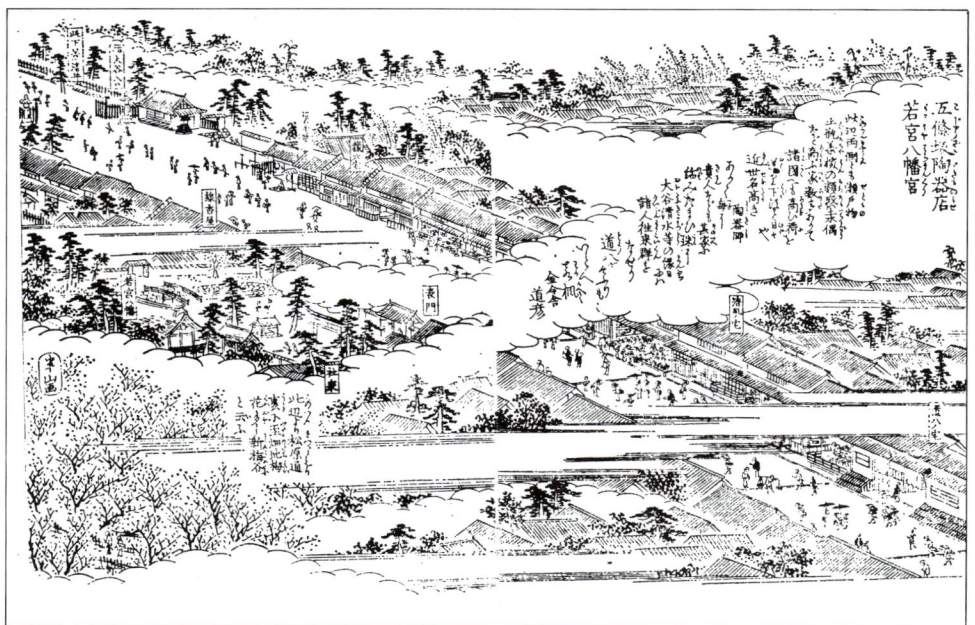

Pottery stores of Gojozaka, in Wakamiya Hachimangu; *Karaku Meishou zue*
五條坂陶器店　若宮八幡宮　『花洛名勝図会』

Gojozaka 五条坂

Wakamiya Hachimangu
若宮八幡宮

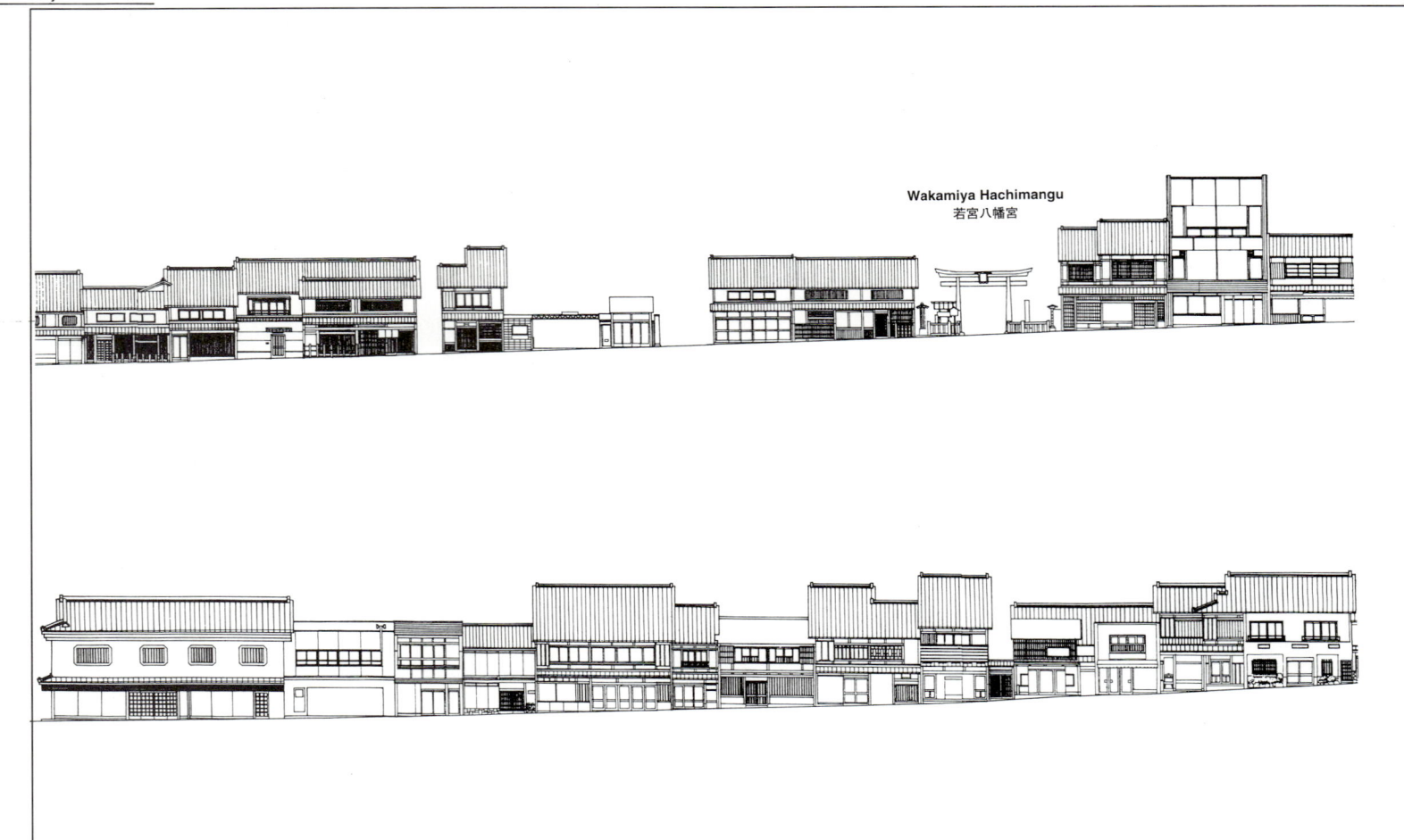

Shopping area of Gojozaka before widening 拡幅前の五条商店街 京を語る会提供

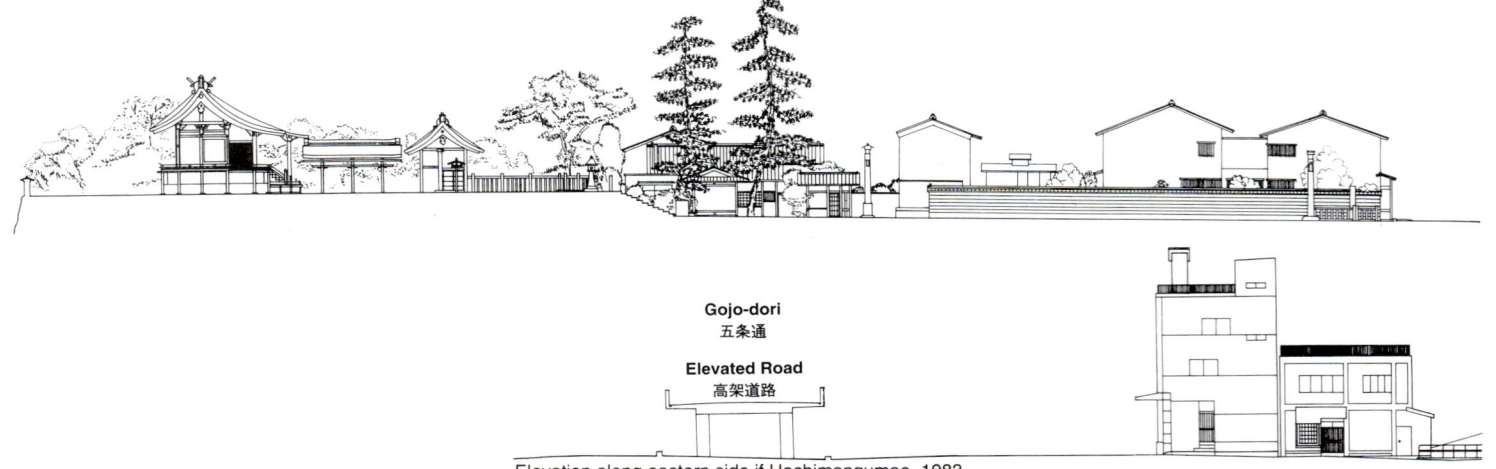

Gojo-dori
五条通

Elevated Road
高架道路

Elevation along eastern side if Hachimangumae, 1983
八幡前(鉄鋳町)東側連続立面図 1983年

Gojozaka 五条坂

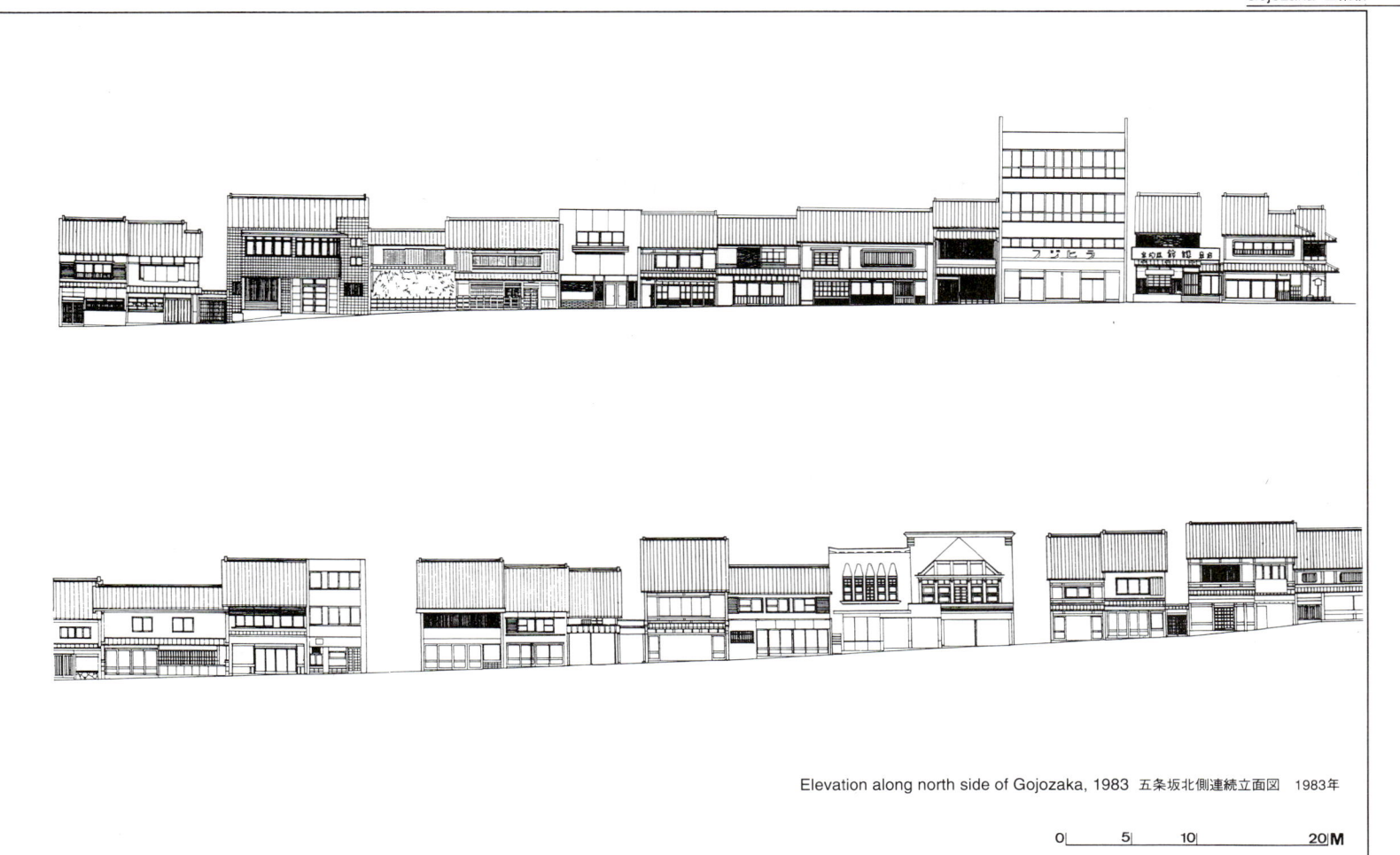

Elevation along north side of Gojozaka, 1983　五条坂北側連続立面図　1983年

Wakamiya Monzen
The street that leads down from Wakamiya Hachimangu Shrine located on Gojo-dori, stretches away to the south. The town houses along this road are very traditional in style and are well known owing to the existence of the former house and workshop of the potter Kawai Kanjiro, who was a leading figure in the arts and crafts movement in Japan.

若宮門前通の町並み
五条通にある若宮八幡宮は門前通が五条通から南へ伸びる．伝統的町並みと，民芸運動で知られた河井寛次郎旧宅がある．

Former Kawai Kanjiro House
河井寛次郎旧宅

Gojozaka 五条坂

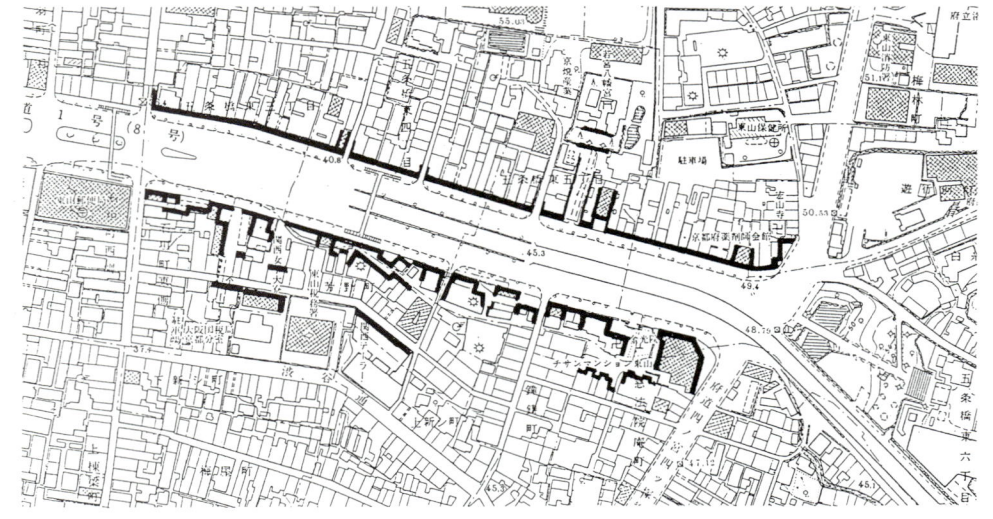

Façade contributing to the composition of the streetscape along Gojozaka
五条坂の町並み景観を構成する壁面の分布

Widening of Gojozaka: Left - Plots and proposed new width Right - After widening
五条坂の道路拡幅　左：地籍図と道路拡幅位置　右：拡幅後の状況

Kamigamo Shakemachi 上賀茂社家町

Kamigamo Shakemachi - Roof Plan, 1979　上賀茂社家町屋根伏図　1979年

Kamigamo Shakemachi

The procession for the Aoi Matsuri wends its way from the former Imperial palace along the banks of the Kamo River up to the Kamigamo Shrine. This shrine has, since its establishment in the Heian period, been the place where the forebears of the Kamo family, former overlords of the area around Kamigamo, have in turn celebrated their ancestors through a festival held at the shrine. It is thought that some special circumstances promoted its erection in the Heian period, possibly its close proximity and relationship to the Emperor's garden being the reason. The festival symbolizes and celebrates the profound interaction between Kyoto and its environs and the natural areas beyond.

Members of the Kamo family have served as Shinto priests at the Kamigamo Shrine since ancient times. This has given rise to a hamlet in front of the shrine, which consists of residences for the priests interspersed with farmhouses. The quiet, delightful appearance of this hamlet is still evident today. Along the Myojin River, which flows from within the precincts of the shrine, the lines of houses belonging to the shrine, with their continuous clay walls, produce an immediately impressive scene to the eye. Since Edo times, construction of gateways and so-called wooden stepped entrances (*shikidai*) to this kind of house have been allowed. There are tow entrances, namely the *shikidai* and another formed by large wooden doors leading on to clay floored areas inside called *doma*. The partitions similarly are distinguished by the area they enclose. There are those which lead on from the entrance and face into the guest rooms and those that face onto the clay floored *doma*. Special features of the exterior include the decorative sculptures, called *gegyo*, that adorn the roof. The clever use of certain forms, such as an inverted divining stick, and spaced rafters lend themselves to produce a visually pleasing structure. The waters of the Myojin River are divided into two. One water flows into a pond in the rear gardens, where it finds use in ritual cleansing by the priests before flowing on back in the river again. The other flows on to on to the rear, and forms the main water supply for daily use. Waste water permeates into a soak-away within the site and this helps to ensure the cleanliness of he water as it gradually filters away. The houses along the river have also been singled out for conservation and inclusion in one of the country's outstanding areas of architectural beauty.

Kamigamo Shakemachi 上賀茂社家町

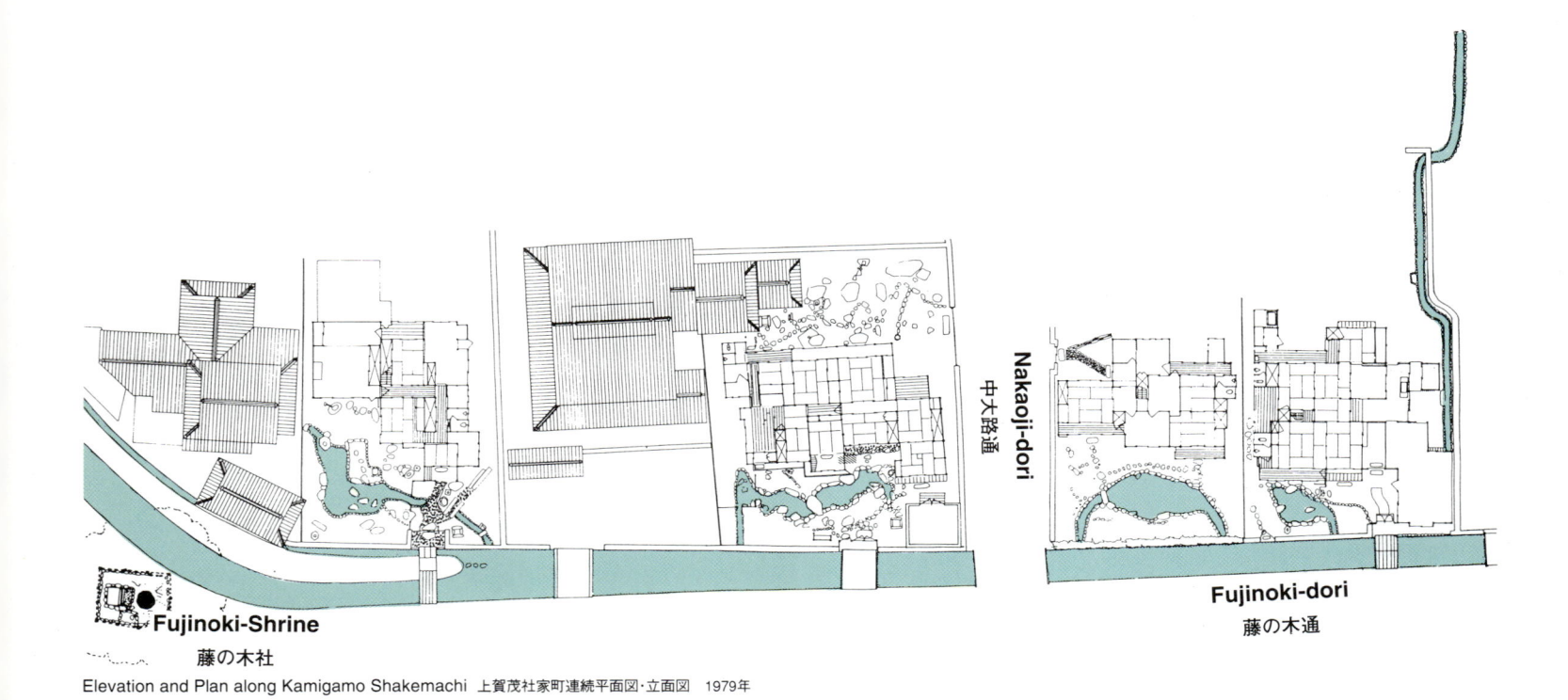

Fujinoki-Shrine
藤の木社

Nakaoji-dori
中大路通

Fujinoki-dori
藤の木通

Elevation and Plan along Kamigamo Shakemachi　上賀茂社家町連続平面図・立面図　1979年

Kamigamo Shakemachi 上賀茂社家町

上賀茂社家町

葵祭りの行列は内裏から賀茂川づたいに上賀茂神社に詣でる．上賀茂神社は平安京建設の以前から上賀茂付近を支配していた豪族，賀茂氏の祖神を祭る神社である．平安京建設時に余程の事情があったのだろうか，朝廷との特別な関係がうかがわれる．葵祭は都と洛外の自然・田園地帯との密接な関係を象徴してもいる．

上賀茂神社は古来，賀茂氏一族の人々が神官を務めてきた．神社門前付近に，この神官たちの住居である社家と農家が混在して営まれてきた集落があり，静雅なたたずまいを今日に伝えている．神社境内から流れ出た明神川に沿って，土塀の続く社家の家並が印象的な風景を見せる．江戸時代にも社家は門と，式台と呼ばれる玄関を構えることが許されてきた．式台と，土間へ入る大戸の二つの入口が並び，間取りも式台から座敷に続く表向きの部分と，土間側の内向き部分に二分されている．外観の意匠的な特徴は屋根の妻飾りで，彫刻を施した懸魚，人の字形に木を組んだ亥叉首（イノコサス），梁（ハリ）と貫（ヌキ）などが美しい構成を見せる．明神川の水は社家に引き込まれて二手に分かれ，一方は表庭の池に入って神官の禊ぎにも用いられ，また明神川に戻される．もう一方は生活用水で，裏の小川に流れる．汚れた水は地中の穴に浸透させるので，水流は清らかさを保っていたという．明神川沿いの家並も国の重要伝統的建造物群保存地区に選定されている．

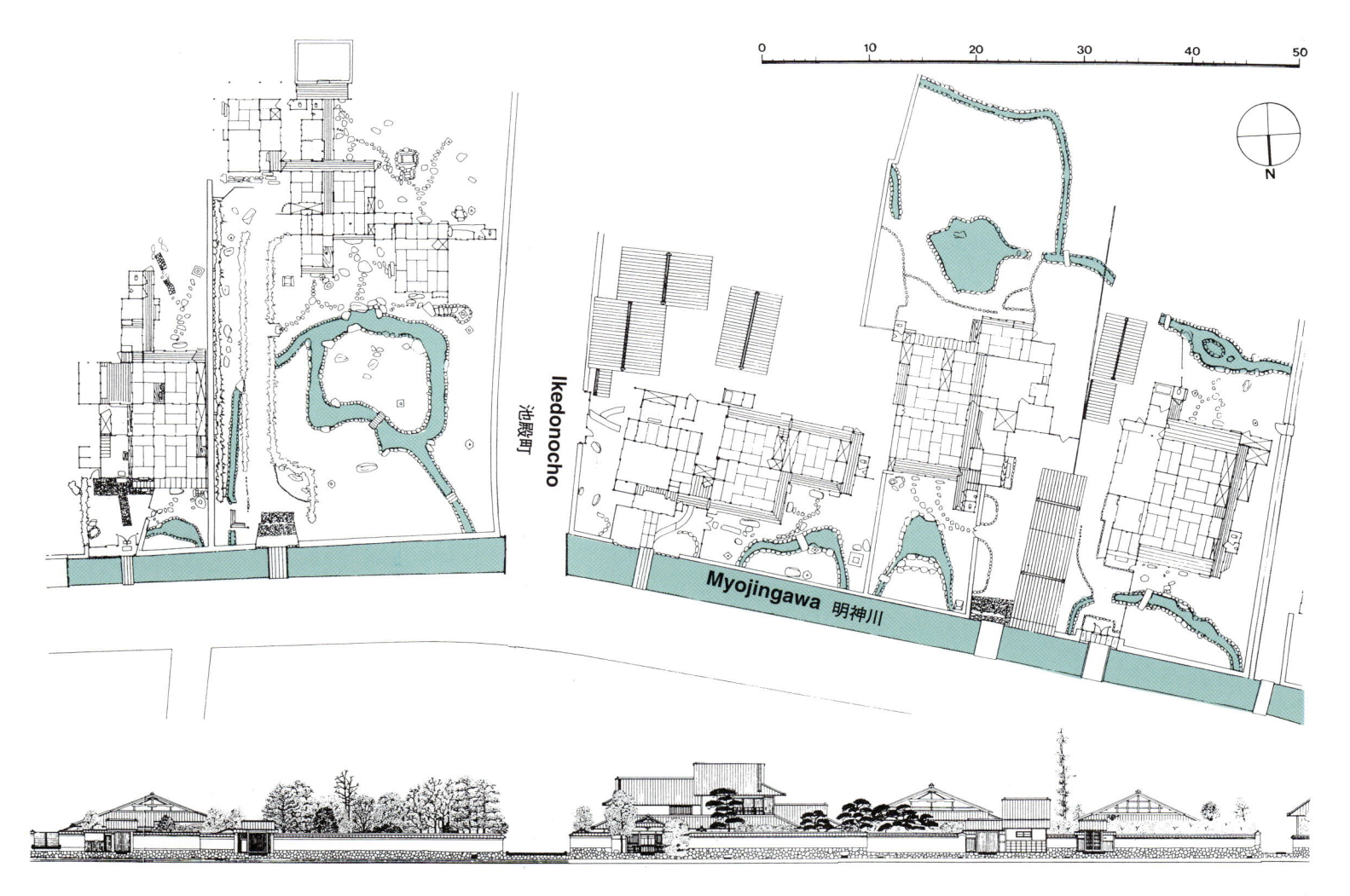

Kamigamo Shakemachi 上賀茂社家町

Kamigamo Shrine 上賀茂神社

Myojingawa
明神川

Drainage
放水口

Intake
取水口

Misogiishi
みそぎ石

Myojingawa River and Shake Houses; *Shin Miyako no Sakigake*
明神川と社家 『新・都の魁』 京都新聞社刊より

The areas leading up to shrines and temples in Japan are described as being *monzen machi*, "districts in front of a gate". Sometimes the approaches within such a defined neighborhood are wide and sometimes they are a compact, limited space with dog-leg turns over an equally defined distance. Such neighborhoods thus seem to welcome pilgrims and visitors alike, who are somehow bound to make their approach with a special sense of expectation. Whether the people living in such quarters are aware of the traditions or not, such districts either have a streetscape full of atmosphere, or on occasions have an air of refined elegance. In fact, Buildings in such neighborhoods are often much more well maintained and conserved than in some other places. Honganji has its own cluster of streets in Teranouchi-cho which came into being when the temple was established and many of these neighborhoods whose very existence is bound up with the facilities they have clustered around for so long still exist on the way up to such temples as Kozanji and Jingoji in Takao as well as at Seiryoji and the same is true at Jakkoin in Ohara. Although the site of a former Imperial villa, Shugakuin, too, has its own clustering hamlet. Many years ago, the path up to the Zen temple of Nanzenji ran through fields and commercial tea shops lined the way creating a scene of particular character. Nearby, the highly representative turn of the century neighborhood of distinctive residences developed by the landscape gardener Ogawa Jihei, provides new-approaches which are beautified by the way the gardens of the houses extending beyond the bounds of their fences. Despite the fact that the routes up to Daikakuji, Ryoanji and the Bishamondo in Yamashina are flanked by neighborhoods dating from relatively recently times, there is an air of quality and moderation about the lines of hedges that are an integral part of the scene. Inevitably, therefore, it is the fostered sense of history and air of refinement existing in such neighborhoods, which can be perceived.

社寺の門前や参道には特別な景観がある．日本の社寺の参道の道自身の形を注意して見ると，門前の一定区間の道幅が広かったり，一定の長さで道を鍵折れにしてまとまった空間に限定していたりして，参詣に先立つ序曲的空間とでもいうべきか，特別な意識を向けていて興味深い．その伝統は門前に住む人々も承知していたのだろうか，門前には風格のある，或は時に上品な風情のある町並み景観が形成され，またそれらは他の町並みに比べてよく保全されている所も少なくない．本願寺の門前には寺院とともに形成された寺内町の町並みがあり，高雄の高山寺・神護寺や清涼寺，修学院，あるいは大原の寂光院の門前などには古い時代からそれらと生活を共にしてきた門前の集落が今日に続いている．南禅寺参道にはかつては野の中を寺院へ向かった道すがらの茶店の風景がある．また寺院に隣接して明治時代を代表する庭師小川治平が屋敷群を開発し，塀の外にまで庭園的空間を広げて，その中を通り抜ける道が美しく新しい脇参道となっている．大覚寺，竜安寺，山科の毘沙門堂などの正面の参道は近代になって町並みが出来た所だが，各戸が生垣を連続して節度を感じさせる品のよい景観を形成してきたのは，さすがに歴史に培われた洗練された環境への感性をうかがわせる．

Traditional Neighborhood - Religious and Imperial
門前参道の町並み

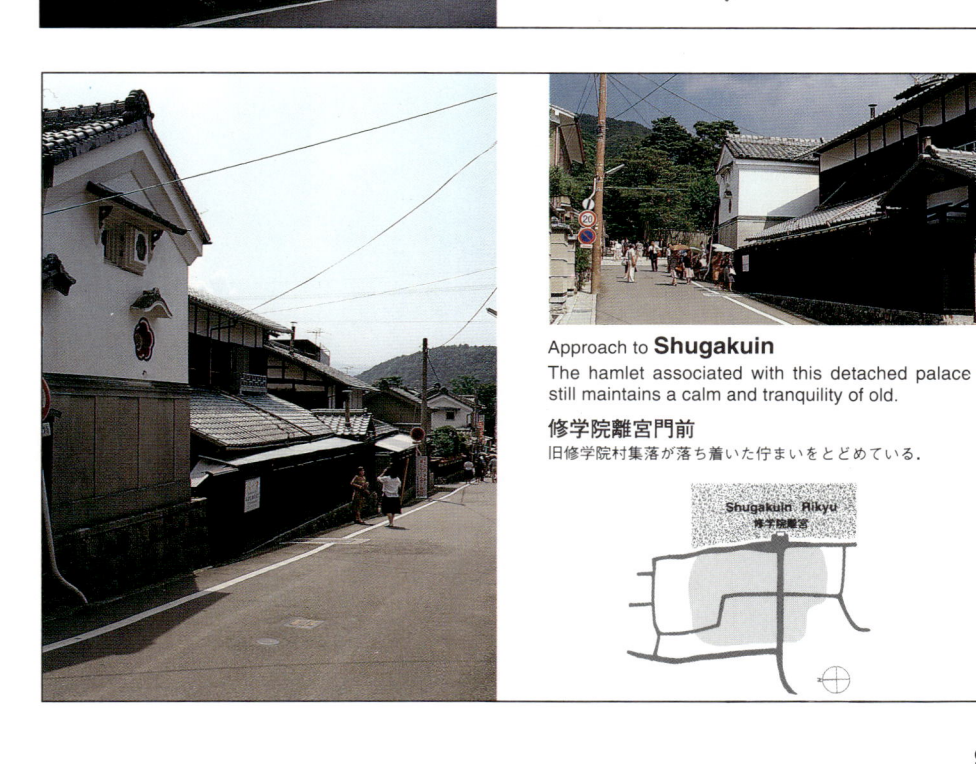

On the way up to the **Kibune Shrine**
With a history dating back to the Heian period, this hamlet stands in the vally as if to welcome visitors to the shrine.

貴船神社門前
平安時代以来の歴史をもつ集落が谷間に参拝客を迎える．

Approach to **Shugakuin**
The hamlet associated with this detached palace still maintains a calm and tranquility of old.

修学院離宮門前
旧修学院村集落が落ち着いた佇まいをとどめている．

On the way up to the Imamiya Shurine
The shops lining the street here contribute significantly to the atmosphere.

今宮神社門前
向かい合う名物のあぶり餅屋が門前の風情を伝える.

Approach to the Shinnyodo
Here the relationship between the Munetada Shrine and Mt. Yoshidayama is significant.

真如堂門前
吉田山の宗忠神社と向き合った景観構成.

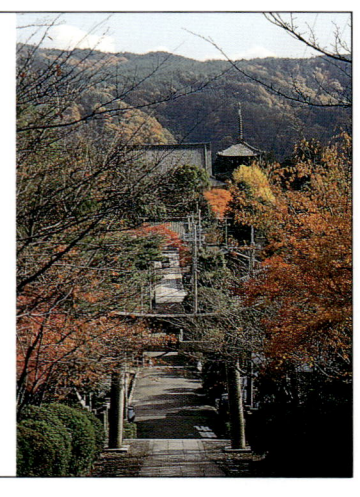

Approach to the Nanzenji
The exclusive eating houses lining the street here still maintain an atmosphere reminiscent to the tea houses of the past. The street on the right leads to Nanzenji through a housing area developed by Ogawa Jihei during the Meiji period.

南禅寺参道
参道沿いの料亭がかつての茶店の風情をとどめる. 右写真は明治時代に小川治平が開発した邸宅群を通り抜けて南禅寺に至る道.

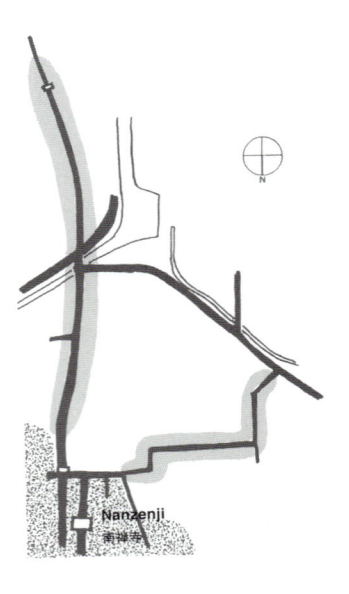

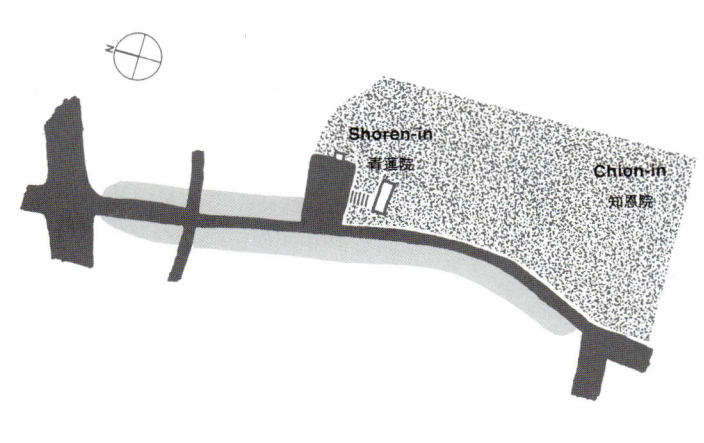

Approach to Shorenin
The pleasant mix of modern Japanese style houses, machiya and trees here, adds interest to the route between Heian Jingu and Maruyama park.

青蓮院門前
このあたりは近代の和風住宅や町家が樹木の緑とともに在り、平安神宮から円山公園に至る散策路となっている。

Jinaicho district near Nishi Honganji Temple
When Honganji was moved at the beginning of the 17th century, people also moved from Osaka and settled in this area which even today maintains its religious atmosphere. The area around Higashi Honganji is the same.

西本願寺寺内町
近世初頭、本願寺と共に大阪から移転してきた人々の町で、宗教の町の雰囲気を伝えている。東本願寺門前にも寺内町がある。

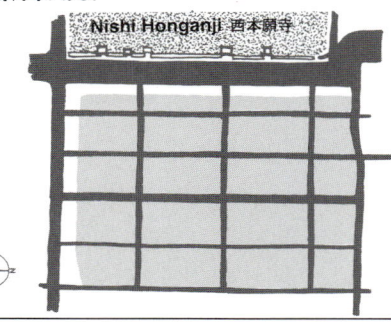

Approach to the Bishamondo
The streetscape here is comparatively new.

毘沙門堂参道
生垣が続く，近代に熟成された参道の家並み．

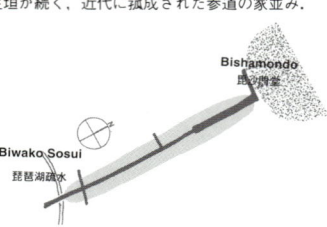

On the way up to Daigoji Temple
The historical streetscape along Otsukaido is highly contributive to this area.

醍醐寺門前
大津街道の歴史的町並みが門前景観を形づくっている．

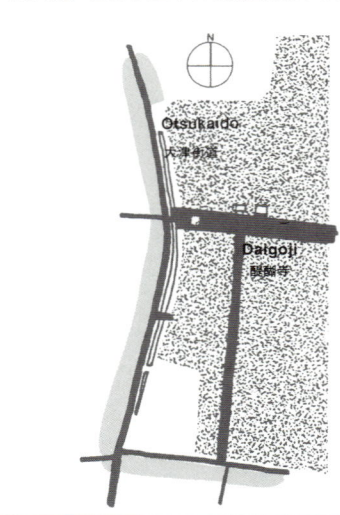

On the way up to Seiryoji Temple
Depicted in Rakuchu Rakugai paintings, this area has a long history.

清凉寺門前
洛中洛外図にも描写された歴史ある門前の町並み．

On the way to Seiryoji Temple from Togetsukyo Bridge
渡月橋から清凉寺に向かう参道

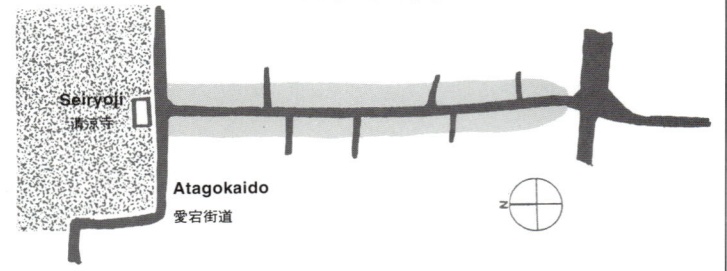

Daikakuji Temple
Although relatively modern in origins, this route up to the temple has atmosphere.

大覚寺
近代に形成された風格ある参道景観

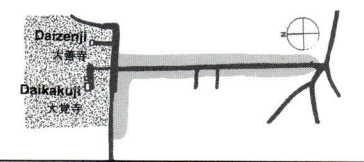

On the way up to **Ninnaji Temple**
This area between the temple and Omuro Station is highly representative of such approaches to religious buildings.

仁和寺門前
御室駅との間のまとまった参道空間

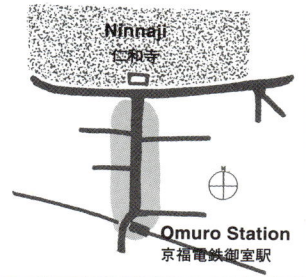

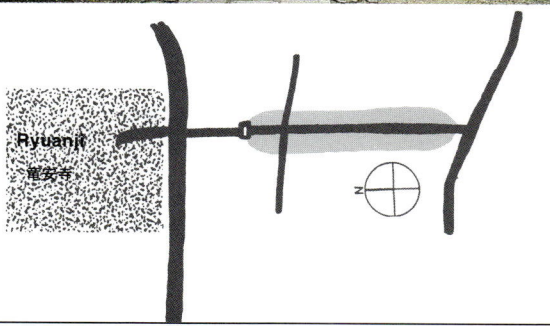

Approach to **Ryoanji Temple**
While blessed with the enduring natural benefits of the environs of Kyoto, the streetscape with its hedges is of relaively recent origins.

竜安寺参道
洛外の緑の中の参道を継承して、近代に生垣の家並みを形成している．

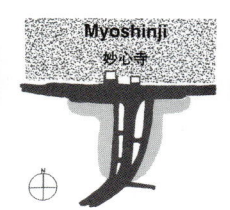

Approach to **Myoshinji Temple**
Both the street and houses along it in front of the temple are of recent origin.

妙心寺門前
門前の広い参道も家並みも近代に形成された．

Saga Toriimoto 嵯峨鳥居本

Hiranoya 平野屋

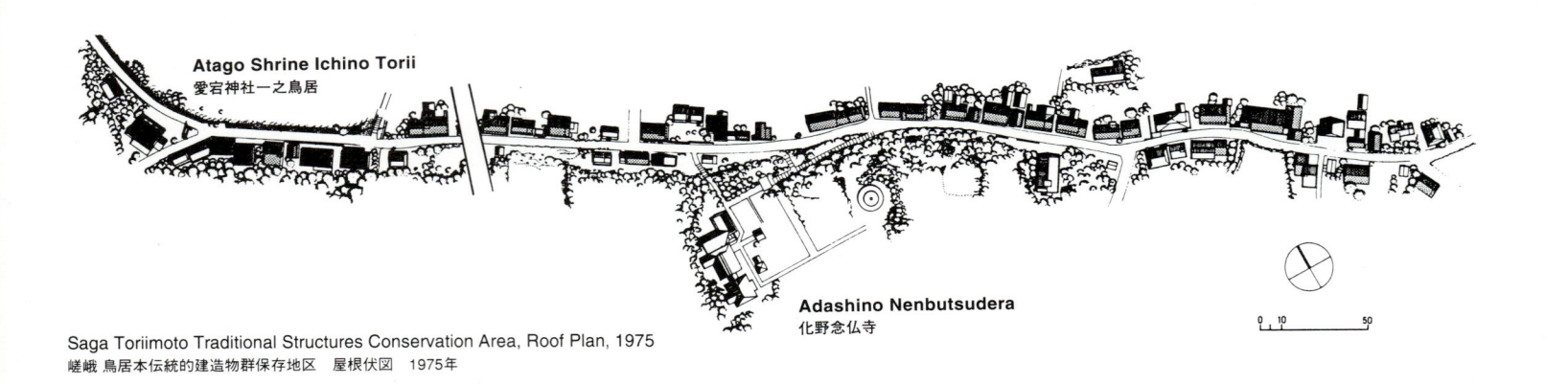

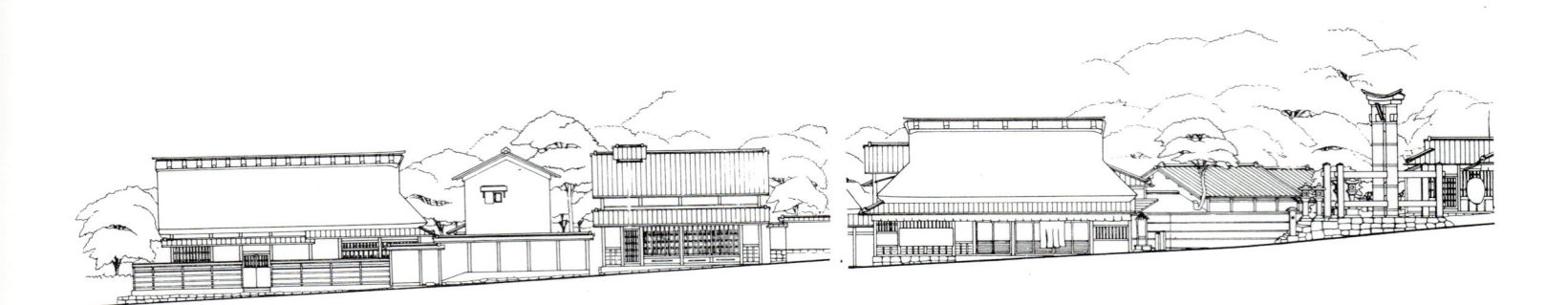

Atago Shrine Ichino Torii 愛宕神社一之鳥居

Adashino Nenbutsudera 化野念仏寺

Saga Toriimoto Traditional Structures Conservation Area, Roof Plan, 1975
嵯峨 鳥居本伝統的建造物群保存地区　屋根伏図　1975年

Highway Streetscapes
街道の町並み

Saga Toriimoto

The Atago Shrine which lies atop Mount Atago was, as the home of the god who administers fire, honored during the Edo period with a monthly prayer gathering and, such was the sincerity of the believers that they even composed a folk song to further enshrine their belief. For the people who lived in the wooden quarters of the city, fire is a constant threat to their existence. Atagokaido, is the road which runs from the Togetsukyo Bridge in Arashiyama, past Seiryoji Temple and the gate of Nisonin Temple up to the Kiyotaki Falls. As the road nears Atago Shrine we come across Ichinotorii, a *torii* being the 'gate' marking the entrance to the grounds of a shrine. Just preceding this lies a village along the road called Toriimoto, which stretches out some 600 meters east of the Ichinotorii. This village and surrounding area, too, has been designated as a special conservation area of particular architectural importance.

In the middle of the area lies Adashino Nenbutsudera Temple. From here on upwards lie houses built in a farmhouse-style. Stretching on downwards toward Kyoto are houses that mimic the style within Kyoto and the juxtapositioning of these styles is of some interest. Moving along the gently winding path of the slope, rows of houses are broken by clusters of trees and open patches of land producing an interesting contrast of areas of shade and sunlight. In addition, along the road stand untended graves, signs, miniature shrines and *torii*, which all in their own way lend a certain charm and attraction to the area. Moreover, one of the main features of this area is that each spot forms its own picture-like scene, partly because of the contrast between the *torii* and the thatched tea shops. Pictures dating from the Edo period that depict this area show scenes that have changed hardly at all when compared to the present. Following the first real increase in tourists to the area, the local residents, fearing that the area would suffer as a consequence of its popularity, began to take steps to ensure its preservation. In summer during Urabon, which is an all souls festival, the villagers light candles on Mandara mountain, in the shape of a torii, to light the way of the souls of the dead back to their place of rest.

嵯峨鳥居本

愛宕山頂の愛宕神社は火を司る神として、江戸時代には「愛宕さんへは月参り」と俗謡に歌われるほど信仰が盛んであった。木造都市に住む人々にとって、火はただならぬ存在であった。愛宕街道は嵐山渡月橋から清涼寺、二尊院門前を経て清滝に至る。街道が山にさしかかる手前に愛宕神社一之鳥居があり、その前に街道に沿って鳥居本の集落がある。一之鳥居から東へおよそ600メートル程の間に町並みが続き、国の重要伝統的建造物群保存地区に選定されている。

町並みの中程に化野念仏寺があり、そこから上では農家風の民家があり、下の京都寄りの部分では京の町家に似た家屋があって、その移り変わりが面白い。緩やかな曲線の坂になっている街道を行くと、家並と樹木や開けた場所が交互に連続し、樹陰に入っては日なたに出て変化がある。また道端の無縁仏や道標、祠、鳥居など、各々に意味ありげな舞台装置がそろっている。また、鳥居と草葺の茶店の取り合わせなど、各所にいかにも絵になるような景観があるのもこの町並みの特徴である。鳥居付近を描いた江戸時代の絵は現在の景観と殆ど変わらない。観光客が増加し始めた頃、景観の俗化を恐れて集落に住む人々は町並み保存に踏み切った。夏の盂蘭盆会には、集落で曼陀羅山に鳥居形の送り火を灯す。

In the vicinity of Ichinotorii 一之鳥居付近

Elevation of Saga Toriimoto, 1975 嵯峨鳥居本連続立面図 1975年

Saga Toriimoto　嵯峨鳥居本

Process of Streetscape Adjustment. Left - 1975, Right - Present.　町並み修景過程　左：昭和50年　中：修景図　右：現況

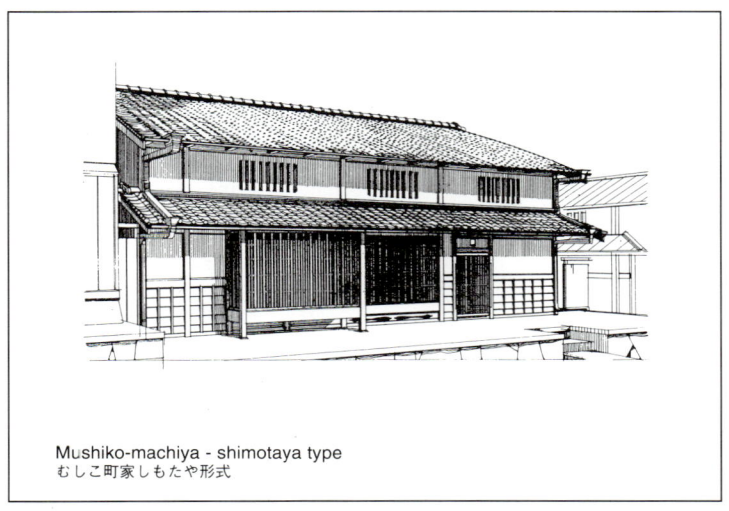

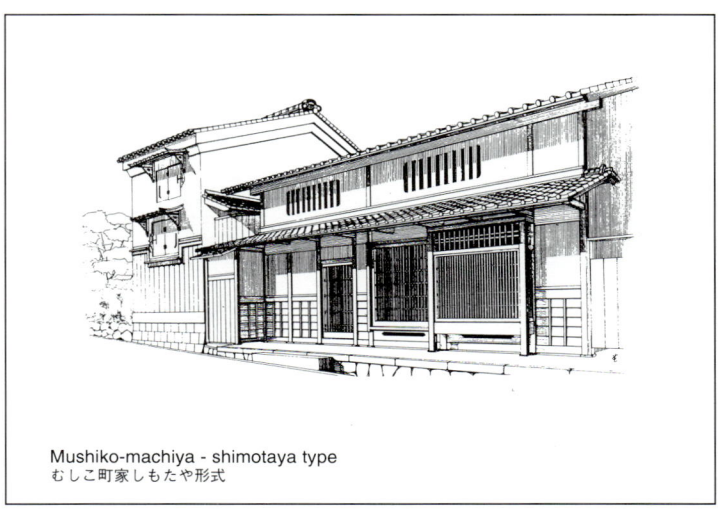

Mushiko-machiya - display window type
むしこ町家飾窓付店舗形式

Mushiko-machiya - "walk-in" style shop with doma
むしこ町家土間店舗形式

Mushiko-machiya - shimotaya type
むしこ町家しもたや形式

Mushiko-machiya - shimotaya type
むしこ町家しもたや形式

Reed thatched gate with bracketing and planted hedge
腕木門(茅葺き屋根)と生垣

Kuzuya shimotaya type
くずやしもたや形式

Types of Exteriors　建物外観型透視図

Saga Toriimoto 嵯峨鳥居本

Atagoji Toriimoto by Uda Tekison, 1968 104 愛宕路鳥居本 宇田荻邨筆 1968 シーグ出版株式会社協力

Saga Toriimoto 嵯峨鳥居本

Hiranoya 平野屋

Machiya of Toriimoto 鳥居本の町家

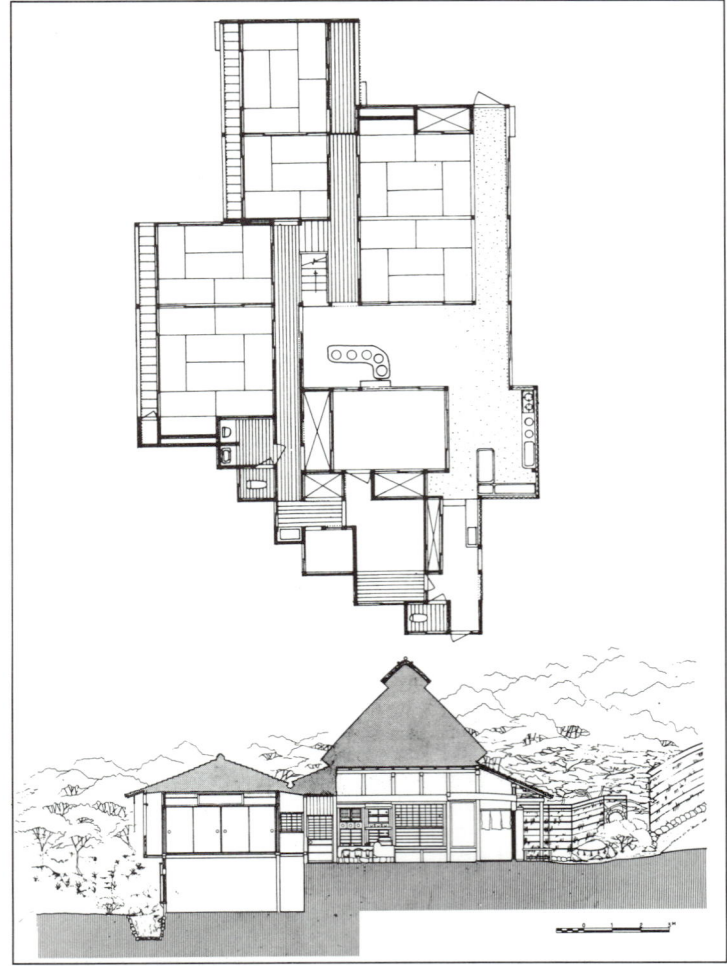

Hiranoya, Plan and Section 平野屋 平面図・断面図

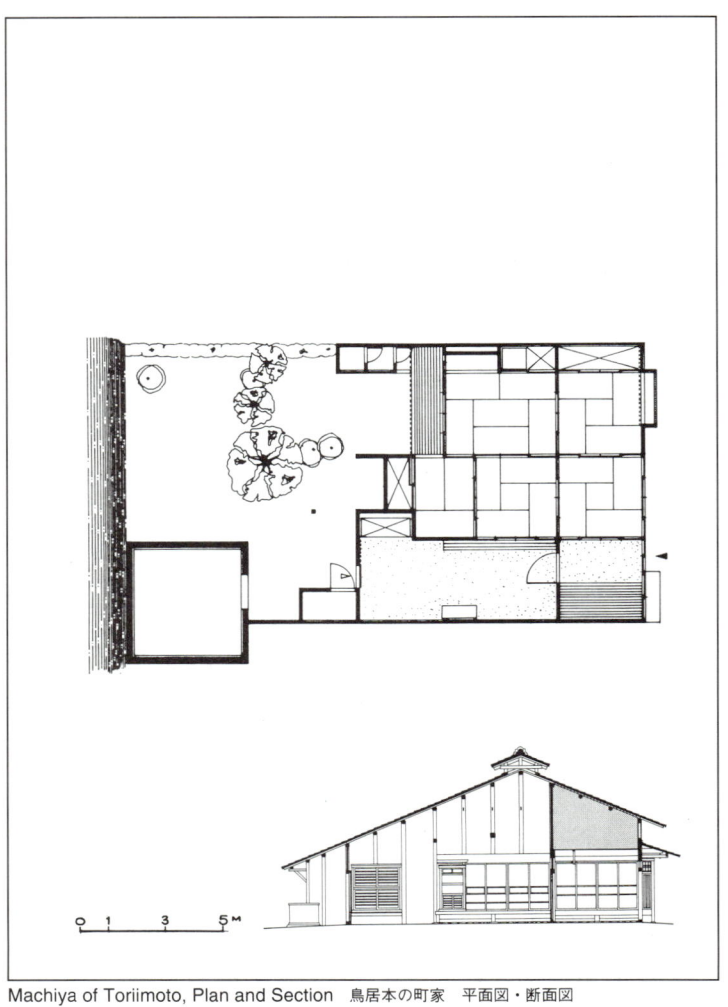

Machiya of Toriimoto, Plan and Section 鳥居本の町家 平面図・断面図

Saga Toriimoto 嵯峨鳥居本

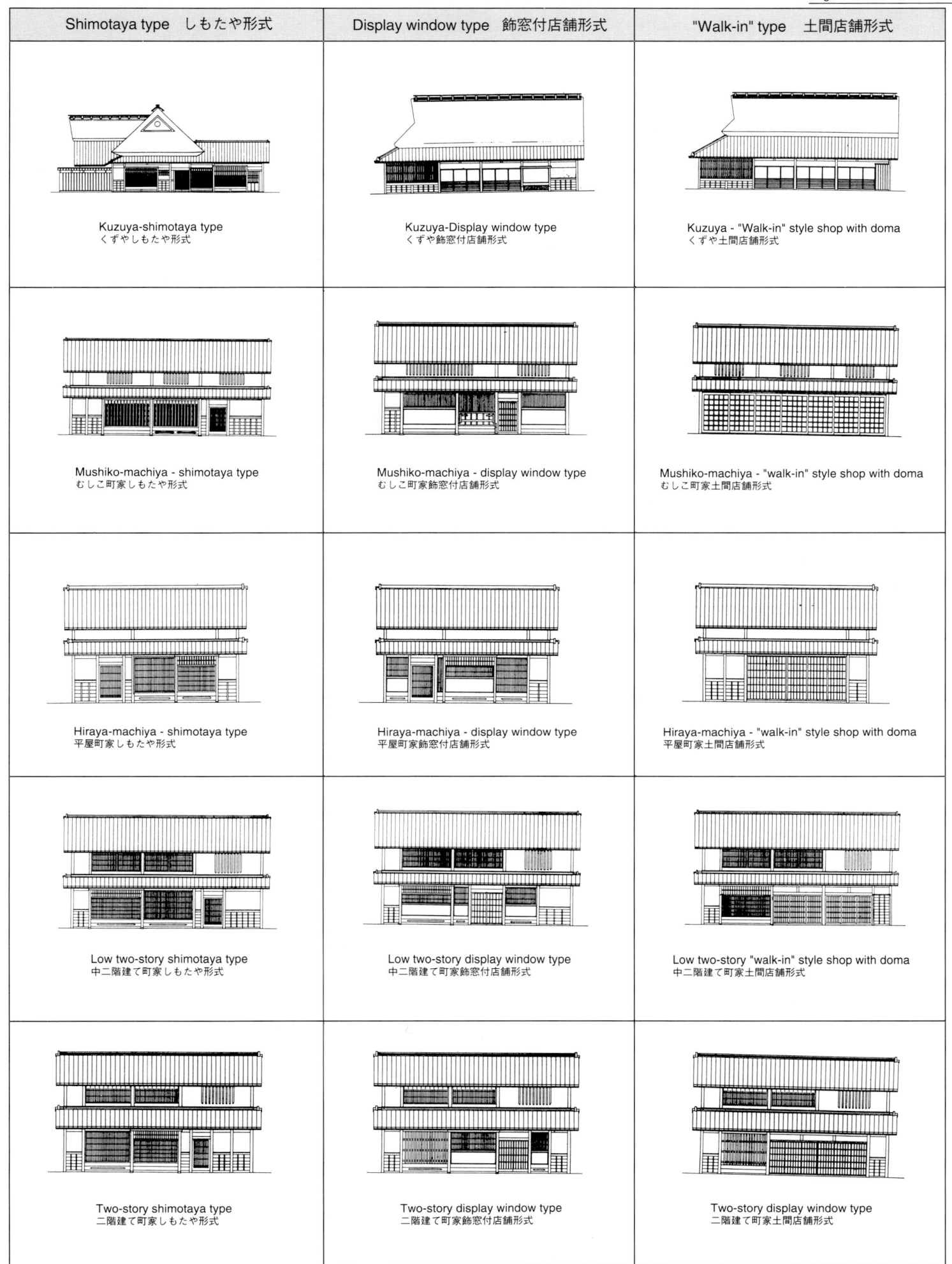

Shimotaya type　しもたや形式	Display window type　飾窓付店舗形式	"Walk-in" type　土間店舗形式
Kuzuya-shimotaya type くずやしもたや形式	Kuzuya-Display window type くずや飾窓付店舗形式	Kuzuya - "Walk-in" style shop with doma くずや土間店舗形式
Mushiko-machiya - shimotaya type むしこ町家しもたや形式	Mushiko-machiya - display window type むしこ町家飾窓付店舗形式	Mushiko-machiya - "walk-in" style shop with doma むしこ町家土間店舗形式
Hiraya-machiya - shimotaya type 平屋町家しもたや形式	Hiraya-machiya - display window type 平屋町家飾窓付店舗形式	Hiraya-machiya - "walk-in" style shop with doma 平屋町家土間店舗形式
Low two-story shimotaya type 中二階建て町家しもたや形式	Low two-story display window type 中二階建て町家飾窓付店舗形式	Low two-story "walk-in" style shop with doma 中二階建て町家土間店舗形式
Two-story shimotaya type 二階建て町家しもたや形式	Two-story display window type 二階建て町家飾窓付店舗形式	Two-story display window type 二階建て町家土間店舗形式

Types of Exteriors　外観類型図表

Kuramakaido 鞍馬街道

Kurama

Mount Kuramayama has been famed for its springtime cherry blossoms since the Heian period. At the peak of one of the off-shoots of Buddhism, Jodo or Amidism, Yase and Ohara, situated to the north of Kyoto, became the center of this sect and, in the middle ages, Kuramadera Temple became the focal point for worshippers of the god Bishamonten with believers coming in an endless procession to worship. The temple was first built in 796, and it was from this time too that the hamlet directly associated with the temple developed. Kurama-kaido, the main road which traces a path along the bottom of the valley, bends sharply at the main gate of the temple to bring us face to face, for a moment, with the temple buildings before rising on up the valley. The open spaces in front of each gateway, in their own esoteric way, are particularly attractive. The hamlet of Kurama has been developed as a useful midway point between areas, almost a haven. In the old days, fish from Wakasa, along with wood and charcoal, the pickle *konomezuke* and a kind of potato called *tokoro* from Hanase and Kuta, are just some of the well known items that were assembled here for distribution in Kyoto.

In quite a few ways, Kurama is rather distinctive and different in style from Kyoto. The roof eaves, for instance, are deep and the clay floors that offer onto the gardens are much wider, in order to facilitate work being done there. Heavier columns and more unevenly formed window screens are usual, and wooden screens standing proud of the windows are rare. There are also many houses with *udatsu - see page 47 -* and other features, such as awnings with wooden covers and shingles prevail. Moreover, the buildings reflect the fact that the hamlet was a stopping place along the highway, as it is common to see one-storey barns running parallel to the main two-storey buildings facing on to the main road here. Further along the street stands the residence of the Takizawa family, a house which was built around 1760, and has been designated as a building of outstanding cultural significance.

The houses along the Kurama River nearly all rely on the flow of clean water from the river for the purposes of such things as washing. There is also a flight of steps leading down to the river, reinforcing the strong ties the community has with the river.

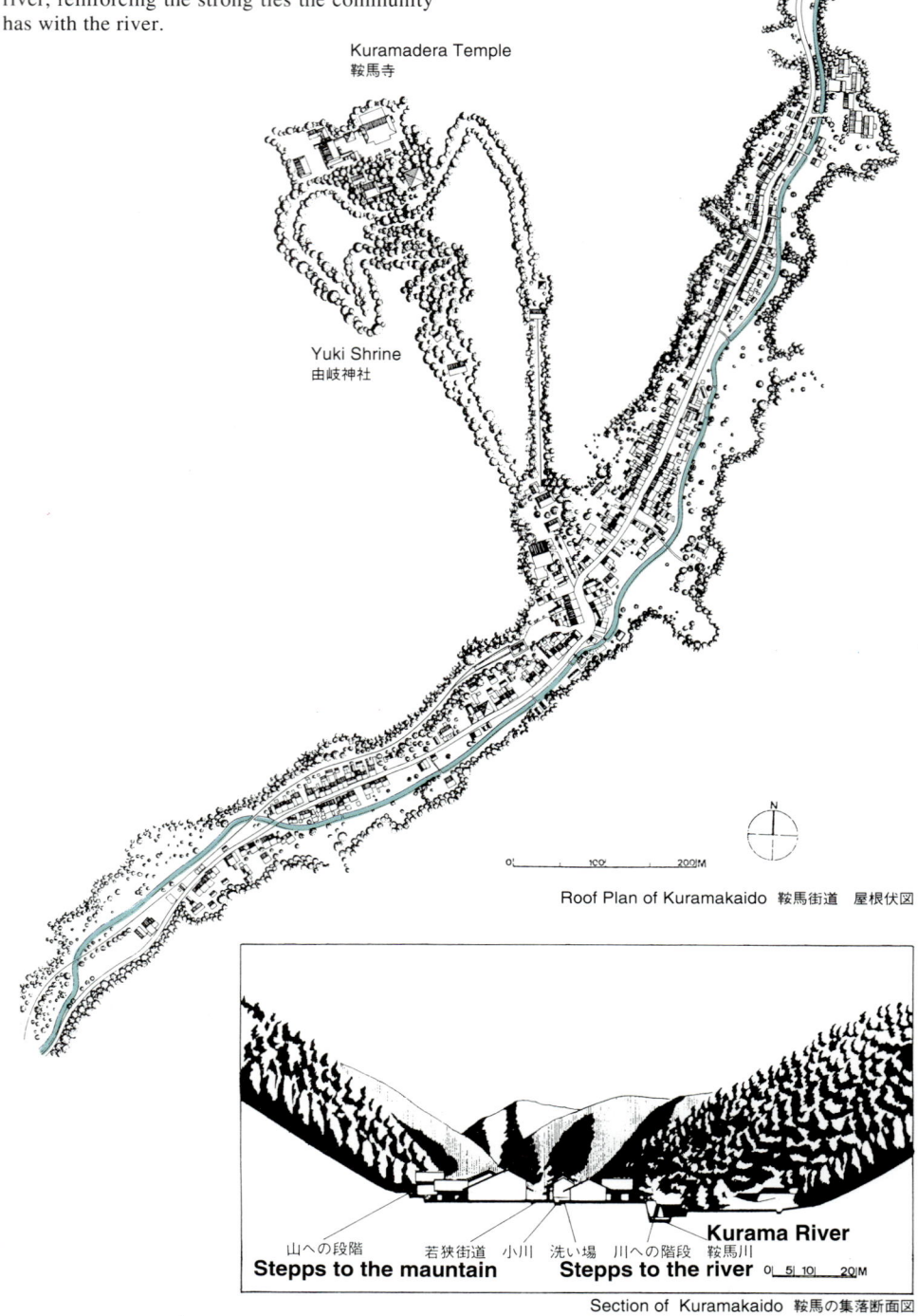

鞍馬

鞍馬山は平安時代から春の桜で名高く，浄土信仰盛んな頃には八瀬，大原とともに「洛北浄土」とされ，また中世には鞍馬寺の毘沙門天が信仰を集め，参詣者が跡を絶たなかった．鞍馬寺の創建は古く延暦十五年(796)と伝え，その頃から門前の集落が営まれてきたという．谷筋を上る鞍馬街道は，鞍馬寺の山門前で鍵折れて一時寺の方へ向き，再び谷沿いに上って行く．門前の空間は社寺各々に工夫があって興味を引く．鞍馬集落は街道の中継地としても発展し，「船のない港」ともいわれた．若狭の魚，花背，久多の木材や薪炭，或は木芽漬（コノメヅケ）や野老（トコロ）などのこの地の名物が京の町へと運ばれていった．

鞍馬の町並みは京の町中とは幾らか趣が異なっている．軒が深く，通り庭の土間を広くして，作業の場を確保している．骨太の柱，粗い格子が多い，出格子が殆どない，卯立（ウダツ）のある家が多い，1階の庇に板葺や柿葺（コケラブキ）も見られるなどの特徴がある．また2階建ての主屋に並んで，平屋の納屋が道に面している例が多いのも街道の中継地であった事情を反映している．集落の上よりにある宝暦十年(1760)建造の滝沢家住宅は重要文化財に指定されている．

町並みの鞍馬川の側の家はたいていが洗い物などに使用できるよう清流を引いており，川へ下りる階段もあって，町並みと川の関係が深い．

Roof Plan of Kuramakaido 鞍馬街道 屋根伏図

山への段階　若狭街道　小川　洗い場　川への階段　鞍馬川
Stepps to the mauntain　　**Kurama River**　**Stepps to the river**

Section of Kuramakaido 鞍馬の集落断面図

Kuramakaido 鞍馬街道

Street Elevation Along Kuramakaido, 1979 鞍馬街道連続立面図 1979年

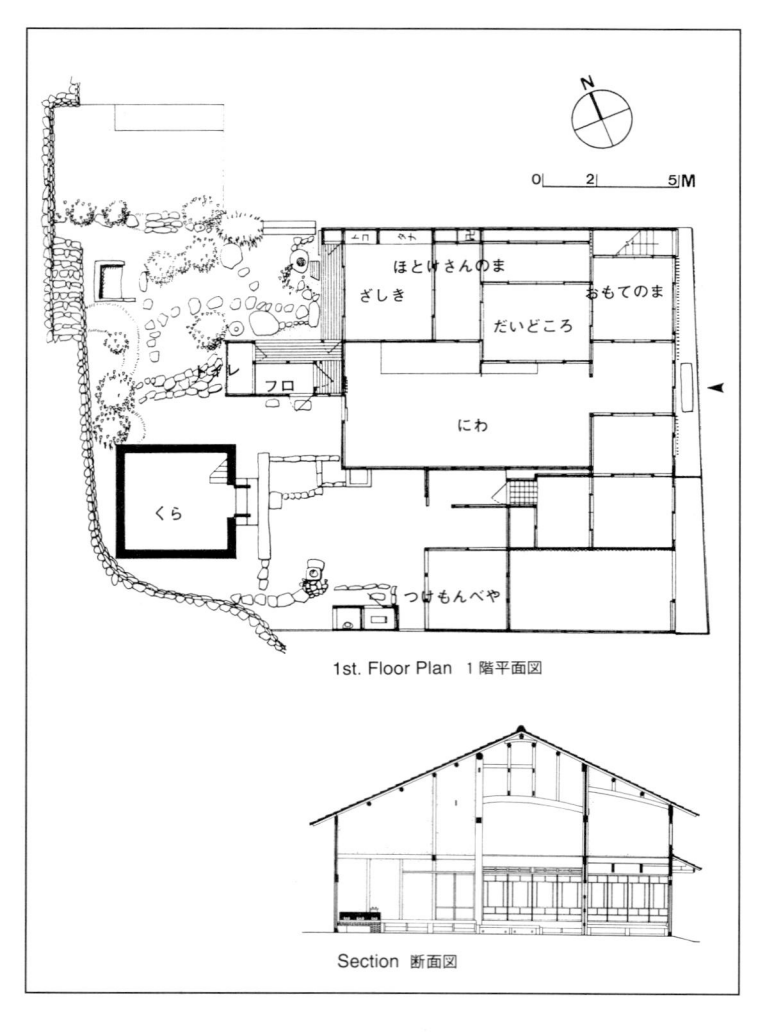

Kuramakaido 鞍馬街道

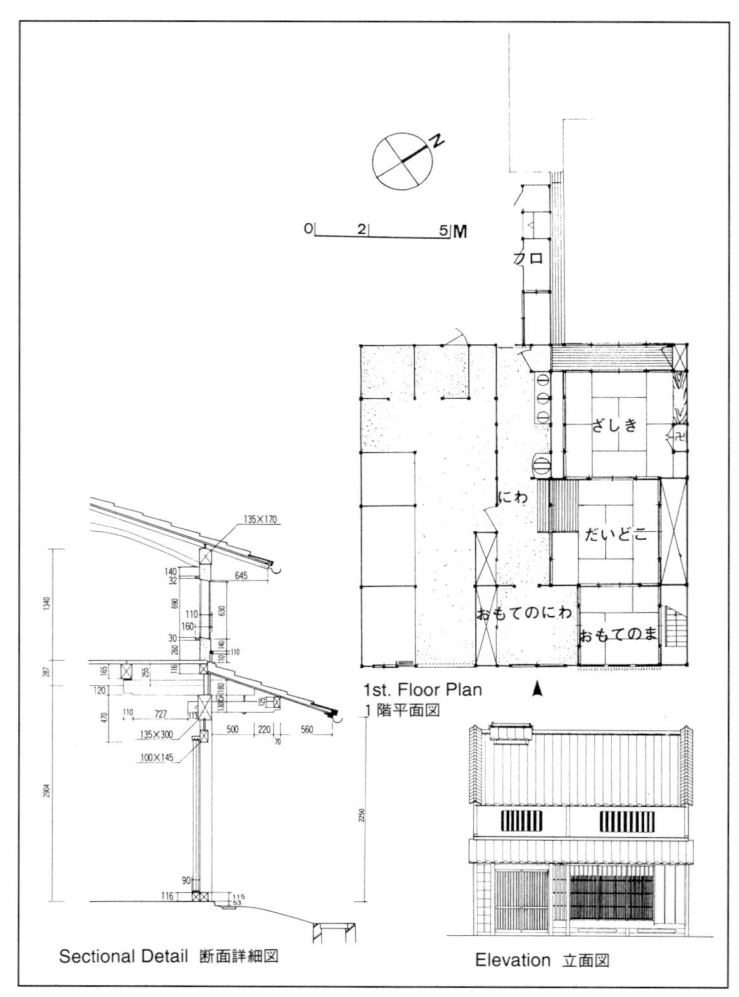

1st. Floor Plan 1階平面図

Section 断面図

Sectional Detail 断面詳細図

1st. Floor Plan 1階平面図

Elevation 立面図

Kuramakaido 鞍馬街道

Section 断面図

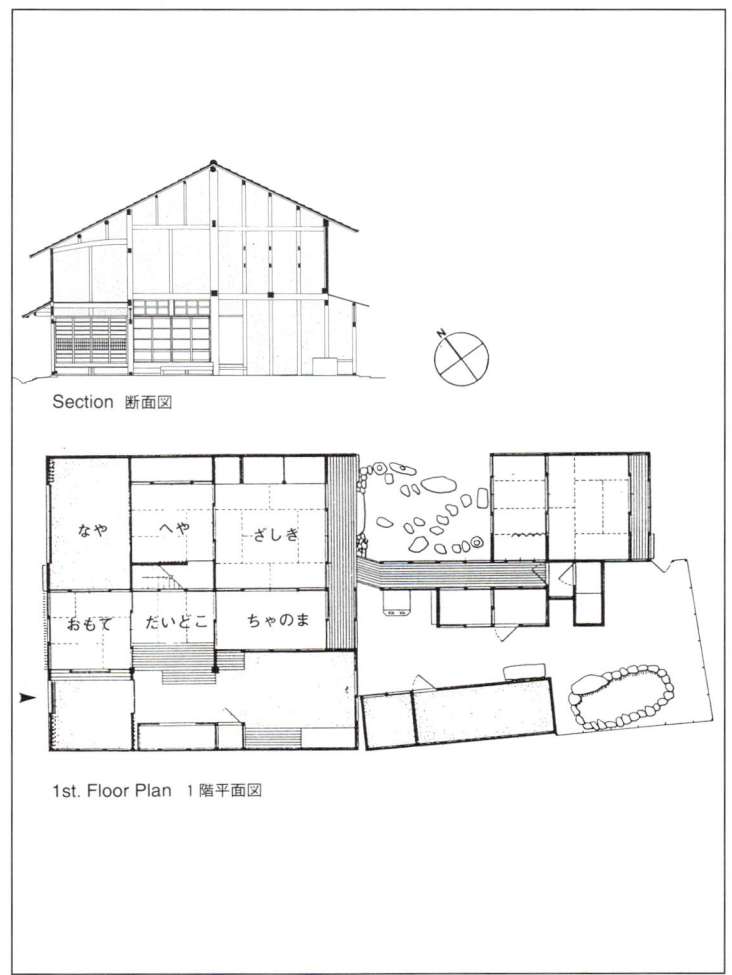

1st. Floor Plan 1階平面図

Section 断面図

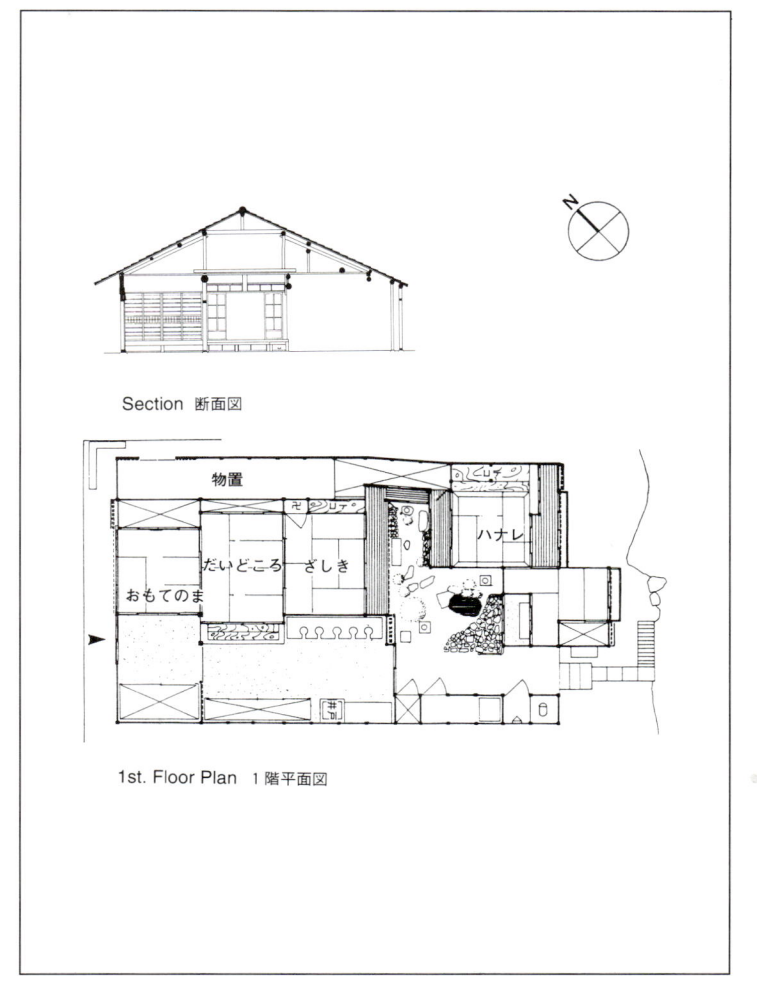

1st. Floor Plan 1階平面図

Kuramakaido 鞍馬街道

Takizawa House 滝沢家住宅

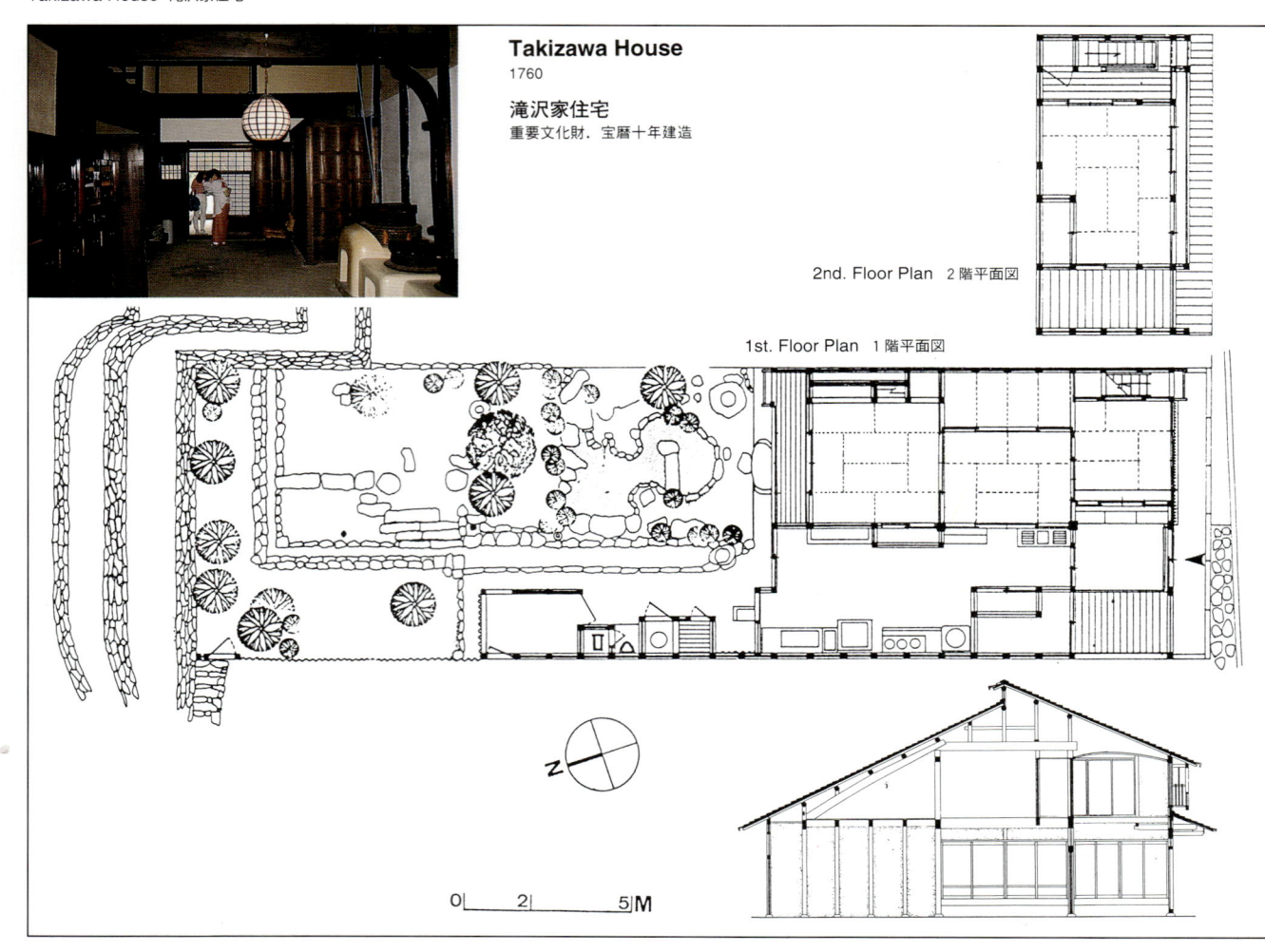

Takizawa House
1760

滝沢家住宅
重要文化財．宝暦十年建造

2nd. Floor Plan 2階平面図

1st. Floor Plan 1階平面図

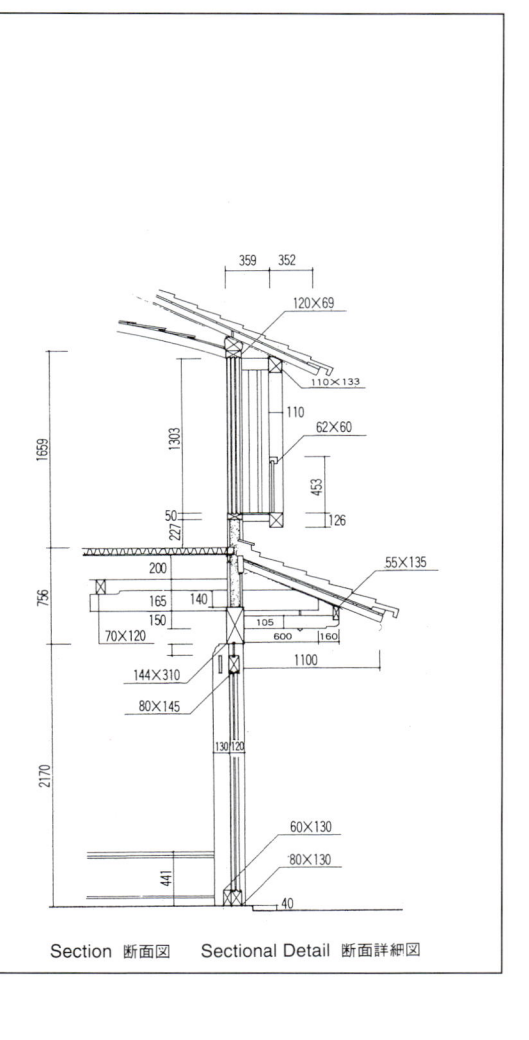

Streetscape of Katagihara, the post town along the old San-in Highway　旧山陰道の宿場町樫原の町並み

Section　断面図　　Sectional Detail　断面詳細図

Former Katagihara Honjin, Tamamura House　旧樫原本陣　玉村家

Otsukaido 大津街道

Approach to Daigoji Temple　醍醐寺門前

In the vicinity of Daigoji Temple　醍醐寺付近

In the vicinity of Ishida　石田付近

Festival at Rokujizo - Daizenji Temple　六地蔵(大善寺)の祭日

Fushimi: Its Townscape
伏見

Fushimi lies at the intersection of the main thoroughfares that lead from Kyoto to Osaka and Nara. Toward the end of the sixteenth century, Toyotomi Hideyoshi built a castle atop Mount Fushimi that commands a grand view of the roads in the area. At the foot of the western slop a village was established to serve the castle's needs. In the early days of the Edo period, the castle was destroyed and one side of it was given over to a peach orchard. It is owing to this that Hideyoshi's period of rule became known as the Momoyama, or literally "peach-mountain" period. The Takase River was excavated so as to facilitate transport by flat-bottomed boats from the Yodo River and Kyoto. Even after the castle no longer existed, the village continued to develop as a center of porterage and trade. During this time of boats, the area around the southern shores of Kyobashi and Minamihama became a bustling place of inns and storehouses. Much later on in about 1929, it came under the wing of the Fushimi local authority, but two years later it became part of Kyoto. To date, Fujimi has enjoyed a fairly independent and distinctive history compared to Kyoto proper.

One of the most memorable things about Fushimi are the groups of saké storehouses which create large continuous plastered walls with their inimitable vertical wooden slats. The saké making industry grew remarkably during the Meiji period. Looking at the layout of the buildings of the saké makers, the main building has been built so as to face on to the main road, with the saké store rooms enclosing it both behind and to the sides. The entrance to the main building of this kind of facility is large and along with a line of tatami matted rooms there is a stone floored area, too. In the center of the house there is a large well which serves for washing the rice in autumn. The saké storehouses all resemble each other, but the actual spaces were the saké is made and the storage rooms differ in terms of their function. Even in this local area where the buildings are fairly general in style, the *maku-kake* beam which clearly defines and emphasizes the horizontal of the façades is not made of a single timber as it is in Kyoto proper, but is made up of a number of wooden strips. Also, the mullioned windows reveal many columns inset into the walls and the gables are dressed with round tiles called *kazekiri*. The feeling the finishes and style give to the buildings is quite different to that found in Kyoto itself.

In the vicinity of Minamihama 南浜付近

伏見は京，大阪，奈良方面からの通行路が合流する位置にあたる．16世紀末，これらの通行路をよく見晴らせる伏見山上に豊臣秀吉は城を築き，西麓に城下町を建設した．江戸時代初期に城が破却されると，やがて城跡は一面の桃畑になり，そこから秀吉の頃が桃山時代と呼ばれるようになった．高瀬川が開削され淀川と京を舟運で結んだこともあって，城がなくなって後もかえって交通と商業の町として発展した．舟運の時代，京橋，南浜あたりに旅籠や問屋が並び賑わった．昭和4年(1929)に伏見市政をしいたが，2年後には京都市に合併されている．伏見は元来，京とは別個の個性と歴史をもつ町なのである．

伏見の町並みを先ず印象づけるのは漆喰壁に竪板張りの大きな壁面を連ねる酒蔵群である．その酒造業は明治時代になって抜きんでて発展した．造酒家の屋敷構えを見ると，主屋を道に面して建て，酒蔵がその背後左右に囲むように位置している．主屋は間口の広い町家で，中には畳の部屋の列と並んで広い石畳の土間があり，中程に大きな井戸があって，秋には洗米の仕事場になった．酒蔵は形はどれも似ているが，造り蔵，貯え蔵など棟毎に別の機能がある．一般の町家も，幕掛けが京のように一本の材でなく板張りであったり，二階の虫籠窓のある壁面に多くの柱を見せていたり，或は屋根の端に風切りと呼ぶ丸瓦の線を通すなど，その町並みは京とは少し違った個性がある．

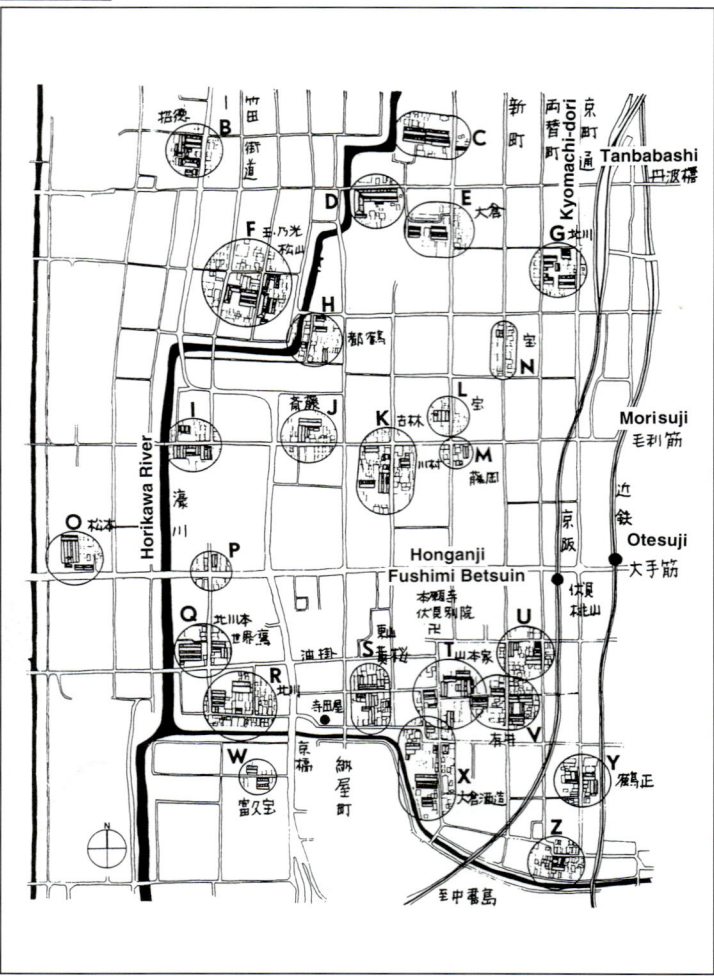

Fushimi 伏見

Distribution of Saké Storehouses in 1983　昭和58年頃の酒蔵の分布

Hoko (Toyotomi Hideyoshi) Fushimijo no Zu - Fushimi Castle　豊公伏見城ノ図

Minamihama; *Yodogawa Ryogan Ichiran*, 1856
江戸時代の南浜『淀川両岸一覧』安政三年刊

Saké storehouse along the Takase River　高瀬川と酒蔵

Saké storehouse along the Horikawa River　濠川と酒蔵

Saké storehouse in Minamihama　南浜の酒蔵

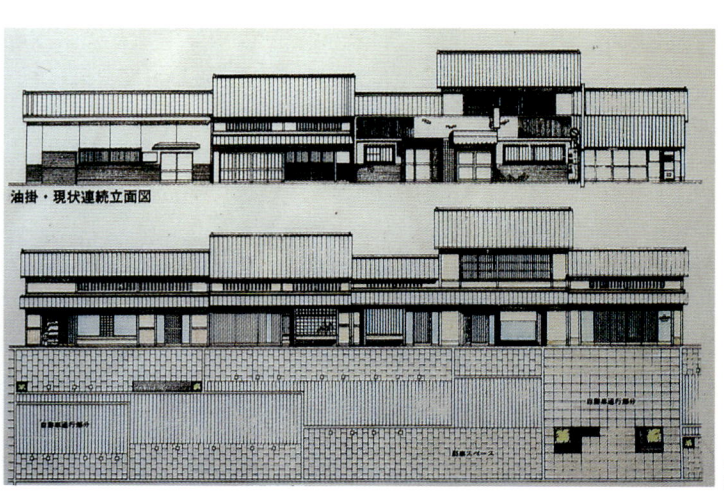

Aburakake Adjustments
油掛修景図

Fushimi 伏見

Gekkeikan Okura Memorial Museum　月桂冠大倉記念館

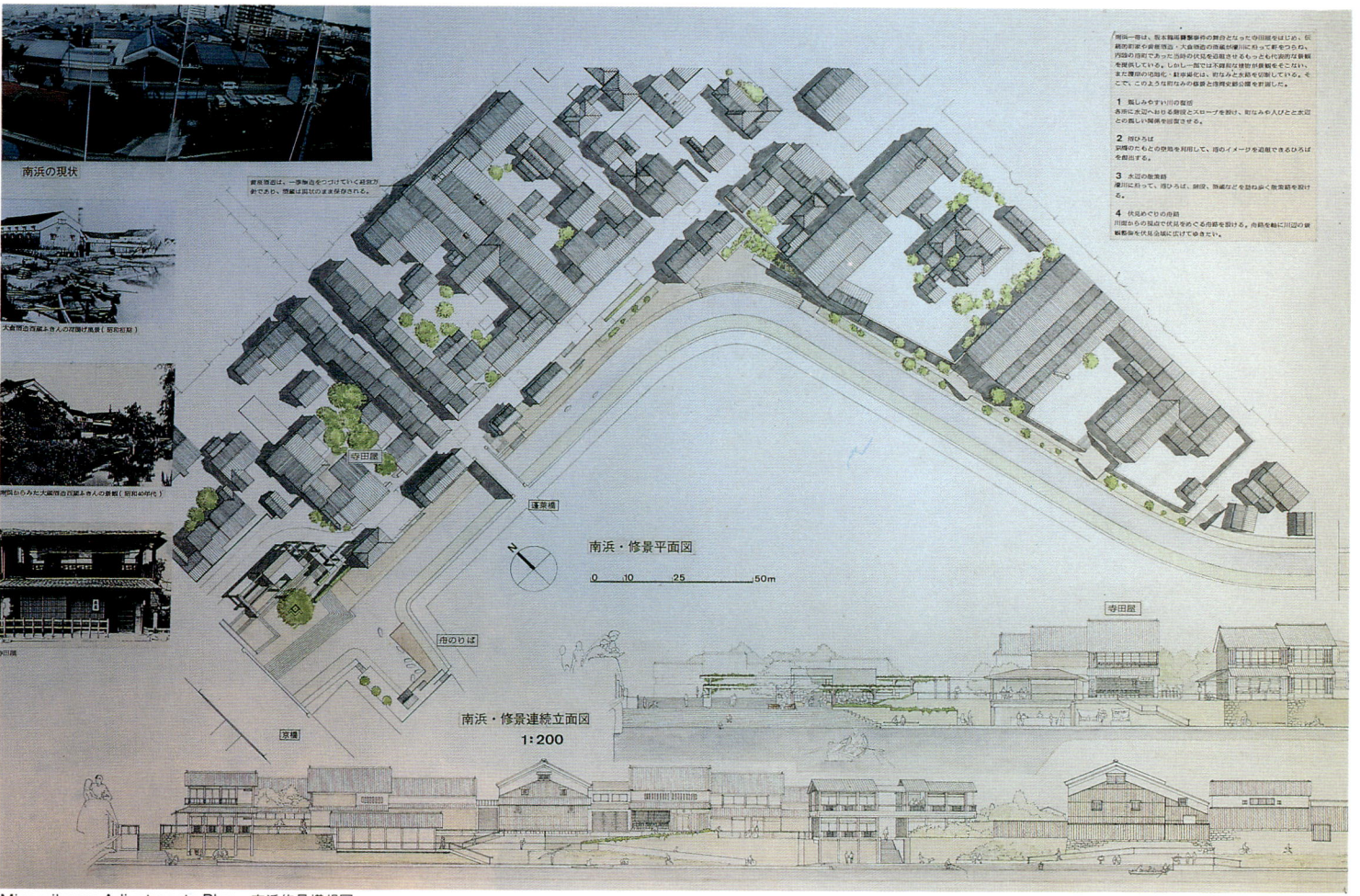

Minamihama Adjustments Plan　南浜修景構想図

Fushimi 伏見

In the vicinity of Minamihama　南浜付近

Saké' storehouse roofs　酒蔵の屋根

Machiya with an omoteya-zukuri layout　表屋造りの町家

Section　断面図

Moribashi-dori　毛利橋通

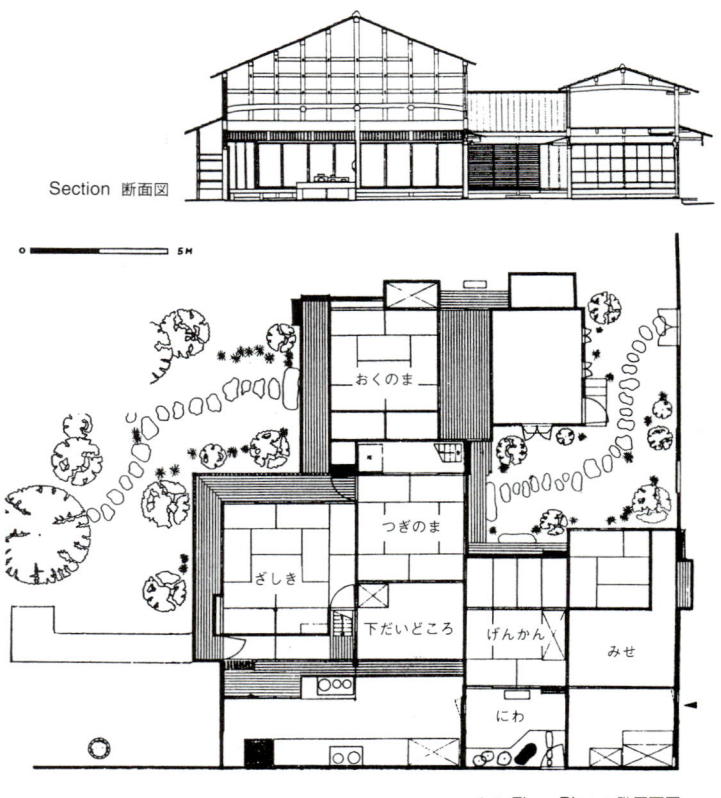

1st. Floor Plan　1階平面図

Machiya with an omoteya-zukuri layout　表屋造りの町家　古建築ゼミ作図

V
Rivers – Urban Design Features
河川の都市意匠

Kamo River

The valley basin on which Kyoto stands, slopes gently from northeast to southwest. The manner in which the Kamo River flows into the Takano river is quite peculiar and it is agreed that the course of the river was diverted in this way sometime during the construction of Kyoto in the Heian period. The waters of the Kamo River are considered to be pure, and ritual purification of the body in connection with eating to celebrate the ascendency of a new emperor and entrance into service at Ise shrine, are carried out there. The occurrence of incredible changes in river levels made it impassable and caused the people of Kyoto grave concern. The width of the river bed, much of which is dry for long periods, has created lots free space, which was utilized in the middle ages for the holding of events in connection with the arts among other things. In fact, a number of well know gardeners, followers of Ashikaga Yoshimasa, have emerged from among the people who lived in this area.

Early on in the seventeenth century, Izumo no Okuni, who started off kabuki dancing, danced on the dry area of the river at Gojo, with the result that within the space of a few years, many Kabuki and Noh performances were being held in small theaters in the area. This hive of activity was accurately depicted in the *Funaki Rakuchu Rakugai* Painting. Late in the seventeenth century, a new embankment was built and the small theaters were moved up on to the top of it. These theaters stretched from Shijobashi to Gion Shrine, and they were later made over to teahouses forming a continuous pleasure area. A theater called Minamiza, whose beginnings can be traced back to this time, is responsible for conveying some of the traditions associated with the Shijogawara of long ago, and the situation is very much to same today. During the festival, Gione, a portable shrine, mikoshi, is taken for temporary rest in Otabisho in Shijo-Teramachi from 7th to 17th June in the lunar calendar. People take particular enjoyment from the cool breeze off the river in summer and events and plays held along the dry area of the river serve to entertain the populous who gather on the temporary staging beside the river provided as places for eating and drinking. In 1690, Matsuo Basho visited this area, and wrote a poem extolling its virtues. This particular event continued on through until the area was renovated in the nineteen twenties. Those teahouses and eating establishments that could not find a place along the river, were given special permission to build staging across the river during the summer. This became known as Pontocho which still reflects the strong ties the inhabitants of this area have had with the Kamo River since the middle ages.

鴨川

京都盆地は北東から南西へかけて緩く傾斜している．鴨川が高野川に合流する流路は不自然で，平安京建設時に川筋を移動したというのが定説になっている．平安時代には，鴨川の水が神聖なものとされ，大嘗会の神斎や伊勢の斎宮の折，身を清める禊の行事が鴨川で行われた．無理な流路がたたってか，鴨川は度々氾濫して都人をなやませたが，その広い河原は自由な場所を提供し，中世には何時しか広場的な機能をもち，芸能を育む所ともなった．河原に住んで河原者と呼ばれた人々の中から，足利義政に重用された善阿弥など有能な作庭家も出ている．

17世紀に入る頃，歌舞伎踊りを始めた出雲の阿国は五条河原で舞っていたが，数年後には四条河原で歌舞伎や能が盛んに演じられるようになり，河原に芝居小屋が並んだ．その賑わいの様子は舟木家本洛中洛外図に描かれて生彩を放っている．寛文年間(1661—1672)に新堤が完成すると芝居小屋は岸上に移された．四条橋から祇園社の間に芝居小屋が建ち並び，やがて茶屋街と一体となって遊興の地が形成された．その中で今に続いている南座は，遠く中世以来の四条河原の芸能の伝統を伝えているわけである．一方，河原での楽しみ方も完全には消えなかった．祇園会の神輿が四条寺町の御旅所に移る旧暦6月7日から17日の間，「四条河原納涼」といって，河原で見せ物や芝居が催され，人々は川床に並べられた床几で酒と食事を楽しんだ．元禄三年(1690)には芭蕉も訪れて「川風や薄柿着たる夕涼み」の句を残している．この習わしは大正時代の河川改修まで続いた．河原での営業が出来なくなった茶店や料理店には，特別に夏の間だけ川の上に床を張り出し営業することが許された．先斗町の納涼の床である．これもまた，中世以来の京の人々と鴨川の親しい関係を今に伝えている．

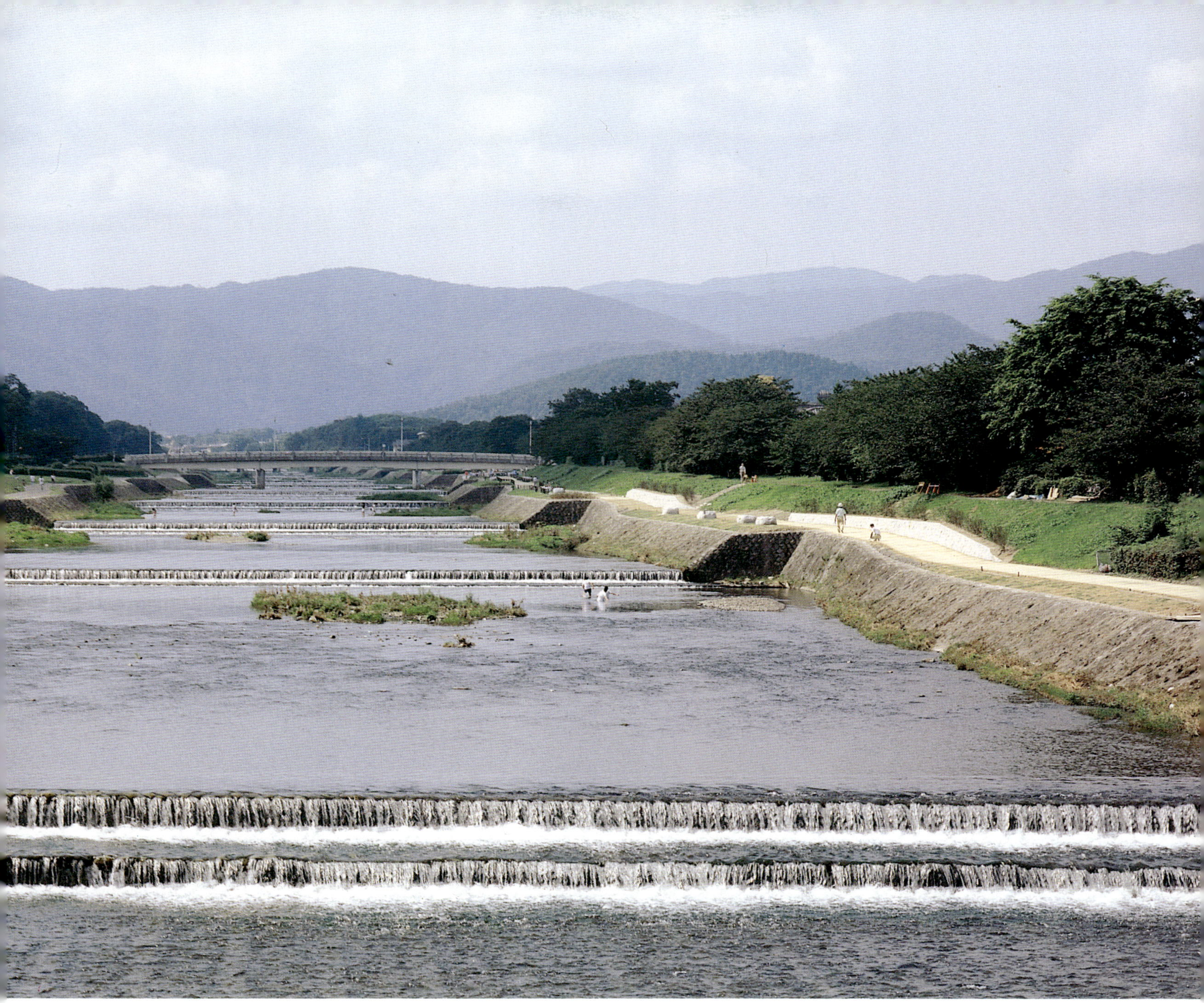

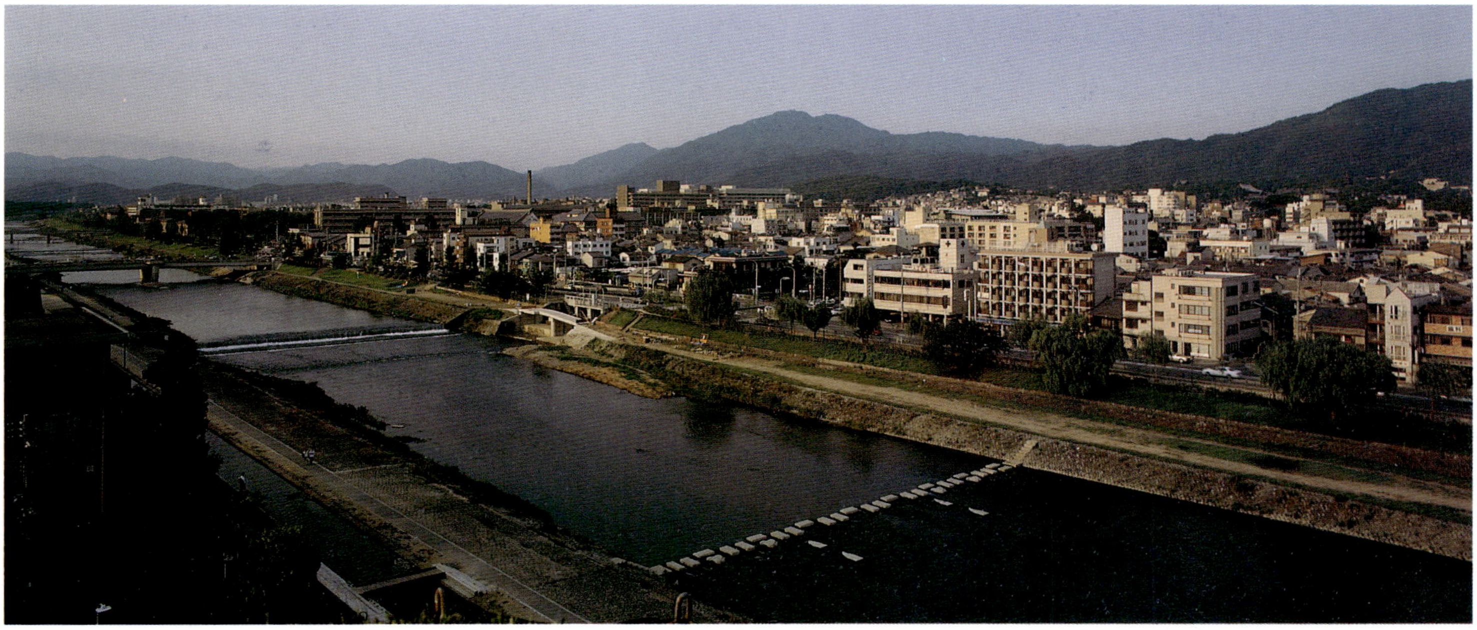

Kamo River　鴨川

Left-hand section of a 17th century screen painting of a summer's evening along the Kamo River.　賀茂川納涼図屏風左隻　17世紀　麻布美術工芸館寄託

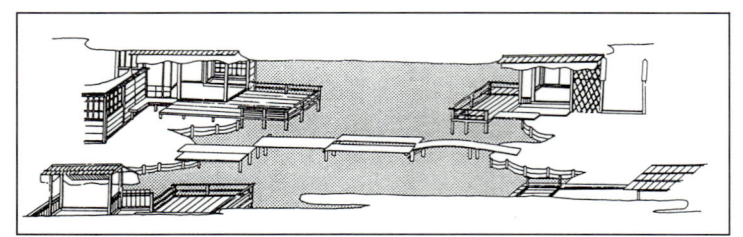

River-side buildings from the Shijokawara scroll
四条河原図巻中の川辺の建物（サントリー美術館蔵より作図）

Kamo River in the vicinity of Shijo during the Muromachi period; section of the Machida Rakuchu Rakugai-zu　室町時代の鴨川四条付近　町田家旧蔵本洛中洛外図部分　国立歴史民俗博物館所蔵

Kamo River　鴨川

Right-hand section of a 17th century screen painting of a summer's evening along the Kamo River.　賀茂川納涼図屏風右隻　同左

Kabuki at Shijokawara; section of the Funaki Rakuchu Rakugai-zu, early 17th century　四条河原の歌舞伎　17世紀初期　舟木家旧蔵本洛中洛外図部分　東京国立博物館所蔵

Kamo River 鴨川

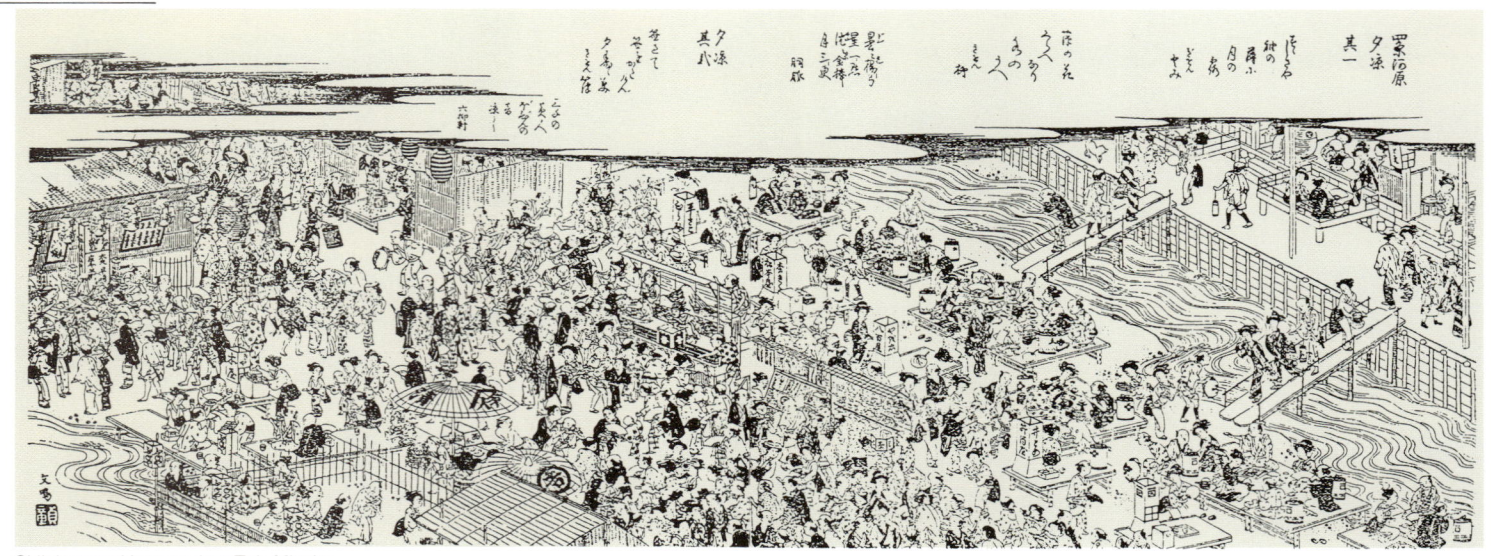

Shijokawara Yusuzumi no Tei; *Miyako Meisho Zue*, 1780
四条河原夕涼之体 『都名所図会』 安永九年刊

Shijokawara Yusuzumi by Ando Hiroshige, early 19th century
四条河原夕涼　安藤広重筆　19世紀前期

Shijokawara Yusuzumi no Zu by Gengendo Matsumoto Yasuoki, early 19th century
四条河原夕涼之図　初代玄々堂松本保居筆　19世紀前期　神戸市立南蛮美術館所蔵

Megane-e of Shijokawara Yusuzumi by Maruyama Okyo
眼鏡絵　四条河原夕涼　夜景　伝円山応挙筆

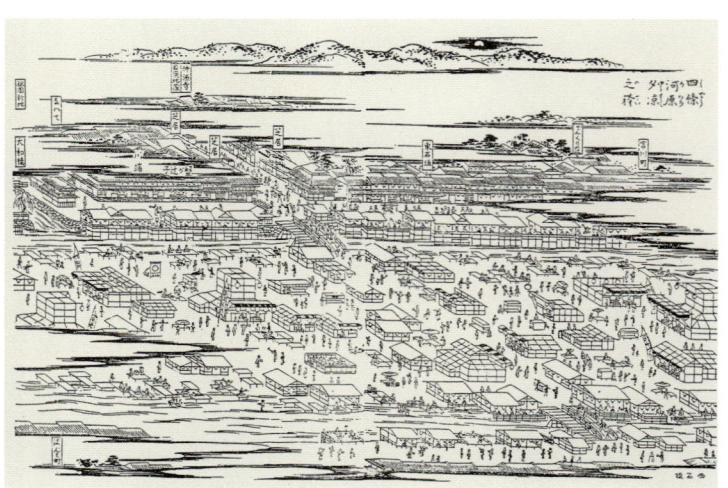

Shijokawara Yusuzumi; *Miyako Rinsen Meishou Zue*, 1799
四条河原夕涼　『都林泉名勝図会』　寛政十一年刊

Kamo River 鴨川

Heian Shokei Zu by Tomioka Tessai, 1917
平安勝景図　富岡鉄斎筆　1917年　清荒神清澄寺所蔵

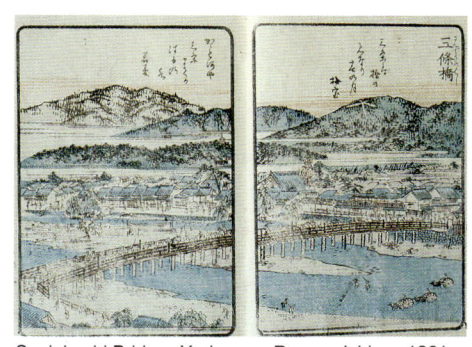

Sanjobashi Bridge; *Yodogawa Ryogan Ichiran*, 1861
三条橋　『淀川両岸一覧』　安政三年刊

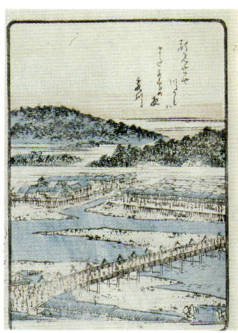

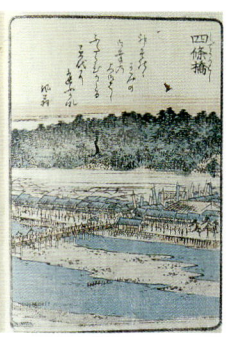

Shijobashi Bridge
四条橋　同左

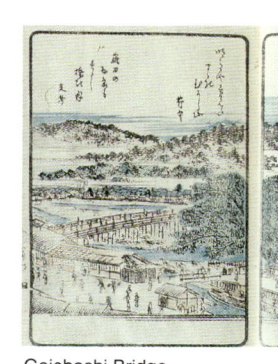

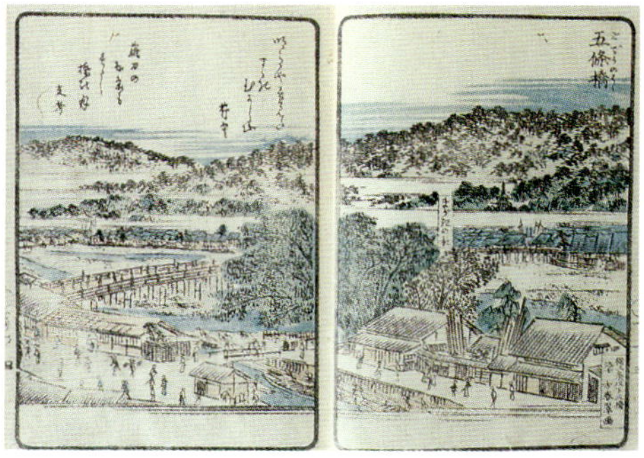

Gojobashi Bridge
五条橋　同左

Right - Machiya along the left bank of the Kamo River. A half of the building is standing on the original dry riverbed.
右／鴨川東岸の町家　建物の半分は元の河原の上に建っている。

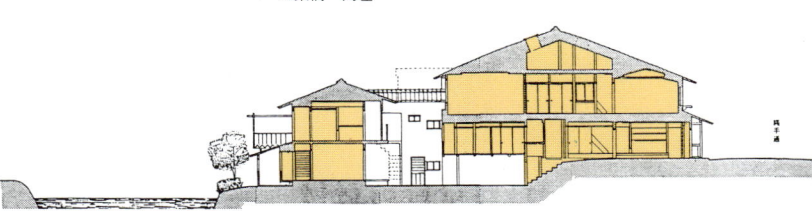

Shijokawara Yusuzumi no Yuka, 1882
四条河原夕涼みの床　明治15年頃　京を語る会提供

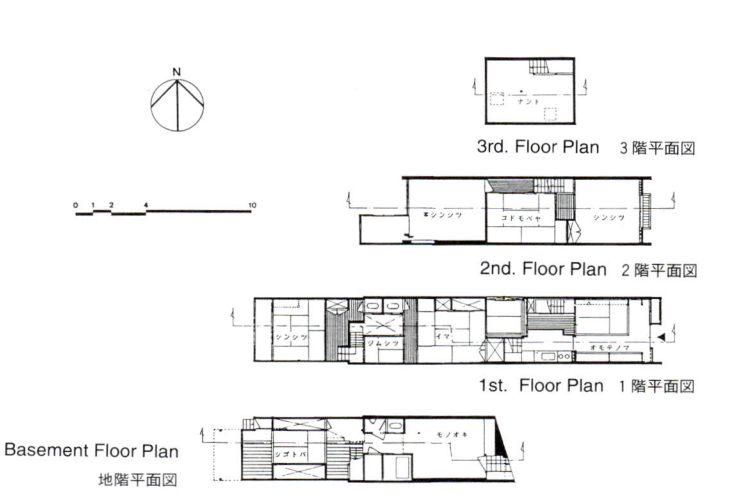

3rd. Floor Plan　3階平面図

2nd. Floor Plan　2階平面図

1st. Floor Plan　1階平面図

Basement Floor Plan
地階平面図

Kamo River　鴨川

The river and Pontocho in the morning. At the present time, the decking is put up by the restaurants here so that customers can enjoy the evening breezes after the heat of the day in the summer months of July and August.　鴨川と先斗町の朝風景．納涼の床は現在は7,8月に設けられる．

Kamogawa no Yudachi by Uda Tekison　鴨川の夕立　宇田荻邨筆　1954年　京都府蔵 (京都文化博物館管理)

Kamo River 鴨川

Pontocho at Dawn by Fujimoto Shizuhiro, 1986　先斗町蒼刻　藤本静宏筆　1986年

Saisoki in a winter veil　雪の西石垣

Kamo River and houses of Saisoki　鴨川と西石垣の町並み

Kamo River 鴨川

Kamo River, in the vicinity of the Botanical Gardens　賀茂川　植物園付近

A watery playground　鴨川で遊ぶ子供たち

An avenue of cherries with the Daimonji in the mountains behind.
大文字を背景に桜並木がつづく．

Pontocho and the river after a fall of snow　雪景色の先斗町と鴨川

Takase River

At the time of the building of Daibutsuden to the foot of Mount Higashiyama, the Kamo River was cleared and dredged to accommodate river craft to haul wood for the construction. In order to provide a safe canal to the river, Suminokura Ryoi and his son Yoichi, applied for permission to the government led forces in 1611. The Takase River canal thereafter took three years to completion. Near Nijo, a shallow canal whose waters stem from the Kamo River, led down in a straight southerly direction, crossed over the winding Kamo River, passed along the western side of Fushimi to join the Yodo river. This made transportation between Osaka and Kyoto extremely easy. The names of the traders and porterers who plied their wares up and down the river live on in the names of the villages that sprung one after the other along the river. The length of the river was known as Kiyamachi (lit: timber marchant village) as it dealt primarily in wood and charcoal. On the western side of the river stood houses belonging to warlords, with boat landings nearby. But, today, only Ichino-funairi, on the upper reaches of the river remains to remind us of this.

If we look at the *Miyako Meisho Zue*, the middle of the Edo period, then the area between the Kamo River and Takase River around Sanjo was crammed with houses, but around Gojo Bridge, the rivers flanced a single row of houses lined either side of the river. However, above the bridge itself there were houses but below it there was only the embankment. Up river, bargees can be seen pulling their vessels up stream. In the same book, a famous eating house called Ikesu can be seen on the west bank of the river. On the first and second stories, the guests can be seen indulging themselves in the rooms that face on to the river, taking in the pleasures to be derived from a direct view of the river. At present, the hostelries to found along the Takase River no longer face on to it, which is both a shame and rather strange in light of his historical value. One building however, Times Building, designed by Tadao Ando, like the old Ikesu, positively makes use of the river aspect and establishes an interesting relationship with it.

In the vicinity of Sanjo Agaru　高瀬川　三条上ル付近

高瀬川

東山麓の大仏殿建設の時，鴨川を整備して船を通し，資材が運搬された．これを安定した運河にしようと，慶長十六年(1611)角倉了意，与一親子は幕府に申請し，およそ3年をかけて高瀬川運河を開設した．二条付近で鴨川から取水した浅い運河はおよそ一直線に南下し，屈曲してくる鴨川を越え，伏見の町の西を通って淀川に結ぶ．大阪方面と京の間の運送が一挙に便利になった．川筋には物資を扱う商人の同業者町が順次形成され町名に残っているが，川筋一帯を木屋町というのは材木，薪炭が主な物資であったことを物語っている．川の西側には藩邸が並ぶようになり，各々に「船入り」を設けた．今では最上流の「一之船入り」だけが残っている．

江戸時代中頃の「都名所図会」を見ると，三条あたりでは鴨川との間に人家も多いが，五条橋付近になると両河川の間に一列の家並があるのみで，それも橋の上流で途切れ下流では堤防があるばかりになっている．その堤防を上流へと人夫が高瀬船を引いている．同じ書に高瀬川西岸の「生洲(イケス)」という料理屋の図があり，川に向けて1・2階の座敷を開いて客をもてなし，運河沿いの立地を生かし楽しんでいる．現在では高瀬川沿いの飲食店が川に対して益々背を向けるようになり，歴史の川の風情を楽しまないのは惜しくもあり不思議でもある．ひとり安藤忠雄設計のタイムズ・ビルが「生洲」に似て川との関係を積極的に取り入れている．ただ，石垣を取り除いたのは惜しまれる．このあたりは川床の石畳が美しい．

Ikesu, in the Sanjo Kita area of the river; *Miyako Meisho Zue*, 1780
生洲　高瀬川三条北に在った．『都名所図会』安政九年刊

Boats on the Takase river in 1895　高瀬川の舟運　明治28年　『京都府史』

In the vicinity of Ichi no Funairi, Literally meaning the "first boat docking place". 一之舟入付近

Looking toward Ichi no Funairi from the river 高瀬川から一之舟入を見る

An intake at Kamogawa Nijo 鴨川二条の取水口

Time's, designed by Tadao Ando. タイムズ 安藤忠雄設計

Cherries along the river 高瀬川の桜

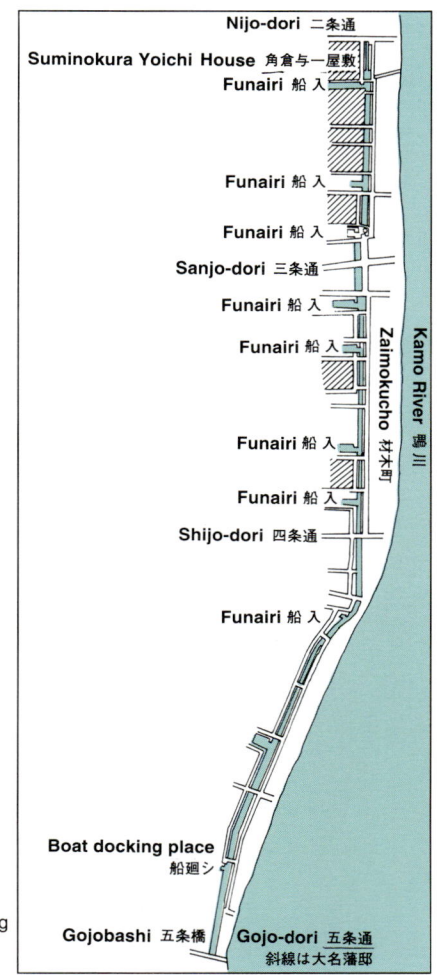

The river and its banks during its busiest period.
舟運盛期の高瀬川とその沿岸

Takase River 高瀬川

Nijo-dori	二条通
Suminokura Yoichi House	角倉与一屋敷
Funairi	船入
Funairi	船入
Funairi	船入
Sanjo-dori	三条通
Funairi	船入
Funairi	船入
Funairi	船入
Funairi	船入
Shijo-dori	四条通
Funairi	船入
Boat docking place	船廻シ
Gojobashi	五条橋
Gojo-dori	五条通

Zaimokucho 材木町
Kamo River 鴨川
斜線は大名藩邸

131

Shirakawa River 白川

Shirakawa River

As it flows down from Higashiyama, the Shirakawa river follows the line of the streets of Yamanakagoe. It gets its name from the fact that it brings sand down from the granite rocks upstream to form a white riverbed. In the Heian period, the area around Okazaki was called Shirakawa and such was the beauty of this "white river" flowing amid the greenery that it soon found favor as a resort for the weekend homes of the aristocracy. Toward the end of the eleventh century, the retired emperor set up the administrative apparatus necessary for continuing his rule in his retirement and in doing so, ensured that it became the center of activity. Beginning with Hoshoji Temple with its nine storried octagonal pagoda (a site now occupied by Okazaki Zoo), six further temple were built in turn. The site of this was used at the turn of the century for exhibitions and to commemorate the city's 1,100 years since its foundation and for the building of Heian Jingu shrine. Later this was followed by a prefectural library, a municipal museum and other cultural facilities. To the north of the Sanjo-dori, the gardens of Heian Jingu, among others, were designed and planted by Ogawa Jihei whose former home also faces the river. The garden of the house next door is also the work of this landscape gardener, who was one of the most accomplished of modern times. An inscribed stone at the approach to the bridge over the river, tells us that if we go down along the river we will arrive at Chionin Temple. Along the length of this route, a shallow stream of water flows along the center of the road, with houses standing in a line on either side. However, since the days of the Heian period, a lake dug for the garden of a palatial residences has been used as a source of water in this district, supplying the more important areas. From an old painting of this district we can see that a shallow river flows down the middle of such famous streets as Nishinotoin-dori and Muromachi-dori. Now lines of trees stand beside the river which is a little wider than before. The area near Shirakawa River conveys an impression of an area that was exceptional in its beauty as a place to live. From here the river passes on through Gion and into the Kamo River.

In the vicinity of Shirakawa Sanjo 白川三条付近

A house along the river 白川畔の家

白　川
ヤマナカゴエ
山中越えの街道と並んで東山から下ってくる白川は，花崗岩の砂を流して河床が白いことからこの名称がある．平安時代には今の岡崎付近が白河と呼ばれ，樹間に白川の流れる美しい地に，貴族の別荘が営まれるようになった．11世紀末には白河上皇が院庁をここに置いて院政政治の中心になり，また八角九重塔のあった法勝寺（現在の岡崎動物園付近）をはじめ六勝寺が建立された．その跡地一帯は明治時代に博覧会場として利用され，建都1100年を記念して平安神宮が造営され，その後府立図書館，市立美術館などの文化地区となっている．三条通りの北には平安神宮神苑などを作庭した近代を代表する庭師小川治平の旧宅が川に面している．その隣の並河家の庭も小川治平の作である．旧東海道三条通に架かる白川橋畔に残る石標が，白川沿いに下れば知恩院に至ると案内している．この間は浅い流れが道の中央を流れ，両側に町家が並ぶ．ところで平安時代以来，寝殿造りの苑池に水を供給することもあって町中の各所に川が流れていた．洛中洛外図にも西洞院通，室町通など，浅い川が通りの中央を流れる様子が描写されている．並木があり川幅も少し広い点が異なるが，白川のこの付近は意外な所で往時の洛中の川のある景観構成を伝えているともいえる．ここから白川は祇園を通り抜けて鴨川に合流する．

Shirakawa River 白川

Here the river flows at the back of Shinmonmae-dori. 新門前通の裏を流れる白川

Shirakawa Sanjo - the river here flows past Ogawa Jihei's former home. 白川三条　小川治平旧宅の横を流れる白川

Kitano no ura no Ume by Irie Hako, 1911
北野の裏の梅　入江波光筆　1911年　京都市立芸術大学所蔵

Horikawa River and Kamiyakawa River

Two canals, the East Horikawa river canal and the West Horikawa river canal, were constructed straddling Suzakuoji in a symmetrical fashion in the Heian period. Later, the eastern canal simply became called the Horikawa River, and was still in the existence up untill 20 years ago. The West Horikawa river is today called the Kamiyakawa river, but its origins are all but forgotten.

It is said that prior to the construction of the Horikawa river canal, the Kamo River followed the same course. In the Heian period, fairly pure waters flowed and the river banks became an assembly point for luxurious villas of the aristocracy. To the south of the Imperial Palace, part of the immense Shinsenen gardens remain in what is now Horikawa-Nijo. The area along the river is rich in riverbed water and this feeds a number of extremely good wells and the premises of tea ceremony schools nearby.

The Horikawa river with its riverbed paved with stone flags flows between lines of willow trees, and remained undisturbed for years, until 1975, when half of it was built over for the purposes of a road widening scheme, thus creating and underground canal. Activities mainly led by people wanting to preserve cultural aspects of the city have led to part of the river being retained to the north of the street now known as Oike-dori.

The West Horikawa river is called the Kamiyagawa River because of the existence of an official paper mill run by the Heian court. Around the time of its construction in the Heian period, the emperor Kanmu moved four deities from Yamato some distance to the south, to a site near the river where he built the Hirano Jinja, a shrine at which to pray for the prosperity of the new city. On the opposite side to this shrine stands another, Kitano Tenmangu. Both of the approaches to these shrines are swathed in heavy greenery, creating an extremely beautiful route that crosses the Kamiyagawa River. In the Edo period, this was in fact a very famous and popular sight-seeing route. Heian Kyoto tends to sweep off to the left, so that the Kamiyagawa River veers of to the west. Hideyoshi used this river as an external moat and built the Odoi, a defensive barrier, and the site still exists on the upper reaches of the Kamiyagawa River.

堀川と紙屋川

平安京には朱雀大路を挟んで対称的な位置に東堀川と西堀川の2筋の運河が建設された．東堀川はその後「堀川」と呼ばれて，わずか20年程前まで同じ位置で存続していた．西堀川の方は今では「紙屋川」と呼ばれ，その由来は忘れられようとしている．

堀川はおよそ平安京建設以前の鴨川の位置にあたるといわれ，平安時代には清流が流れ，川沿いには貴族の邸宅が集まっていた．大内裏の南に存在した広大な神泉苑は，その一部が堀川二条に今も残っている．川沿いの地域は伏流水も豊かでよい井戸水を提供し，茶の湯の千家も堀川の近くに居を構えている．柳並木に挟まれて石畳の川床が一直線に続いていた堀川も昭和50年代に惜しくも自動車道拡幅のために大半が暗渠化されたが，文化人を中心とする運動で御池通以北が残った．

西堀川は，平安朝の官営製紙工場である紙屋院があったことから何時しか紙屋川と呼ばれるようになった．平安京建設の頃，桓武天皇は大和から四神をこの川のそばに移して平野神社を創り，新都の繁栄を祈願した．平野神社の対岸には北野天満宮があり，両社を結ぶ参道が深い緑に包まれた紙屋川を渡る美しい配置構成があり，江戸時代は観光ルートであった．平安京は左京に偏ったため，紙屋川は町の西はずれになり，秀吉はこの川を外堀にして内側に御土居を建設した．紙屋川上流にはその御土居が現存している．

Horikawa River 堀川　1974年

Kamiyagawa River 紙屋川

VI
Views – City and Environs
京の眺望景観

A view of the city from Daimonji. 大文字より市中を望む.

Cityscape Design and Features

A overall bird's eye view of Kyoto gives the scene a particular significance. In the past, most of the world's cities were depicted in this way from some high vantage point, which not only provides a clear overall impression but this way of viewing a city is also perhaps the best way of understanding the general framework of almost any area, planned or natural.

From the tops of Higashiyama, Kitayama and Nishiyama, three peaks among the surrounding mountains that enclose Kyoto, it is possible to look down over the city and enjoy for ourselves the view that is spread out below. At the time of the building of the Heian capital, it seems that the position of Suzakuoji - *oji* meaning wide street - was decided by looking directly southwards from the top of Mt. Funaoka. At that time, the dignified and orderly nature of the grid of city streets must have been clearly visible.

When the two- and three-storey buildings of the Zen temples were first introduced into Japan and took up their positions as elements of the land- and cityscape, people no doubt gained great pleasure from the scene, such as could have been seen from the pagoda-like tower on Mt. Kameyama called *Kichoto*, one of the *jikkyo* or "meaningful landmarks" associated with Tenryuji temple. Seen from here, the streets of Kyoto would have stretched into the distance. The Rakuchu Rakugai depictions of the city and its environs that appeared towards the end of the middle ages, show the city as viewed from some high vantage point, and would no doubt have been admired by the people of the city as such. In these renderings, which also show in fine detail activities along the streets and at street corners, the artists have evolved a way of reconstructing the scenes they observed in well know quarters of the city, combined with the actual views they would have observed from mountain tops and towers or other vantage points above the city. These depictions combining the visual experiences of both street scenes with scenic bird's eye views, give a hint as to the form of the present city.

It is well known that even now the view from the precincts of Kiyomizudera temple on Mt. Higashiyama is quite outstanding. Of a series of drawings showing famous places in Kyoto in the Edo period published in the *Kyohabatae* in 1685, there are ten views of Kiyomizudera temple. Of these, six are views looking down from the temple itself: *Rakuyobanko* is a beautiful rendering of the buildings densely lining the streets; *Kamogawaittai* shows the area to the east of the Kamo River; *Tokoinu* is also a fine depiction of the scene to the east through rain and smoke; *Seimonchobo* is the view from the west gate of the temple; *Ganryoseisetsu* is a snow scene of Mt. Atago; and *Kitakuboai* shows the area of Arashiyama and Mt. Kameyama in evening light. The last two works are distant snow scenes of mountains in the west, both of which are well in excess of 10 kilometers from Kiyomizudera. Another series of views, the *Miyako Rinsen Meishou Zue* done in about 1799, introduces eight views of Ryuanji temple which also make use of distant scenes. They depict respectively, the temples on Mt. Higashiyama, the shrine Iwashimizu Hachimangu, castle remains in Fushimi, the length of the Yodo River, the pagoda of Toji temple, a evening scene at Myoshinji temple, a scene of twisted pines and cloud covered mountains, and finally the autumn colors of temples nearby. All of these scenes are views taken from a room in the temple, which means that they have most probably been viewed from across the stone garden there. However, the eight scenes differ somewhat from the previous ten scenes in that they depict features of the scene from the temple in specific seasonal conditions, so that they suggest the time of year that it is best to view these scenes.

It seems that in the Edo period, Kyoto's town folk ventured up Higashiyama to look down on

Kenninji Temple and the center of the city　建仁寺と京都都心部

眺望の名所とその意匠

町の全体を俯瞰する眺望景観は特別な意味を持っている．古来，世界の多くの都市は高所から俯瞰した都市図をつくってきたし，都市の全体像を示すにも理解するにも最も適した視点であろう．

東山，北山，西山の三山に囲まれた京都は都市の全体像を実際に俯瞰することができたし，その眺望景観を楽しんできた都市である．そもそも平安京建設にあたっては，船岡山から真南を見すかして朱雀大路の位置を決めたとされる．整然とした碁盤状都市の威容が眺められたことであろう．禅宗寺院が二階建てあるいは三階建ての楼閣建築を日本に初めて招来したことは，人々に眺望景観の楽しみを教えたものと想像される．天竜寺の十境のひとつ亀頂塔の上からは京の町が遠望された．中世末に現われた洛中洛外図は京の全体像を俯瞰景で表現し，見る人を楽しませた．街角の細部まで描く洛中洛外図は，画家が町の各所で観察した風景を再構成する方法と，山上や塔の上などから実際に見た眺望景観の描写とを複合して制作したものであろう．街角の景観と眺望景観の二つの視覚経験が複合して都市の全体像がイメージされた事実は，現代の都市景観形成にも示唆を与えている．

東山の清水寺は今でも境内からの眺めがよいことで知られるが，江戸時代の京名所案内記のひとつ『京羽二重』(貞享二年(1685)刊)が紹介する「清水十景」は，そのうち6景は清水寺境内からの眺望景観であって「洛陽萬戸，鴨川一帯，東郊烟雨，西門眺望，宕嶺晴雪，亀阜暮靄」を挙げている．最後の二つ，西山の愛宕山の雪と，嵯峨の亀山は清水寺から10キロメートル以上離れた景観を遠望している．京の町の幾萬かの家並も，鴨川の東に広がる郊外が雨に煙るのも，八景に挙げるに足る美しい景観であった．『都林泉名勝図会』(寛政十一年(1799)刊)が紹介する竜安寺の八景も遠景を多く取り入れている．「東山の仏閣，八幡の源廟，伏見の城跡，淀川長流，東寺の宝塔，花園の暮鐘，雲山虹松，隣院の紅葉」を挙げ，「これみな方丈よりの遠景をもって風色となす」とあるから，石庭の向こうに遠景が望まれたのであろう．ところで八景は十境とちがって特定の季節天候の中で見た風景を取り上げる所に特徴があり，風景の見方を教えるものでもあった．

江戸時代，京の人々は東山から町を見おろしながら宴席を楽しむことができた．東山には寺院が並んでいたが，各寺院は山腹に幾つもの坊舎を従え，これらの坊舎は見晴らしのよい座敷を宴席に提供していた．『都林泉名勝図会』はこれらを絵入りで詳しく紹介している．これを見ると，円山安養寺の端之寮は山の斜面に張り付いた3階建ての建物であったし，多福菴也阿弥には町の眺望を借景にした庭園があり，正法寺の珠阿弥では舞台造りの座敷で家族づれが眺めを楽しんでいる．図(140頁左下)の座敷の向こうに広がる町を見れば，山下には八坂ノ塔と方広寺大仏殿の大きな屋根があり，京の町の甍の波の向こう南方には東西本願寺，東寺五重塔，北方にはいまや天守閣のない二条城が見えている．また月光の下で町の夜景を楽しむ名所もあった．清水円養院は雪月名所と記し，図(同頁中段右)には庭の床几で宴を開く人があり，その向こうに京の町の夜景がある．

ちょうどその頃の京の町の眺望をかなり写実的に描いた彩色画として，19世紀初めの黄華山筆「洛中洛外一望図」(II. 43頁に掲出)が伝えられている．低い町並みの中に突出して目立つものといえば内裏付近の邸宅群と社寺の屋根である．王朝と宗教の都市としての印象が京の眺望景観にはあったし，この特徴は永く20世紀中頃まで続いた．さて，中でも方広寺大仏殿は巨大さが目立っていた．二条城天守閣は寛延三年(1750)に，大仏殿は寛政十年(1798)に，両者とも落雷で焼失していたが，「洛中洛外一望図」も『都林泉名勝図会』も，焼失後間もな

137

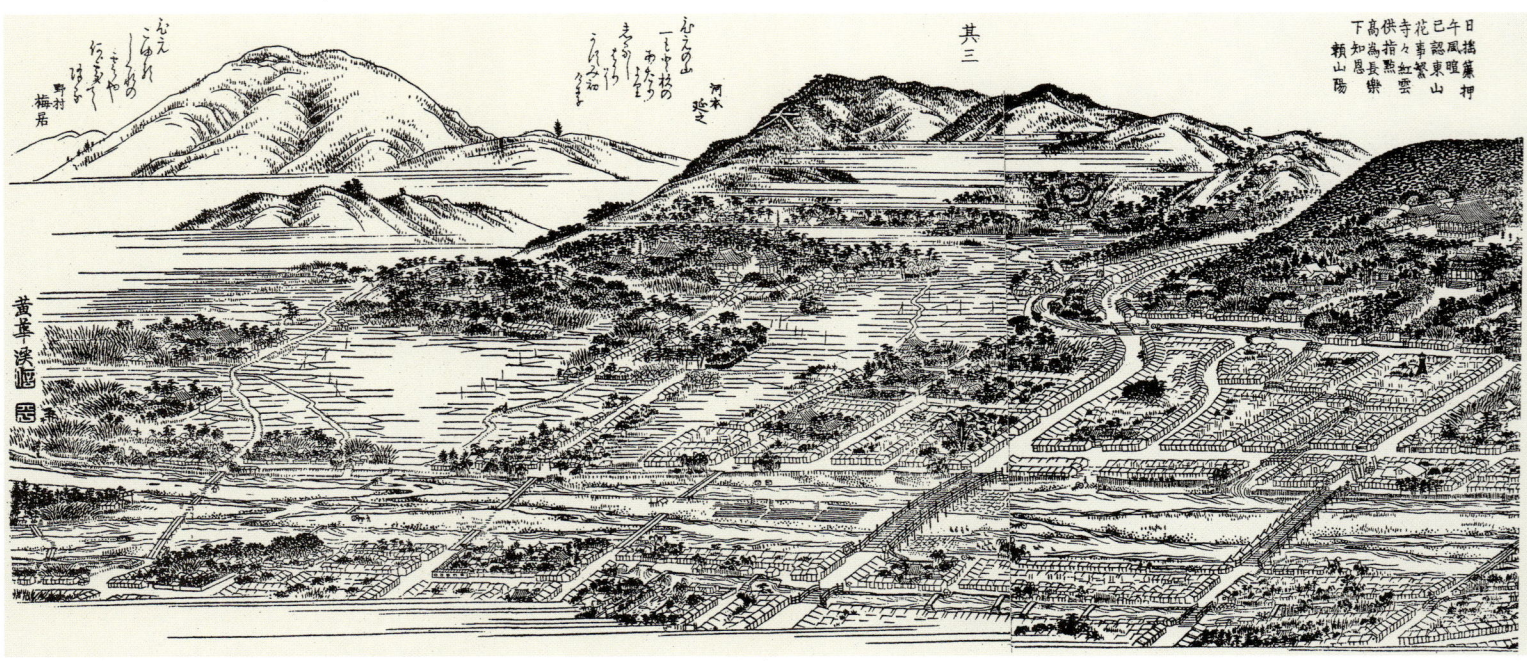

An over view of Higashiyama; *Karaku Meishou Zue*,1864 東山全図 『花洛名勝図会』 元治元年刊

The western outskirts of the city are visible beyond the main build-up area. 京都市街の向こうに洛西を望む

to the city while enjoying a meal. A number of temples stood on the mountain and each one had a number of residences for the priests set back into the mountain. Because they commanded a good view of the city, these residences were often lent out for banqueting purposes. The *Miyako Rinsen Meishou Zue* shows this quite clearly in loving detail. A closer look shows the Hashinoryo, a building belonging to Maruyama Anyoji temple as a three-storey building built into the sloping face of the mountain. It also shows the gardens of Tafukuan Ya'ami with the city as a piece of 'borrowed landscape'; and at Shohoji temple's Shuami, families are shown looking down from the vantage point offered by the stage-like structure. The town can be seen spreading out beyond where the people are seated and at the foot of the mountain, there is the huge roof of the Daibutsuden at Hokoji temple and the Yasaka pagoda. Beyond the wave-like roofs of the city, the buildings of Higashi and Nishi Honganji temples and the five storey pagoda of Toji temple can be seen, while to the north stands Nijo Castle with its now non-existent tower. Recorded as places well known for their snow scenes and moonlight scenery, people are shown enjoying a meal seated on benches in the garden of Enyoin, a sub-temple of Kiyomizudera, with a nightscape of the city beyond.

The *Rakuchu Rakugai Ichibozu* painted at the beginning of the 19th century by O Kazan, is a fairly realistic colored rendering showing most of the city at that time. Thrusting out from amid the low houses, the buildings of the aristocracy around the Emperor's residence stand out along with the roofs of the temples and shrines. Such views of Kyoto convey a definite impression of it as a city of imperial and religious leanings, a feature which continued at least until the middle of the 20th century. Other outstanding features include the gigantic form of the Daibutsuden at Hokoji temple. The tower of Nijo Castle was completed in 1750 and the Daibutsuden in 1798. Both were subsequently destroyed by lightening however, although the Daibutsuden is clearly shown in both the *Miyako Rinsen Meishou Zue* and the *Rakuchu Rakugai Ichibozu* renderings. It must have been a great loss therefore when it was lost to the flames.

There was also an amusement area which brought pleasure to all who viewed it shown in these scenes of Kyoto. In the same *Miyako Rinsen Meishou Zue* there is a picture entitled *Yoshidayama*, which from atop a hill decked in autumn foliage looks down on the teahouses among the pine trees further down the hill and shows in life-like fashion, here and there, people passing a pleasant time on straw mats that have been spread out for the occasion. In addition, from the depictions in the *Karaku Meishou Zue* done in the nineteenth century, we can see that the view of the area known as Keage on Mt. Higashi Iwakurayama must have been particularly good as it has been mentioned in writings and it seems that Toyotomi Hideyoshi built a tower for the purposes of taking advantage of the view here, too. There just happened to be an excellent level area from which to view the city and in autumn it was the scene of feasting held prior to the gathering of the matsutake mushroom, while in spring it was renowned for its azaleas.

It is also difficult to forget the views offered by looking from the city up at the surrounding mountains. The sight of snow laying on Higashiyama and Kyoto made a deep impression on the artist Yosa Buson and one of his better known works, *Yashoku Rodaizu* sprang from this. This is not representational art but a scene that has passed through the fertile imagination of the artist, and shows rows of houses leading up a gentle slope from Gojozaka to Kiyomizudera, in a style that is instantly reminiscent of the real thing. The holding of Urabone in summer, when fires are lit in the shape of characters to light the way of the spirits back to their resting place, confirms the close ties the city has with the mountains in the outskirts. In an excellently situated spot on Higashiyama that stretches a finger out into the city, fires are lit to form the characters for "big", or *dai*. This "Daimonji" can be seen from almost

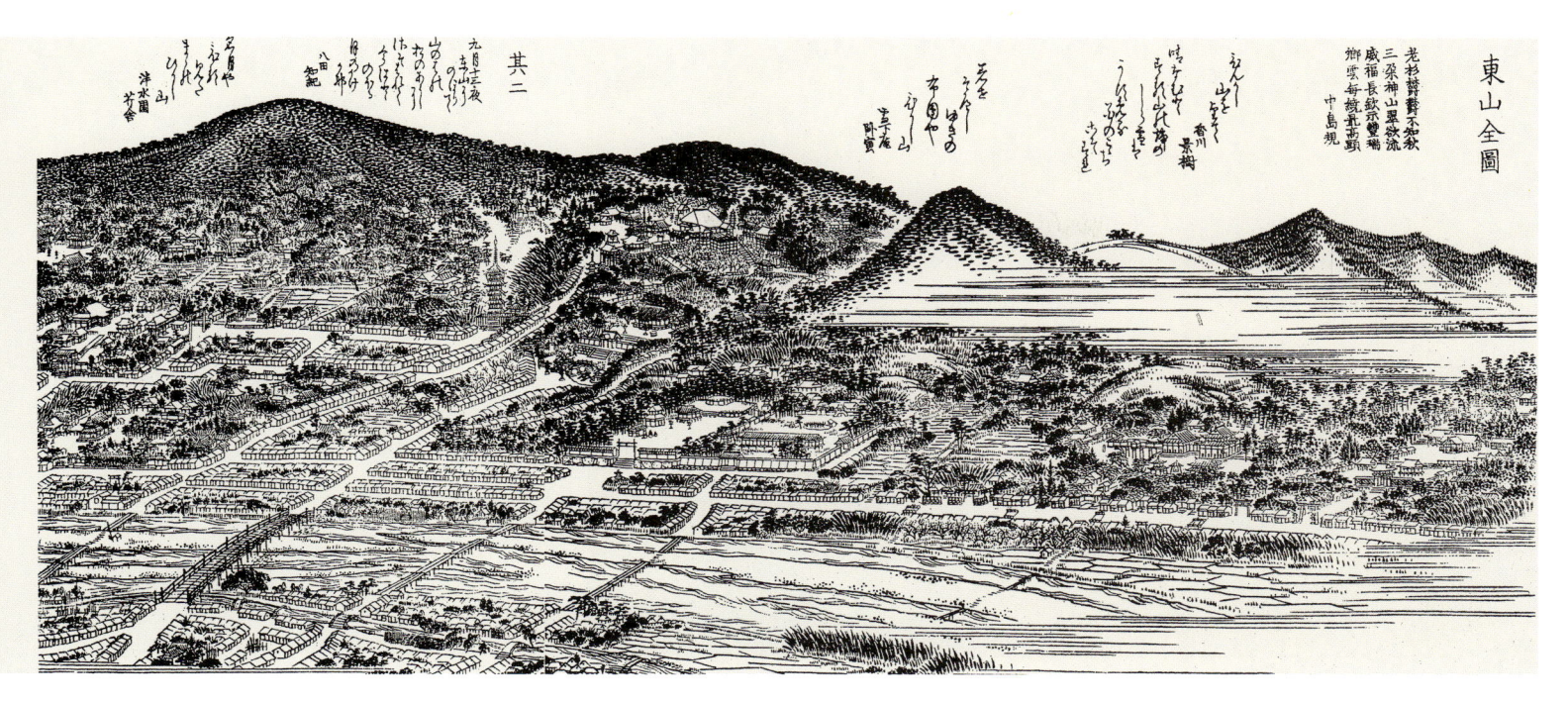

Higashiyama from the Yasaka Pagoda　八坂ノ塔から望む東山

Looking toward the center of the city from the Yasaka Pagoda　八坂ノ塔から望む市中

い大仏殿だけはまだ存在した時の景観を描いている．大仏殿焼失は残念な出来事にちがいない．

京の町の眺望を誰もが楽しめる見晴らしのよい行楽地もあった．前述の『都林泉名勝図会』に「吉田山遊宴」の図があり，紅葉の季節に眺めのよい岡の上で，低い松林の間に茶店もあれば，そこかしこに筵(ムシロ)を敷いて宴を開く人々を活写している．また，幕末の『花洛名勝図会』によれば，蹴上の東岩倉山(ケアゲ ヒガシイワクラヤマ)は「洛中唯一望にありて絶景の勝地なり」とあり，豊臣秀吉がここに楼閣を建て京を眺望したと伝えているから余程眺めがよかったのだろう．ちょうど京の町をよく眺望できる位置に平坦な所があって，秋には松茸狩りの宴を開き，春は躑躅(ツツジ)の名所であった．

いっぽう，町から三山を眺める仰望景観も忘れることはできない．東山と京の町に雪の積もる夜景は与謝蕪村に深い感銘を与え，その代表作と評価される『夜色楼台図』が生まれた．この図は写実ではなく，現実を元に画家の想像した風景を描いたものと言われるが，緩い斜面を登る家並みの様子は五条坂から清水に至るあたりをいかにも思わせる．夏の盂蘭盆会の送り火の行事も，三山と京の町が眺望景観で結ばれていることを再確認させる．東山の中でも高く京の町の方へ張り出した形のよい場所に「大文字」を火で書く．それは京の町

の殆ど全ての町から見ることができたし，逆に大の字の中央に登れば京の町が一望できる．大文字は鴨川から仰ぎ見るとちょうどよい仰角位置にあり，鴨川の河原か橋上から見たものである．『花洛名勝図会』冒頭の「東山全図」は東山と鴨川の間に広がる幕末期の鴨東の家並を描ききっている．山川の自然と一面の家並みの眺望景観，その中に目を引く高い建物といえば，権力の象徴でも経済の象徴でもなく，宗教施設であった．それもまた京の都の景観が，人の心に安らぎを与え，多くの人を惹きつけてきた魅力の一つだったであろう．

残念なことに，近代に入ってからはこれら京の町の眺望の名所を私たちは失ってきた．東山山腹の寺院群は明治時代に衰え境内を随分縮小し，数軒の料亭がかつての坊舎の位置にその伝統をひいて営業してはいるが，坊舎は殆どなくなってしまった．正法寺だけは境内へ登れば今も町が一望できる．東岩倉山の眺望のよかった台地は明治時代に墓地になって行楽地ではなくなり，吉田山は最近の十数年の間に松林から鬱蒼とした照葉樹林に変わり眺望もできなくなった．鴨東地域の建物が高くなるにつれ，現行の美観地区指定による高さ規制ではやがて東山山麓の寺院の屋根も隠れ，八坂ノ塔さえ最上部一層しか見えなくなるだろう．鴨川の橋上からの大文字送り火の鑑賞も，加茂大

橋からの視線はかろうじて守られるが，三条大橋や四条大橋などこれより川下の橋から大文字を眺める視線を遮る高さのビル建設が許容されている．眺望の勝地を失うのと同時に昨今は屋根景観が乱れ，鑑賞すべき景観の方も失いつつあり残念な事態を生じている．それでも三山に囲まれた京都は各所に意外な所に町を眺望する地点があり，また近年はビルの上から町や東山などを眺望する機会が増えている．眺望景観の美しい都であった伝統を想起し，その継承への努力が始められるべきではないだろうか．

Yaami Hotel, Maruyama, Photographed at the turn of the century
円山　也阿弥ホテル　明治時代　石田 明撮影　大日本スクリーン提供

Yoshidayama Yuen　吉田山遊宴

Illustrations from; *Miyako Rinsen Meishou Zue*, 1799
京を眺望する東山中腹の寺坊　都林泉名勝図会　寛政十一年刊

Maruyama Anyoji Hashinoryo　円山安養寺　端之寮

Maruyama Anyoji Tahukuan Yaami　円山安養寺　多福菴也阿弥

Kiyomizudera Enyoin　清水寺　円養院　雪月名所

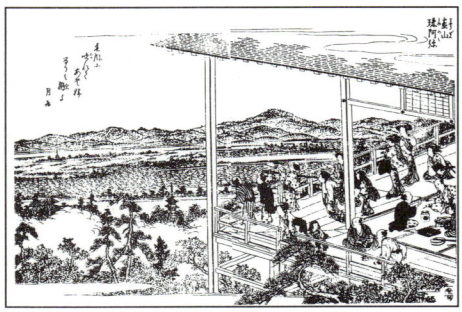

Ryozen Shohoji Shuami　霊山正法寺　珠阿弥

Maruyama Anyoji Chojuin　円山安養寺　長寿院

Maruyama Anyoji Tahukuan Yaami
円山安養寺　多福菴也阿弥の座敷

all districts of Kyoto, and conversely, if we climb up to where this character is, then the whole of Kyoto can seen at a glance. When seen from the Kamo River, the angle is such that a particularly good view is given. On the first page of the collection of *Karaku Meishou Zue* pictures, the drawing of Higashiyama depicts the houses to the east of the Kamo River during the nineteenth century as they spread out from between Higashiyama and the Kamo River. One tall building in the scene that demands the eye's attention is not some symbol of power or wealth, but one of religious teaching. It is part of the scenery of Kyoto, and calms the human soul, and is one of the many things in Kyoto that tend to attract people to the city even today.

Unfortunately, in these modern times these places from which Kyoto was viewed have been lost to us. The temples that once lined the slopes of Higashiyama fell into obscurity from the turn of the century, and the sites were drastically reduced in size. Several restaurants now carry on the tradition to some extent on the site of the former priests quarters, but of the residences all but a few have vanished. Only from Shohoji temple can a good view of the city be enjoyed, after having made the arduous climb to this spot. The excellent observation point offered by Mt. Higashi Iwakurayama became a burial place in the Meiji period and yet another pleasure spot was lost. The dense pine forests on Mt. Yoshidayama have given way to glossy-leafed trees over the last few decades, meaning that the views of old are gone. East of the Kamo River, the buildings have grow in height and owing to the present regulations that designate the area as a special scenic amenity, the height regulations are such that the roofs of the temples at the foot of Higashiyama are cast into shadow. Most likely it is impossible to even to see the pagoda of Yasaka temple except for part of the top half. The prospects of seeing the Daimonji lit in flame from the bridges over the Kamo River and Kamo Ohashi Bridge have barely been retained. Certainly the view from Sanjo Bridge and Shijo Bridge and all those bridges further down river has been cut off following the approval of high-rise building. With the loss of the old viewing places and the present destruction of the building skyline, we are very sadly in danger of losing what should be a magnificent sight. Even so, there are still some places from the surrounding mountains which continue to offer a view of the city below, and we can console ourselves to some extent as the opportunity to view the city and Higashiyama from the tops of some of the higher buildings has increased. Kyoto is certainly a beautiful city that still manages to provide us with some magnificent sights to remind us of its traditions, and surely we should be endeavoring to see that this will be retained for future generations to enjoy, too.

Above - Kyo no Shunsho by Ikeda Yoson, 1929. From the vicinity of Shinkyogoku on a spring evening, there is a view taking in the Kamo River, Gion and Maruyama, too. The roof of the temple, Chionin is also visible.

上／京の春宵　池田遥邨筆　1929年　耕三寺博物館所蔵．新京極辺りより春宵の鴨川、祇園、円山を俯瞰する．知恩院の屋根も見える．

Minamiza Theater all lit up　南座夜景

Yashoku Rodai Zu, by Yosa Buson, 18th century
This is how Buson pictured the elegant lines of Higashiyama on a winter's day. It is possible that the people of Kyoto also saw it in the same way.

夜色楼台図　与謝蕪村筆　18世紀　個人蔵
蕪村の目に映った高雅な東山の雪景色。都人もこのような雪の東山を仰ぎ見たのであろう。

Kiyomizu Shindo shrouded in snow　雪の清水新道

View from Kiyomizudera Okunoin　清水寺奥の院より望む

Higashiyama draped in snow　東山雪景色

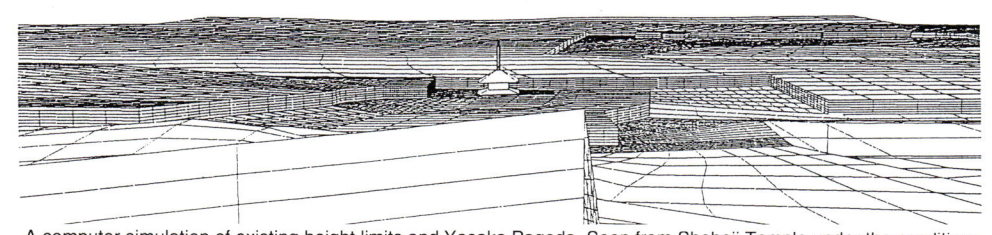

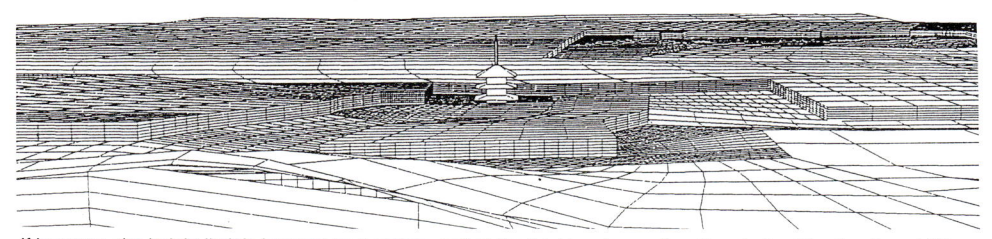

A computer simulation of existing height limits and Yasaka Pagoda. Seen from Shohoji Temple under the conditions of the present height limits, it is only possible to see the top levels of the Yasaka Pagoda when it is surrounded by an area with a 20 meter hight restriction, and thus the sense of it being a multi-leveled structure is completely lost.
八坂ノ塔と現行高さ規制のコンピュータ・シミュレーション　正法寺より望む. 現行の高さ規制では、八坂の塔が20mの高さ規制地区に囲まれて最上層しか見えず、多層塔の雰囲気が損なわれている.

If however, the height limit is lowered by 5 meters, half of the third level as well as the whole of the fourth and fifth levels come into view, and thus it can be ascertained that the Yasaka Pagoda is indeed a multi\leveled structure.
高さ規制を一律5m低くすると、八坂の塔の第3層の半分と第4層、第5層が見え、多層塔であることが認識できる.

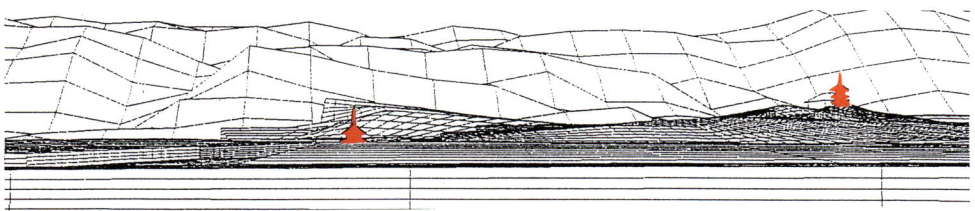

A computer simulation of existing height limits in relation to the Yasaka and Kiyomizudera. The view from the west bank of Kamogawa River. Under the height limit which is in force at the present time, only the very top level of the pagoda is visible. Kiyomizudera stands on the site high up in the right background.
八坂ノ塔, 清水寺と現行高さ規制のコンピュータ・シミュレーション　鴨川西岸のビルから望む. 現行の高さ規制では、八坂ノ塔の最上層のみが見える. 右手後方は、高い敷地に建つ清水寺.

Yasaka Pagoda seen from Shohoji Temple
正法寺から見た八坂ノ塔

View of the Yasaka Pagoda and the area around it from the west bank of the Kamo River.
鴨川西岸のビルから望む八坂ノ塔付近

143

As part of the Obon festival, fires are lit in the shape of a character meaning "big" as a way of sending the souls of the dead back to heaven. Nowadays, this takes place on 16th August. Daimonji Okuribi; *Miyako Rinsen Meishou Zue*, 1799,
大文字送り火『都林泉名勝図会』寛政十一年刊 現在は8月16日盂蘭盆会の夜にともる.

View of the Daimonji from the north side of Kamo Ohashi Bridge
加茂大橋中央北側から大文字を望む

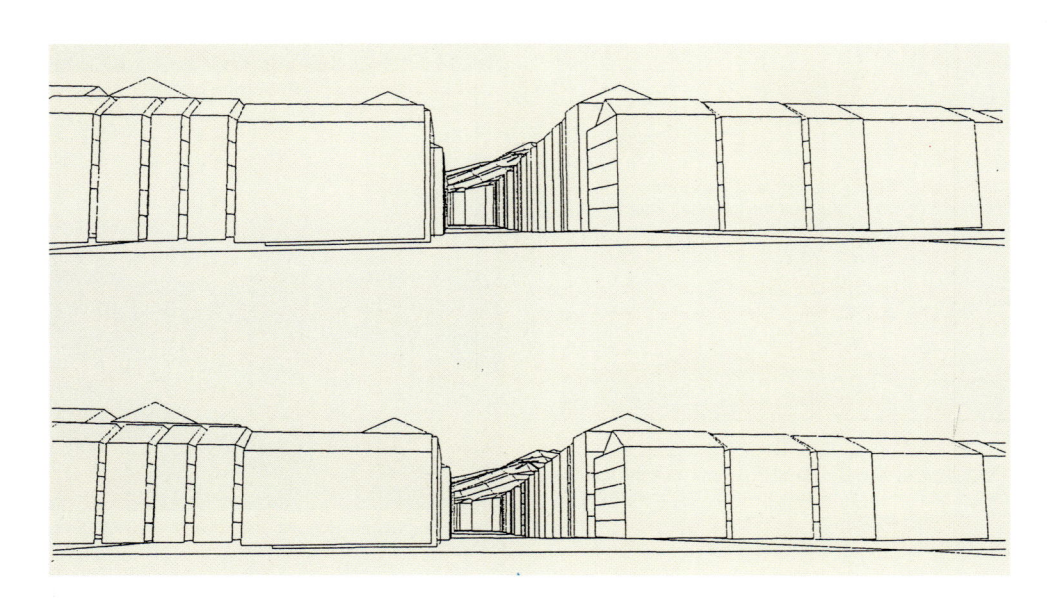

Computer simulation showing the Daimonji and the height limit.
Viewpoint: From the middle of Kamo Ohashi Bridge, looking north
The top simulation shows the situation when a 3 meter slopping roof-line bonus is allowed on buildings which fall within the existing height limit. Under the existing height limit, the Daimonji is completely invisible from bridges further down stream. However, the lower simulation shows the situation when the slopping roof-line bonus is no used on buildings which fall within the existing height limit. The eave line is therefore lower and the whole of Daimonji then becomes visible.

大文字と高さ規制のコンピュータ・シミュレーション
視点場：加茂大橋中央北側
上図は現行高さ規制枠のビルに高さ3mの傾斜屋根を載せた場合．現行高さ規制はこれより下流の橋からは大文字が全く見えなくなる．下図は現行高さ規制枠のビルの肩を削る形で傾斜屋根とした場合．軒高が下がり大文字の文字全体が見える．

VII
Tasks – Present and Future
現代の課題

Toward a Modern Japanese Style City

Over the last few years, the visual amenity of Kyoto's traditional cityscape has been vanishing at a rapid rate. Since the end of the era of the "bubble economy", the amount of building work being carried out has dropped noticeably. Things are a little more rational than there were, but the organization and system which has been responsible for the destruction of the traditionally appointed areas of the city has not been reformed in the slightest.

During the halcyon days of the economic bubble, space within the city confines was no more than a pawn in an economic game. Provided that vacant land remained vacant, the negative effect on the appearance of the city was fairly marginal. However, these areas too fell prey to the financial intrigues of mammon. Speculation promoted the construction of high-rise apartment blocks with the very scenic land they had been built on giving them extra prestige. This was particularly so with regard to sites in close proximity to an environment of some historic value such as that where there are shrines or temples. Investment flowed on down from Tokyo to Kyoto, creating a terrific surge in land prices. And, for those owning land in the more traditional areas of the city, this sudden rise in the value of land meant that their heirs faced the prospect of having to pay hundreds of millions of yen in inheritance tax. In order to cover the ensuing loans, therefore, a splendid city was spoiled as land was made over to developers and speculators. For the most part, the building work was carried out in the name of providing badly needed accommodation. As a result, 15% of Kyoto's residential accommodation is presently unoccupied. Empty office accommodation too stands out like a sore thumb. Even so, building work continued for a short while. But this problem, of course, is the result of the financial system and the way the taxation system is organized.

There is also another major problem, and that is to do with the regulations pertaining to building and planning. For the majority of Japanese people, including the residents of Kyoto, the historic scenery of Kyoto with its densely treed mountain surrounds, has, thanks to the severe conservation system - Ancient City Preservation Act - been preserved for prosperity, but only at the price of making life difficult for residents, requiring them to be more patient and long suffering than usual. The truth of this is clearly reflected by events. The articles of the Ancient City Preservation Act, cover the areas around the old sector of the city and the green hilly areas that are deemed areas of historic and natural beauty. However, what it fails to do is to similarly cover those parts of Kyoto that correspond to the original Heian capital or the inner city areas that date back to the Edo period.

The exceptional scenic areas in the surrounding mountains have been designated as a conservation area, but this is not to regulate development per se, but to attach conditions to the way in which developments are carried out. Conversely, if we look at the town houses in the traditional city center, then it is fair to say that it is basically impossible for one of these town houses to be handed down to the next generation. Areas of particular historical value which developed during the three-hundred year period up to the beginning of this century, have been designated as semi-fire free zones. When rebuilding and imple-

Toward a Modern Japanese Style City
近代都市の日本的様式へ向けて

制度としての京都の景観問題

京都の伝統的な都市景観はこの数年急速に失われている。バブル経済の破綻とともに今はビル建設が減少し、落ち着きを少しは取り戻したかに見えるが、伝統的景観を惜しげもなく破壊する制度と構造が改まったわけではない。

バブル経済の時期には、京都の都市空間が経済活動の道具となった。土地だけならまだ景観への影響は少なかったかもしれないが、その上の空間までが資産運用のための道具となった。投機のため高層マンションが建てられ、その床が買われた。景観の良さがその付加価値となり、とりわけ景観の良い社寺などの歴史的環境の近くに建設が進んだ。東京から資金が京都へ流れ込み、地価高騰が生じたといわれる。都心の地価高騰は町家の住人にしばしば億単位の相続税を課す状況を生み、それを借金で相殺するために立派な町家を壊し、ビルへの建て替えが行われた。いずれの場合も、住居が必要だからという本来の理由で建設されたのではない。その結果、京都では空き家が15％を越える状況になっている。オフィス・ビルも空室が目立っている。一時はそれでもビル建設が進んだ。これは経済構造と税制度の問題である。

もう一つの大きな問題として、建築と都市計画に関する法制度の問題がある。京都の市民を含めて日本人の多くが、緑の山に囲まれた京都の歴史的な景観は、「古都保存法」という厳しい保存制度によって、京都人の不便を忍ぶ我慢の上に保存がはかられている、と信じてきたのではなかっただろうか。事実はそれに反している。古都保存法による保存指定区域は古都周辺の歴史的風土としての山林部であって、元の平安京の範囲も、江戸時代の洛中の範囲も、どちらにも触れもしていない。周囲の三山は風致地区に指定されているが、これも開発そのものを規制できるものでなく、開発の仕方に条件を付けるのが役割である。いっぽう都心の町家について言えば、町家の継承は基本的に禁止されているといってよい。江戸時代から明治時代にかけての歴史的市街地は現在その全てが準防火地域に指定されており、建て替え、大規模な改造、建物用途の変更などに際しては、格子戸や千本格子、板壁など木造の意匠が禁止されている。木の意匠にこだわってきた京都の町並みの歴史の否定である。軒裏までモルタルで塗込め、アルミサッシにしなくてはならない。これを免れるの

menting large-scale changes of building use, lattice-work doors and grills in wood and wooden walls as well as other such wooden design features are strictly forbidden. This is inhibiting the historical face of Kyoto that shows an obsession with wooden features. It is now compulsory to plaster under the eaves and install aluminium window sashes. The only place where it is possible to escape this is in the areas that have been designated as of particular architectural merit or as a cultural treasure. Slatted screens have been forbidden even on the commercial teahouses in Hokomachi and Gion. In truth, this ruling only applies to those parts of the buildings which are "susceptible to the spread of fire". The area affected by this ruling is that which lies three meters away from the center of any bounding road, for the first storey, and five meters with respect to the second storey. However, the exterior of nearly every building falls within the scope of this ruling. It also applies to the Buddhist temples, so that even their looks are no longer sacrosanct. Also, with respect to Buddhist temples, the main sanctuary is usually a wooden structure more than 15 meters in height. Unfortunately the building laws concerning wooden structures limit the height in general to 13 meters so that anything above this is forbidden. In order to circumvent this restriction, special permission must be obtained from the Minister for Construction. For this reason, reinforced concrete and steel framed structures are becoming more common when rebuilding and building anew. Local skills with regard to wooden structures are slowly disappearing. Existing town houses with their lattice-work doors as well as temple architecture, are doomed, without a doubt, to be reduced to mere parodies of their former selves with these inappropriate architectural innovations. The city should of course be protected from the dangers of fire, and to this end there are already any number of woods that would be suitable after fireproofing treatment. Moreover, sprinkler systems to safeguard the walls of buildings are something that has not been developed to the full as yet. Using this as the means for a new method of fireproofing to safeguard the cultural heritage that is the wooden city of Kyoto the time has surely come to revise the existing regulations.

There are also problems with the city planning laws. In historical shopping areas, it is necessary, owing to the city planning laws in operation, to define the business area when we classify the kind of businesses present, and the majority of businesses, even in places where two-storey buildings have been the historic norm, are eligible for high-rise construction because of the high floor area to site area ratios currently in operation. Generally, these land usages and limits for floor area to site coverage are implemented, which is giving rise to a dichotomy in Japan's historical towns. These and rulings associated with the setting up of semifire free zones are national rulings that do not allow the municipal government of Kyoto any latitude. However, the extent of the limits and definition of the areas is a matter for the planning authorities in Kyoto to decide. If we consider the city planning map designating approval for expansion corresponding to the assigning of high floor area to site area ratios into areas beyond the confines of Kyoto proper, it is easy to imagine how the city could quite easily develop into a kind of future city more reminiscent of

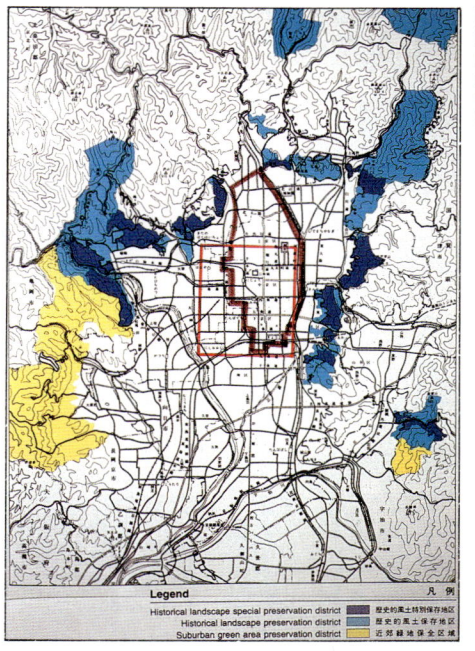

Relationship between areas of historic importance and conservation areas maintained under Kyoto Conservation Laws
古都保存法による保存区域と歴史的街区の関係図

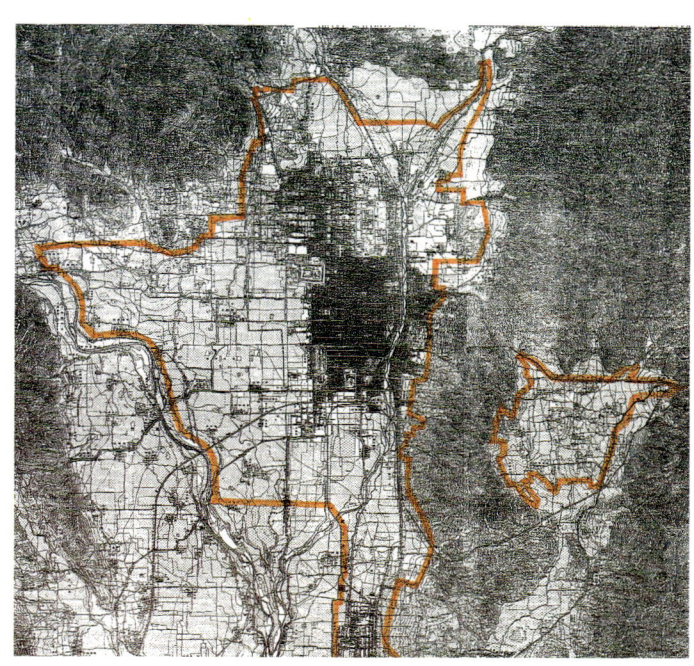

Quasi-fire zones (enclosed by orange line) and historic areas
準防火地域（枠線内）と歴史的街区
ベースマップは明治20年測図仮製地形図

は指定文化財と伝統的建造物群保存地区だけで、鉾町も祇園のお茶屋も格子は禁止である．正確に言えば建物のうち「延焼の恐れのある部分」（敷地境界および道路中心からの距離が1階で3m，2階では5m以内の範囲）についての制度であるが，町家は外観のほぼ全てがそれに該当する．これは寺院の塔頭や子院にも適用され，寺院の景観にも影響を与えている．寺院について言えば，日本の寺院の本堂は木造で高さ15mを越えるものが多いが，建築基準法では一般に高さ13m以上の木造建築の建設を禁止しており，この規模を越える場合は建設大臣の特別な許可を必要とする．このため寺院の建て替えや新築は鉄筋コンクリート造か鉄骨造で行われ，地方の木造技術はいよいよ消えようとしている．現存する格子戸の町家も寺院建築も「既存不適格建築」として朽ちるまでの存続が許されているに過ぎない．都市の防災は進めるべきだが，木材の不燃化処理技術は既にあり，建物外壁用のスプリンクラーの開発も困難ではないだろう．新しい防災技術のもとで，木造の都市文化そのものを抹消しようとしている現行制度を改正すべき時期ではないだろうか．

都市計画制度にも問題はある．歴史的な町の商店街で，既存の職種を認めようとすると大抵の場合は都市計画法による商業地域指定が必要であり，これに指定すれば2階建ての歴史的町並みであっても高層ビルが建てられるような高容積率指定が連動している．一般に，土地用途の指定と建物の容積制限とが連動しており，日本の歴史都市の状況とそれが矛盾している．これと準防火地域の規制は国の制度であり，京都市の行政では自由にならない．しかし，どの範囲をどのような地区指定にするかは京都市の政策である．歴史的市街地に高容積を割当て，洛外を広く市街化区域に指定した都市計画地図を見れば，ビル化した市街地と郊外に広がる住宅地というアメリカ的な未来都市像が浮かび上がる．

新・洛中洛外都市構想
京都の未来都市像をどのようなものに描くべきだろうか．京都独自の未来像を設定し，その実現へ向けて諸制度を整備してゆく必要があるだろう．でなければ歴史的環境を殆ど持たない日本の他の大都市と同じ方向に向かってしまう．基本的な態度として，京都は歴史的環境を否定する革命的未

American suburbia than historic Kyoto, with city streets lined with buildings spreading into peripheral areas of housing.

New Kyoto and Environs City Concept

What kind of future should we expect for Kyoto? In order to decide on an independent future image for Kyoto, it is necessary to rethink various regulations if we want to realize anything worthwhile. Unless this is done, Kyoto will finally look like Japan's other cities which now have very little left of any historical importance and interest. As a basic approach to this problem, Kyoto should not let its historical heritage be lost to an uncertain fate, but it should take the bull by the horns and ensure that its heritage is properly developed for prosperity.

From the numerous Rakuchu Rakugai depictions of the city and its environs, it is quite evident that the city of Kyoto as such is the product of both the streets within the city proper and the outlaying areas of natural landscape, which often has the appearance of parkland. Just as a house has a garden, Kyoto was built with a 'garden' on an urban scale. Despite being a large-scale city, it is in a style that is completely in keeping with its natural surrounds. Taking this form as a working model, I propose that it be taken and used for creating a new *rakuchu rakugai*, or "city center and environs" city concept.

The city center must provide residential as well as business and office facilities, which is already a task of major proportions. In order to this, a safe pleasant environment in which to live has to be provided within the city, not only for single men, but for children and old people as well. We also have to change the fact that cars can pass through all the city streets, as and when they please. A number of streets should be made safe for children to play in, for old people to walk along and for housewives to do their shopping in: completely car-free pedestrian precincts should, in other words, be provided. The bleakness of the present city center reflects well the sagacity of the decision of the inhabitants to move to the suburbs for the sake of their families. In the center of the city, almost every one of the rectangular sites has a plot reduced to open space. In order to ensure some open space and greenery for the streets some way of linking these together should be devised. Most of the traditional housing is destined for rebuilding and, as stated before, it is necessary to guarantee some freedom with regard to rebuilding this cultural inheritance of wooden architecture. To some extent, some of the present traditional housing stock can be expected to last for a number of years yet. Accordingly, buildings built nearby should at least harmonize with the existing houses and cause as little trouble as possible with regard to the scale and form of the existing housing style. This is a stance that has to be acknowledged, because if it is not, then I do not think that it will be possible to create the beauty that is Kyoto. Even though medium-rise buildings are built fronting onto the main thoroughfares, the height of houses beyond this should be no more than three to four storeys high. Any existing four-storey buildings scheduled for reconstruction should only have one extra floor. According to a building survey we carried out in the heart of the city, for instance, covering the street Shijo-dori, Kawaramachi, Gojo-dori and the streets adjoining Karasuma, two-storey buildings (with a floor area to site area ratio of be-

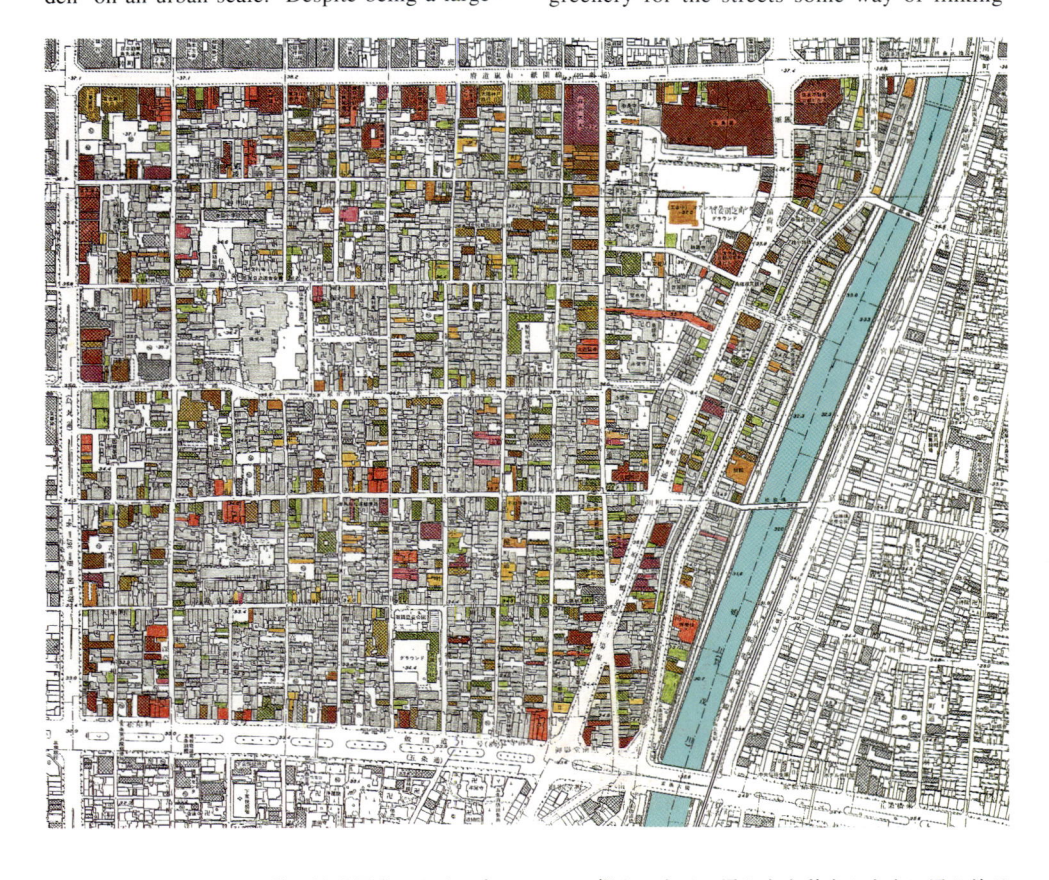

Number of floors of buildings within the city center
都心部街区　建物階数図

- Empty lot　空地
- 2 storied Building　2階
- 3 storied Building　3階
- 4 storied Building　4階
- 5 storied Building　5階
- 6 storied Building　6階
- More than 6　7階以上

来像を描くべきでなく，継承的発展をはかるべきであろう．

洛中洛外図屏風では，洛中という市街地部と，洛外という公園的な自然景観地域の両者から京という都市が成り立っていることが表明された．家が庭を持つように，都市が都市的スケールの庭を作っていたのである．大規模な都市でありながら自然と共存するスタイルがそこにはある．この形を基本とする新・洛中洛外都市構想とでも呼ぶべき未来像を私は提言したい．

洛中，言い替えれば都心市街地に商業・業務機能とともに「住む」という機能を明確に割り当てる．これは実は大変な課題である．そのためには壮年男性だけでなく，子供や老人もいる家庭が安全快適に住める環境を都心部に確保しなくてはならない．都心の全ての通りを自動車が自由に通り抜けできる現状を変え，幾本かの通りは子供や老人が安全に歩け，遊べ，主婦が買物に行けるような歩行者専用道を確保する必要がある．今の状況では，都心の空洞化は家族のために郊外に住むというむしろ市民の賢明な判断を反映している．短冊状の街区の中央部に各戸がいくらかの空地を提供して，緑道と若干の空地を確保し，それを各街区結んで行く方法も考えられる．伝統的町家は大半が建て替えられてゆくだろうが，前述のように木造文化を継承する建て替えの自由が保証される必要がある．いっぽうで何割かの伝統的町家は少なくとも今後数十年存続するはずであり，それらの近隣に建つ建物は既存町家と少なくとも調和し，既存町家の住人に出来る限り迷惑をおよぼさない規模と形であるべきであろう．これは基本的に求められる態度で，これが拒否されるなら，美しい京都の景観創造はありえないと私には思われる．都心の大通りに面した部分では中層ビルを建てるとしても，大通りより内側の街区では町家の建て替えは3〜4階程度とすべきであろう．一定程度4階建てに建て替わった段階で5階建てとすべきであろう．我々が都心部で行った建物階数調査(戸数)では，例えば四条通・河原町通・五条通・烏丸通に囲まれた街区(容積率制限700〜400%，商業地域)でも2階建て79.3%，3階建て9.6%，4階建て5.0%，5階建て3.1%という数字であり，町家の建て替えはまだこれからの課題であること，市民の大半は3〜5階建てへの漸進的な中層化を選択していることがわかる．これを秩序ある変化とするために

tween 400% to 700%, and designated for business use) accounted for 79.3% of those surveyed, three-storey buildings for 9.6%, four-storey buildings for 5.0% and five-storey buildings for 3.1%, which means that the decision to opt for new high-rise buildings has yet to be taken. In order to ensure an orderly change, it is therefore necessary to reduce the floor area to site area ratios.

Making the creation of more public space a condition, these area ratios should be increased in any overall city plan, but the appropriate increase within the center of the city is somewhat at loggerheads with the above idea. In the overall city plan, it is intended to create densely packed high-rise buildings amid the ensuing greenery, an idea that basically works totally against the idea of developing Kyoto's street architecture. There is certainly a lack of trees in the center of the city. But unless the trimming of the trees there are to prevent them growing any larger before their leaves turn and fall creating a mess of leaves that seems to be disliked; and if the number of trees along the rivers is reduced and if nothing is done to prevent the removal to the suburbs of temples which have, up to now, provided areas of greenery, it will undoubtedly be almost impossible to reverse what is happening.

In order, therefore, to ensure the stimulation of the city and its neighborhoods, policies to attract large scale commercial facilities tend to conflict with the idea of a new combined city center and environs city concept.

The New Kyoto Station building, is just one of the projects that is supposed to commemorate the 1,200th anniversary of the founding of the city. But besides the problems presented by a building of such immense scale - 60 meters high by 470 meters long, 95% of its floor area will be given over to commercial use, half of which is for a large scale shopping area. This building has generated a terrific increase in the floor area allotted for department store use, and small scale shops and retailers will surely vanish as a result. It will also mean that the city will become intolerable for old people to live in as people become more dependent on the motor car for shopping. In short, the city is being fobbed off with the American vision of a city, which of course may be fine for America. But perhaps what we should be doing is to reassess the problems and adopt something along European lines where there are delightful rows of individual shops and buildings of similar height and style, intermingled with housing. However, in doing so, we must not fail to incorporate what is essentially the style of Japan and Kyoto.

As far as possible, there should be a consensus to preserve the more natural areas in the environs of Kyoto. This does not just mean conserving a green belt. Following in the footsteps of the inhabitants og Kyoto, who made use of these areas in the past, cultural amenities should be established in the form of parks emulating nature, thrie beauty being something from which to derive some pleasure at all seasons. About 20 years ago, Kyoto zoned all the flat areas from around the valley basin up to the foot of the surrounding mountains themselves, for city use. It has done the same for land stretching as far as Okusaga, Iwakura and Kamigamo in the northwest. Now, these areas, which form an important cultural heritage with respect to Kyoto, are being developed as a residential green belt. While generating unoccupied houses in the city

Buildings encroaching on machiya within the city center　都心の町家街区．町家に迫るビル

Buildings and machiya within the city center　都心の町家とビル

は，容積率制限を小さくするダウン・ゾーニングが必要であろう．

公開空地をつくることを条件に容積率のボーナスを与える総合設計制度が，都心部に広く適用される現状は，上の考え方と矛盾する．総合設計制度は樹木の間に高層ビルが林立する都市像をめざしており，これは基本的に京都の町家街区の継承的発展とは反対の方向へ向かっている．確かに都心部には樹木が不足しているように感じられるが，落葉を嫌って街路樹を紅葉の前に短く剪定するのを改めこれを大きく育てたり，河川沿いの樹木を守り，緑地を提供してきた寺院の郊外への移転を防ぎ活用を図るほうが先決ではないだろうか．

町の活性化のために大規模商業施設を誘致しようという方針も新・洛中洛外構想と矛盾する．建都1200年記念事業の一つである新京都駅ビルも，高さ60m，長さ470mという巨大な規模の問題の他に，その床の95％が商業機能であり，その半分が大規模店舗であるという問題をもっている．この建物は市内の百貨店の増床を促したが，その結果必ず市内の小規模店舗・小売店が消えるだろう．それは，都市の居住者にとって店舗が遠くなり，自動車による買物，老人の住みにくい町への変化を意味する．敢えて言えば，それはアメリカ的な都市像に向いつつあることを意味しており，この現状から，個性的な店舗が軒を並べ，似た高さの建物・住居が並ぶヨーロッパ的な都市に向けて方向転換すべきであろう．ただしそれを日本的京都的スタイルで実行することを考えなくてはならない．

さて，洛外部分はできるだけ樹木の緑の保全が求められる．それは単なる自然保存ではなく，かつての京都人が育てあげた文化的公園的自然として，美しく，四季を楽しめる姿で守りたいものである．20年程前に京都は盆地周囲の三山の山裾まで，平坦部を全て市街化区域に指定した．岩倉，上賀茂，さらには奥嵯峨までが市街化区域となり，今になってこれら京都を取り巻く歴史的な文化財集積地域でもある田園地帯に住宅開発が及んでいる．都心に空き家を生み出しながら，洛外の緑が侵食されている．東京からは市街化区域内の市街化を促進せよという声が聞こえて来る．京都はこれに抵抗すべきであると私は思う．洛外の文化的自然環境を守ったなら，これを市民が誰でも楽しめるようにする必要がある．かつて貝原益軒や司馬江漢が巡ったように，洛外は都心からの歩行距

center, Kyoto is eating up its green outskirts. From Tokyo voices are asking for greater commercial exploitation of the areas designated for commercial use in the city. I think Kyoto should resist this by all the means at its disposal. In conserving the natural environment that makes up so much of the cultural heritage of Kyoto's outskirts, the townspeople should ensure that it can be enjoyed by all. A long time ago, people like Kaibara Ekiken and Shiba Kokan walked these areas which are within walking distance of the center, and they are most certainly within easy cycling distance. I would like to see a network of pedestrianized precincts and cycling paths established and with respect to this we should see which roads were used historically speaking.

The population of Kyoto is fairly stable and the amount of floor space available is sufficient for their needs. How efficiently it is being used is the problem, but it is not always necessary to build high-rises blocks of housing and offices simply to make "improvements". After all, are children raised in high-rise buildings really happy? Surely it would be something of an improvement for people who spend half of their lives in high-rise buildings to have a work place from which they could see an abundance of greenery? Similarly, I can not agree with the insistence for the promotion of the idea of an underground city. Surely Kyoto is a city where people can live close to the ground which has enjoyed a long relationship with flora and fauna. I think that we should respect the land and take Kyoto, that clearly demonstrates a large city's close coexistence with nature, as a role-model for the future. We are always overly concerned with day to day goings on, but it is very important where we place emphasis with regard to the city's future image. I sincerely hope that the Japanese government will allow Kyoto, as a first, some latitude in following an individualistic course in realizing its cultural inheritance vis-à-vis a traditional Japanese city, and that the city planning and building regulations will be left to the discretion of the regional authorities.

Toward a Sensitively Composed Cityscape
Since ancient times, the Japanese people have held all kinds of sensitively composed scenes and environments in high regard, and the close relationship between people in general and nature embodied in such historically appointed environments, have been a continuing source of inspiration to the people who inhabit these islands. For this very reason, therefore, scenes and environments, whether man made, natural or a combinations of both, have a depth of meaning and sophistication which supports their very existence.

It must surely follow that the reason people recognize this degree of sensitivity in any scene is because of the way in which it is composed, and scenes and environments of this métier are therefore capable of touching the very heart of humankind. If, however, objects invested with overtly personalized forms of expression and motifs are dropped ignorantly and unheeding of context into such historically appointed environments by contemporary man, not only are such edifices obtrusive but they also demand our attention so wantonly that we are denied the opportunity to develop our own ideas and impressions. A plan put forward some years ago for the Kamo River serves as a good example of this, as it involved an "improvement" plan, which aimed to change the whole appearance of the river by completely artificial means. To me, it seems totally inappropriate to even attempt such a thing, especially in a city like Kyoto which has such a historically meaningful environment. Surely an effort should be made to bring out the sensitivity of a scene or environment rather than to elabo-

Buildings blocking out the view of religious structures on Higashiyama
東山の寺院を隠すビル

Kyoto Station II 二代目京都駅　京を語る会提供

離圏にあり，まして自転車を使えば近い．歩行者道・自転車道のネットワークで洛中と洛外を結合したいものである．それにはかつての歴史的な街道の利用を検討したい．

京都の人口は安定しており，建物の床はおおよそ現状で足りている．その利用効率が問題であって，ビルや住宅の高層化は必ずしも必要ではない．高層住宅の室内で育つ子供は幸せだろうか，超高層ビルで一生の大半を送る人生は，樹々の緑が見える職場で過ごすより進歩しているのだろうか．その意味では最近主張されている地下都市構想にも賛成できない．京都は樹木と生物が永く生活してきた地表近くに人が生活する都市を実現すべきではないだろうか．地表を尊重し，自然と共存する大都市モデルを示すことこそ，かえって次代を先取りするものと私には思われる．日々の利害が我々を忙殺するが，未来像を何処に据えるかが大きな意味をもつのではないだろうか．日本政府には，京都をはじめ歴史都市が日本的都市文化を継承する独自の道を歩む自由を手にできるよう，都市計画，建築法規の地方分権を認めることを切に希望したい．

都市景観形成の方向──風情ある景観
古来日本人は風情のある景観を尊重してきた．歴史的景観には一般に人と自然の親密な関係と，人に想像を誘う魅力があり，だからこそ景観が深みを帯びて存在している．私たちが風情を感じるのはそういう仕方で人の心に働きかける景観であろう．現代人の余りに個性や作意を表現した造形をそこへ持ち込むと，それは目立つばかりでなく意識をそこへ縛りつけ，人それぞれの自由な想像を妨げてしまう．数年前，鴨川にそういう人為的造形によって川の姿を変える改修計画が発表されたが，京都の歴史的景観にはふさわしいとは思えない．造形に凝るよりも風情の演出にこころすべきであろう．中世の京の文化を代表する能を大成した世阿弥は，芸のしぐさや音曲の具体的な形を「風情」と呼んだ．江戸時代には風情は「身だしなみ」のことでもあった．和風とか風体というように，風には様式（スタイル）という意味があるから，風情という語そのものは，情の，すなわち心の様式ということができよう．精神は事物の形態と共にあると考えられてきたのである．黒瓦の屋根は雨に光り，雪の朝を美しく装飾する．天候や季節

rate it with stiff, unsympathetic creations.

Noh theater was perhaps the most representative art form in Kyoto during the middle ages and Zeami, who was an acclaimed artist of this form of theater, described the physical form of a melody and the gestures of a performance as being full of "sensitivity and meaning". Later during the Edo period, this same sense of sensitivity and meaning became described literally as poise. This is more or less equivalent to "style" or perhaps an embodiment of "taste". And something which has sensitivity and meaning must surely be expressive of a mood or attitude of true poise. After all, a material object is always invested with a spirit and there are numerous examples of this fact.

Taking a pertinent example, the black roof tiles so indicative of Kyoto take on many guises. After rain they glisten like silver, with a dusting of snow they create a pattern of such beauty in morning light, and in other ways they reflect and express both the changing of the seasons and the nuances of the climate. Such design elements are an integral part of the historical land- and cityscapes of Kyoto. Inevitably, therefore, the inheritance of such forms of sensitivity within the cityscape and the development of a creative approach to deal with it, are some of the most important tasks in the area of urban design facing the historic city of Kyoto today.

Environmental Design Based on Local Contexts

Up to now in Japan, the conservation of historical architecture and areas of outstanding natural beauty, has been a process that merely limits preservation to individual buildings or areas and seeks to maintain them in a state of complete stasis. With regard to items falling outside this category, it has become acceptable to develop them without any regard for conservation. If we merely keep things in a state of stasis, residents begin to feel quite strongly about the inadequacy of the situation, added to which there are really very few individual buildings or areas that have been designated as cultural treasures. Other than these the historical roots have vanished completely without trace along with the push of development. If we continue in this fashion, we stand to lose forever the cultural features that comprise the historic city of Kyoto and its superb surroundings. Rather than allow this, the time has come to work out what features make up the city's environment, to understand them and to evaluate them, and to choose the most appropriate methods of conservation and preservation for any given area. Then it will be necessary to develop environmental planning and design methods that will facilitate it. For instance, with regard to the particular historical context of the features of a region (time context), how should we perceive past history, and how should we express it with regard to the future? Also, at the present moment in time, with regard to the scenic context of the surrounding environment (space context), how should we evaluate it and try to add to it? In other words, we should reconsider environmental design based on the context of the local scenic amenities offered. If we proceed from this stand point then, even in the historical city of Kyoto, design work in numerous places will take on the aspect of conservation. In this way, by respecting the traditions of the urban design of Kyoto, it will be possible to unveil developments that show the liveliness of their antecedents, at least that is what I would like to wish for in closing.

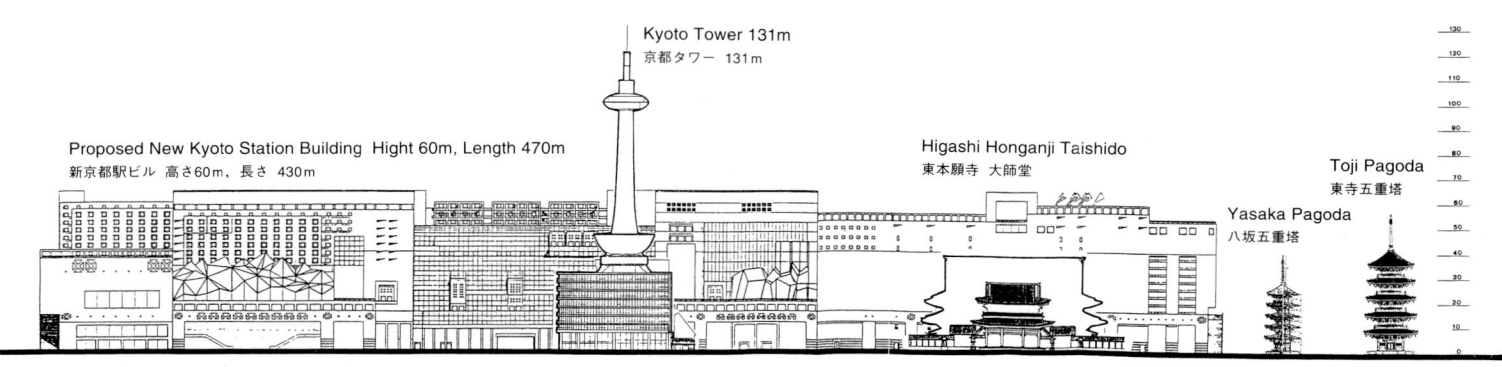

Comparison between historic structures and the proposed new Kyoto Station building
新京都駅ビルと歴史的建造物の規模比較

の状況に呼応し表現するデザインが京の歴史的景観にはある．都市景観における風情の継承と創出は歴史都市京都の大きな課題といえるだろう．

地域景観の文脈にもとづく環境デザイン

これまでのわが国では，歴史的な建築や環境の保存といえば，保存の対象を限定し，それについては完全な凍結的保存をはかり，いっぽうでそれ以外のものについては一切保存を考えず開発を行うのを良しとしてきた．凍結的保存をすれば住人は不便を強いられることになり，それゆえ極く少数の物件を文化財指定し，それ以外は歴史の痕跡を全く残さない開発が進んできた．しかし，それでは京都という歴史的都市環境が持つ文化的特質は失われてしまう．こういう考え方ではなく，都市環境の持つ特質を読み取り，解釈し，評価し，様々な保存の度合と様々な保存手法の中からその場にふさわしいものを選択して，環境の計画・設計を行う方法が必要だろう．言いかえれば，地域の環境が持つ歴史的文脈（通時的文脈）の上で，過去の歴史をどう受けとめ，未来へ向けてどう発言するのか，また現時点での周辺環境の景観的文脈（共時的文脈）の上で，それをどう評価しそこに何を加えようとするのか，という「地域景観の文脈にもとづく環境デザイン」を考えるべきではないだろうか．この立場からすれば，歴史都市においては，あらゆる場所での設計行為が何らかの保存的性格をもつことになるだろう．こうして京都に，その都市意匠の伝統を尊重する活き活きとした継承的発展が展開されることを願って稿を閉じたい．

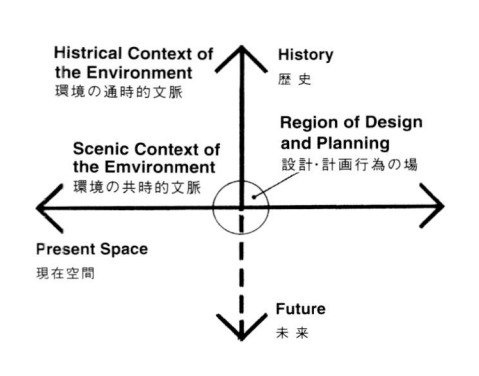

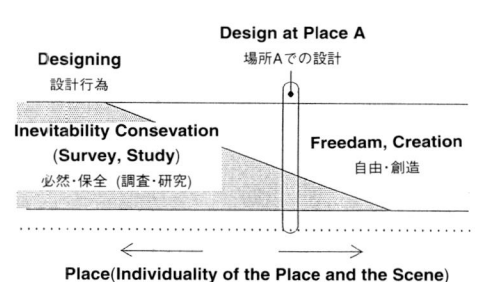

Location Map　本書掲載の場所・地域　位置図

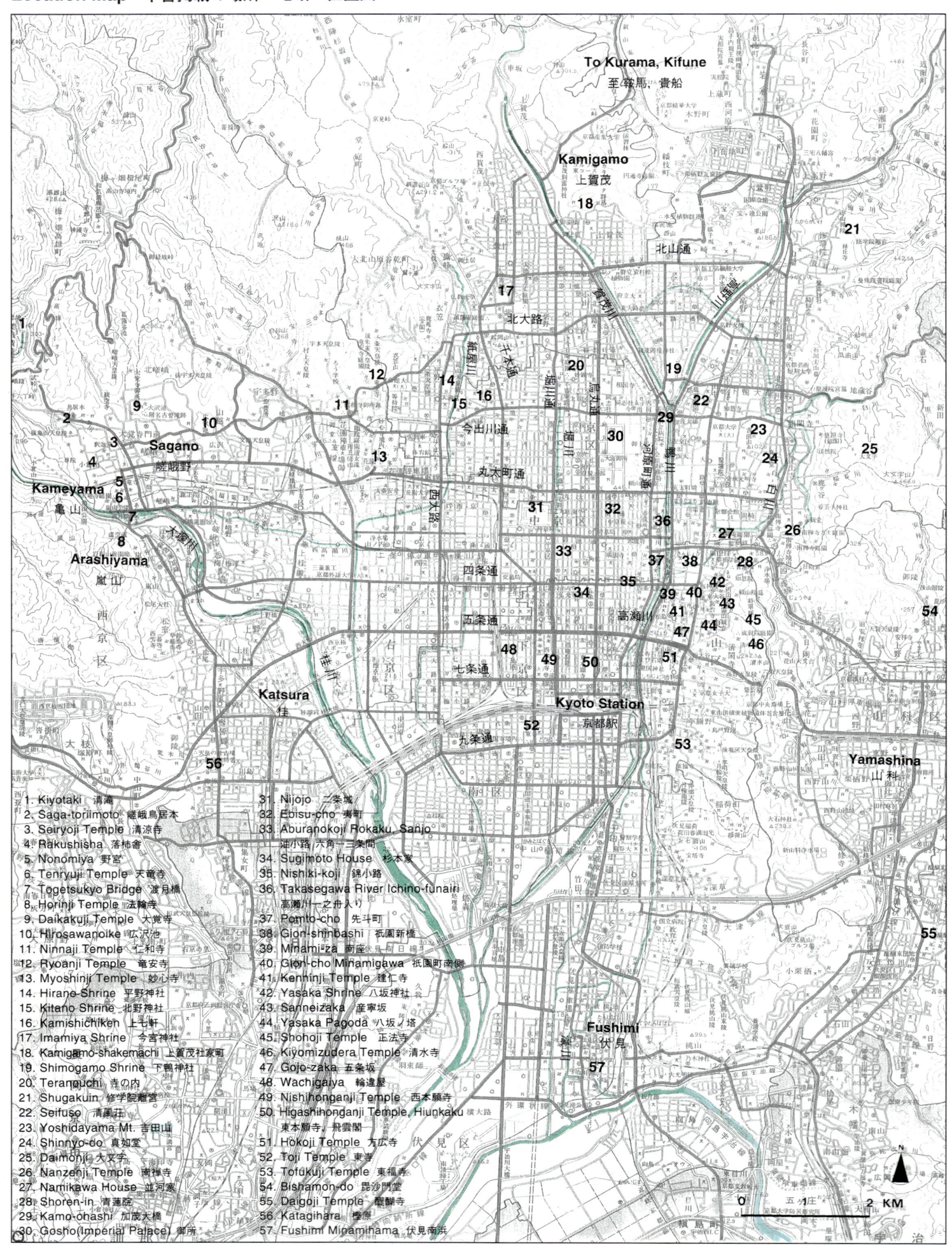

1. Kiyotaki　清滝
2. Saga-toriimoto　嵯峨鳥居本
3. Seiryoji Temple　清涼寺
4. Rakushisha　落柿舎
5. Nonomiya　野宮
6. Tenryuji Temple　天竜寺
7. Togetsukyo Bridge　渡月橋
8. Horinji Temple　法輪寺
9. Daikakuji Temple　大覚寺
10. Hirosawanoike　広沢池
11. Ninnaji Temple　仁和寺
12. Ryoanji Temple　竜安寺
13. Myoshinji Temple　妙心寺
14. Hirano Shrine　平野神社
15. Kitano Shrine　北野神社
16. Kamishichiken　上七軒
17. Imamiya Shrine　今宮神社
18. Kamigamo-shakemachi　上賀茂社家町
19. Shimogamo Shrine　下鴨神社
20. Teranouchi　寺の内
21. Shugakuin　修学院離宮
22. Seifuso　清風荘
23. Yoshidayama Mt.　吉田山
24. Shinnyo-do　真如堂
25. Daimonji　大文字
26. Nanzenji Temple　南禅寺
27. Namikawa House　並河家
28. Shoren-in　青蓮院
29. Kamo-ohashi　加茂大橋
30. Gosho (Imperial Palace)　御所
31. Nijojo　二条城
32. Ebisu-cho　夷町
33. Aburanokoji Rokaku, Sanjo　油小路六角〜三条間
34. Sugimoto House　杉本家
35. Nishiki-koji　錦小路
36. Takasegawa River Ichino-funairi　高瀬川一之舟入り
37. Pontocho　先斗町
38. Gion-shinbashi　祇園新橋
39. Minami-za　南座
40. Gion-cho Minamigawa　祇園町南側
41. Kenninji Temple　建仁寺
42. Yasaka Shrine　八坂神社
43. Sanneizaka　産寧坂
44. Yasaka Pagoda　八坂ノ塔
45. Shohoji Temple　正法寺
46. Kiyomizudera Temple　清水寺
47. Gojo-zaka　五条坂
48. Wachigaiya　輪違屋
49. Nishihonganji Temple　西本願寺
50. Higashihonganji Temple, Hiunkaku　東本願寺、飛雲閣
51. Hokoji Temple　方広寺
52. Toji Temple　東寺
53. Tofukuji Temple　東福寺
54. Bishamon-do　毘沙門堂
55. Daigoji Temple　醍醐寺
56. Katagihara　樫原
57. Fushimi Minamihama　伏見南浜